RESISTANCE TO EVIDENCE

We have increasingly sophisticated ways of acquiring and communicating knowledge, but efforts to spread this knowledge often encounter resistance to evidence. The phenomenon of resistance to evidence, while subject to thorough investigation in social psychology, is acutely under-theorised in the philosophical literature. Mona Simion's book is concerned with positive epistemology: it argues that we have epistemic obligations to update and form beliefs on available and undefeated evidence. In turn, our resistance to easily available evidence is unpacked as an instance of epistemic malfunctioning. Simion develops a full positive, integrated epistemological picture in conjunction with novel accounts of evidence, defeat, norms of inquiry, permissible suspension, and disinformation. Her book is relevant for anyone with an interest in the nature of evidence and justified belief and in the best ways to avoid the high-stakes practical consequences of evidence resistance in policy and practice. This title is also available as Open Access on Cambridge Core.

MONA SIMION is Professor of Philosophy and Director of the COGITO Epistemology Research Centre at the University of Glasgow. Her publications include *Sharing Knowledge* (2021) and *Shifty Speech and Independent Thought* (2021).

CAMBRIDGE STUDIES IN PHILOSOPHY

General Editors
Nomy Arpaly
(Brown University)
Sanford Goldberg
(Northwestern University)

Cambridge Studies in Philosophy is the cornerstone of Cambridge University Press's list in mainstream, high-level analytic philosophy. It serves as a forum for a broad range of monographs on the cutting edge of epistemology, the philosophy of language and mind, ethics, and metaphysics.

Recent Titles

DAVID LEWIS *Papers on Ethics and Social Philosophy*
FRED DRETSKE *Perception, Knowledge, and Belief*
LYNNE RUDDER BAKER *Persons and Bodies*
ROSANNA KEEFE *Theories of Vagueness*
JOHN GRECO *Putting Skeptics in Their Place*
RUTH GARRETT MILLIKAN *On Clear and Confused Ideas*
DERK PEREBOOM *Living Without Free Will*
BRIAN ELLIS *Scientific Essentialism*
ALAN H. GOLDMAN *Practical Rules*
CHRISTOPHER HILL *Thought and World*
ANDREW NEWMAN *The Correspondence Theory of Truth*
ISHTIYAQUE HAJI *Deontic Morality and Control*
WAYNE A. DAVIS *Meaning, Expression and Thought*
PETER RAILTON *Facts, Values, and Norms*
JANE HEAL *Mind, Reason and Imagination*
JONATHAN KVANVIG *The Value of Knowledge and the Pursuit of Understanding*
ANDREW MELNYK *A Physicalist Manifesto*
WILLIAM S. ROBINSON *Understanding Phenomenal Consciousness*

D. M. ARMSTRONG *Truth and Truthmakers*

KEITH FRANKISH *Mind and Supermind*

MICHAEL SMITH *Ethics and the A Priori*

NOAH LEMOS *Common Sense*

JOSHUA GERT *Brute Rationality*

ALEXANDER R. PRUSS *The Principle of Sufficient Reason*

FOLKE TERSMAN *Moral Disagreement*

JOSEPH MENDOLA *Goodness and Justice*

DAVID COPP *Morality in a Natural World*

LYNNE RUDDER BAKER *The Metaphysics of Everyday Life*

MICHAEL J. ZIMMERMANN *Living with Uncertainty*

SANFORD GOLDBERG *Anti-Individualism*

CRAWFORD L. ELDER *Familiar Objects and Their Shadows*

JAMIN ASAY *The Primitivist Theory of Truth*

RICHARD FUMERTON *Knowledge, Thought and the Case for Dualism*

CHRISTOPH KELP AND MONA SIMION *Sharing Knowledge*

ARTŪRS LOGINS *Normative Reasons: Between Reasoning and Explanation*

RESISTANCE TO EVIDENCE

MONA SIMION
University of Glasgow

Shaftesbury Road, Cambridge CB2 8EA, United Kingdom

One Liberty Plaza, 20th Floor, New York, NY 10006, USA

477 Williamstown Road, Port Melbourne, VIC 3207, Australia

314–321, 3rd Floor, Plot 3, Splendor Forum, Jasola District Centre, New Delhi – 110025, India

103 Penang Road, #05–06/07, Visioncrest Commercial, Singapore 238467

Cambridge University Press is part of Cambridge University Press & Assessment, a department of the University of Cambridge.

We share the University's mission to contribute to society through the pursuit of education, learning and research at the highest international levels of excellence.

www.cambridge.org
Information on this title: www.cambridge.org/9781009298513

DOI: 10.1017/9781009298537

© Mona Simion 2024

This work is in copyright. It is subject to statutory exceptions and to the provisions of relevant licensing agreements; with the exception of the Creative Commons version the link for which is provided below, no reproduction of any part of this work may take place without the written permission of Cambridge University Press.

An online version of this work is published at http://dx.doi.org/10.1017/9781009298537 under a Creative Commons Open Access license CC-BY-NC 4.0 which permits re-use, distribution and reproduction in any medium for non-commercial purposes providing appropriate credit to the original work is given and any changes made are indicated. To view this license, visit https://creativecommons.org/licenses/by-nc/4.0

All versions of this work may contain content reproduced under license from third parties. Permission to reproduce this third-party content must be obtained from these third-parties directly. When citing this work, please include a reference to the DOI: 10.1017/9781009298537

First published 2024
First paperback edition 2025

A catalogue record for this publication is available from the British Library

ISBN 978-1-009-29852-0 Hardback
ISBN 978-1-009-29851-3 Paperback

Cambridge University Press & Assessment has no responsibility for the persistence or accuracy of URLs for external or third-party internet websites referred to in this publication and does not guarantee that any content on such websites is, or will remain, accurate or appropriate.

For Chris

Contents

Acknowledgements	*page* xii
Introduction	1
0.1 Game Plan	2

PART I THE EPISTEMOLOGY AND PSYCHOLOGY OF RESISTANCE TO EVIDENCE

1	Resistance to Evidence: Triggers and Epistemic Status	9
	1.1 Resistance to Evidence	9
	1.2 The Social Psychology of Evidence Resistance	11
	1.3 Rejecting Evidence: A Taxonomy	16
	1.4 Conclusion	22
2	Evidence One Has and the Impermissibility of Resistance	23
	2.1 Evidence Internalism	23
	2.2 E = K	25
	2.3 Reliable Indicators	28
	2.4 Virtuous Reasons	31
	2.5 Conclusion	34
3	Evidence You Should Have Had and Resistance	36
	3.1 The Social 'Should'	36
	3.2 Worries for Social Epistemic Normativity	39
	3.3 Problems for the Moral 'Should'	45
	3.4 Conclusion	46
4	Permissible Suspension and Evidence Resistance	48
	4.1 Proper Suspension: The Simple Knowledge-Based View	48
	4.2 Sosa on Virtue, Telic Normativity, and Suspension	51
	4.3 The Respect-Based View of Permissible Suspension	59
	4.4 Gesturing towards a Better Way	62
	4.5 Conclusion	66

x   *Contents*

5   Resistance to Evidence, Epistemic Responsibility, and
    Epistemic Vice   68
      5.1 Responsible Inquiry and Epistemic Character Traits   68
      5.2 Content-Individuating Responsibilist Virtues and Vices   72
      5.3 Psychological Vice Individuation   77
      5.4 Value-Based Vice Individuation   83
      5.5 Conclusion   91

    PART II RESISTANCE TO EVIDENCE AND EPISTEMIC
    PROPER FUNCTION

6   Resistance to Evidence as Epistemic Malfunction   95
      6.1 Epistemic Oughts   95
      6.2 Functions and Norms   99
      6.3 Resistance to Evidence as Epistemic Malfunction   105
      6.4 Conclusion   110

7   Evidence as Knowledge Indicators   111
      7.1 Knowledge Indicators   111
      7.2 Evidence and the Impermissibility of Resistance   116
      7.3 Infallibilism: Evidence and Knowledge   120
      7.4 Conclusion   123

8   Defeaters as Ignorance Indicators   124
      8.1 The Nature and Theoretical Importance of Defeat   124
      8.2 Defeaters as Ignorance Indicators   130
      8.3 External Defeat and Norms of Evidence Gathering   134
      8.4 Conclusion   137

9   Inquiry and Permissible Suspension   138
      9.1 Suspension and the Knowledge Function   138
      9.2 Justified Suspension   139
      9.3 Suspension and the Normativity of Inquiry   142
      9.4 Conclusion   147

    PART III THEORETICAL UPSHOTS

10 Epistemic Oughts and Epistemic Dilemmas   151
      10.1 Obligations to Believe and Epistemic Dilemmas   151
      10.2 What Dilemmas Are Not   152
      10.3 Epistemic Non-dilemmas   155
      10.4 Conclusion   164

11 Scepticism as Resistance to Evidence   165
      11.1 Two Neo-Mooreanisms   165

	11.2 Against Concessive Neo-Mooreanism	167
	11.3 A New Radical Neo-Mooreanism	173
	11.4 Conclusion	177
12	Knowledge and Disinformation	178
	12.1 Information and Disinformation	178
	12.2 Against Disinformation Orthodoxy	180
	12.3 A Knowledge-First Account of Disinformation	184
	12.4 Conclusion	190
	Concluding Remarks: The Way Forward in Policy and Practice	192
	Evidence Resistance	192
	Disinformation	195
Bibliography		197
Index		215

Acknowledgements

I have benefitted from extraordinary levels of support from my peers and mentors for this research. I would like to especially thank Jessica Brown, Herman Cappelen, J. Adam Carter, Sandy Goldberg, Peter J. Graham, John Greco, Jonathan Jenkins-Ichikawa, Chris Kelp, Jennifer Lackey, Matt McGrath, Susanna Schellenberg, Ernie Sosa, and Tim Williamson for the feedback on this material and all the support. I would also like to thank Bob Beddor, Sven Bernecker, Cameron Boult, Fernando Broncano-Berrocal, Matthew Chrisman, Juan Comesaña, Paul Faulkner, Claire Field, Giada Fratantonio, Lizzie Fricker, Miranda Fricker, Jane Friedman, Mikkel Gerken, Olav Gjelsvic, Kathrin Gluer-Pagin, Emma Gordon, Patrick Greenough, Thomas Grundmann, Michael Hannon, Frank Hofmann, Matt Jope, Tim Kearl, Maria Lasonen-Aarnio, Clayton Littlejohn, Jack Lyons, Lilith Mace, Aidan McGlynn, Anne Meylan, Lisa Miracchi, Jesus Navarro, Gloria Origgi, Orestis Palermos, Carlotta Pavese, Richard Petigrew, Duncan Pritchard, Bernhard Salow, Susanna Siegel, Martin Smith, Amia Srinivasan, Julia Staffel, Rachel Sterken, Kurt Sylvan, Alessandra Tanesini, Joe Uscinski, Daniel Whiting, Asa Wikforss, and Christopher Willard-Kyle for the very helpful discussions. I am sure that I have missed people who deserve to be acknowledged by name and hope they will accept my apologies. Many thanks also to two anonymous referees for Cambridge University Press who gave me excellent comments on the book.

I would also like to thank the organisers and audiences of the Cambridge Moral Sciences Club, University of Cambridge; the Urbino Summer School in Epistemology; Philosophy Visiting Speaker Seminar, University of Aberdeen; Arche Epistemology Seminar, University of St Andrews; Bled Philosophical Conferences, Bled; Episteme Conferences, Negril; *The Power and Limits of Rational Reflection Conference*, University of Luxembourg; the British Society for Theory of Knowledge Meeting, Glasgow; Bad Beliefs, Conspiracy Theories,

Testimony and Resistance to Evidence GAP11 Satellite Workshop, Berlin; Epistemic Explanations: Investigations into the Epistemology of Ernest Sosa, University of Miami; COGITO–LANCOG Workshop, University of Lisbon; the American Philosophical Association Pacific 2022 BSTK Session, Vancouver; *The Social and Political Dimensions of Epistemic Risk Conference*, University of Seville; Nicod Philosophy Colloquium, Institut Jean Nicod; Philosophy Colloquium, University of Warwick; Jowett Society, University of Oxford; European Epistemology Network Meeting 2022, Glasgow; Talk Series on Conspiracy Belief, University of Bochum; Young Academy of Europe; Colloquium in Theoretical Philosophy, University of Zurich; Book Symposium on Ernest Sosa's 'Epistemic Explanations'; 2021 APA Pacific Division Meeting, Portland; Arché Conceptual Engineering Seminar, University of St Andrews; Visiting Speaker Seminar, University of Stirling; the *Asian Journal of Philosophy* Launch Conference; 'Climate Justice, Risk, and Wellbeing' Conference, COP26 UK Universities Innovation Showcase, Glasgow; Thomas Grundmann Summer School, University of Cologne; Epistemic Normativity Workshop, University of Leeds; ALEF Workshop in Analytic Philosophy, Babeș-Bolyai University; Perception: Epistemology and Mind Workshop, University of Glasgow; Research Seminar, University of York; *The 2019 Joint Session of the Aristotelian Society and the Mind Association*, Durham University; Closure and Transmission Workshop, University of Edinburgh; Edinburgh Epistemology Graduate Conference, Edinburgh; Visiting Speaker Seminar Series, University of Reading; Philosophy Club, University of St Andrews; Philosophy Seminar, University of Southern Denmark. I got excellent feedback from these audiences over several years, and the view has thereby improved significantly.

A few chapters of the book draw on previously published work: Chapters 2 and 6 partially draw on my Young Epistemologist Prize-winning paper 'Resistance to Evidence and the Duty to Believe' (*Philosophy and Phenomenological Research*, 2023). Chapter 5 relies on my contribution to 'Epistemic Virtues and Virtues with Epistemic Content' (with C. Kelp, C. Boult, and J. Schnurr, in J. Greco and C. Kelp (eds.), *Virtue Theoretic Epistemology: New Methods and Approaches*, 2020) and on my 2023 *Inquiry* paper 'Tanesini on Truth and Epistemic Vice'. Chapter 10 draws on my 'Scepticism about Epistemic Dilemmas' (in K. McCain, S. Stapleford, and M. Steup (eds.), *Epistemic Dilemmas: New Arguments, New Angles*, 2021). Chapter 11 relies to some extent on 'Closure, Warrant Transmission, and Defeat' (in M. Jope and D. Pritchard (eds.), *Epistemic Closure and Transmission*, 2022). Finally, Chapter 12 relies on my *Episteme* paper 'Knowledge and Disinformation' (Simion 2023b). I want to thank the editors of these journals and volumes, as well as the anonymous referees, who provided me with excellent comments on these articles.

The research results outlined in this book have been made the subject of two major outreach initiatives; I want to thank all those involved in enabling me to showcase my results in these ways: (1) a 2022 White Paper titled 'Trust, Disinformation, and Evidence Resistance', written and submitted in response to the UK Parliament Call for Evidence: 'Fighting Disinformation with Trustworthy Voices' (with C. Kelp). The White Paper is published on the UK Parliament website (https://committees.parliament.uk/writtenevidence/111503/pdf/); (2) a 2022 documentary film titled *Scotland, African Voices: The Covid19 Vaccine Debate* (co-developed with Josephine Adekola, PI). The documentary aims to address health inequalities and save lives by encouraging vaccine take-up in the Scottish African, Caribbean, and Black community and by highlighting the social-epistemological obstacles amongst the barriers to vaccination for these communities. The full documentary is available here: https://youtu.be/h1yNAZffpOg. The trailer is available here: www.youtube.com/watch?v=9Ie8SMVvy1Y.

The research in this book has been very generously funded by a Horizon 2020 European Research Council (ERC) grant for my project 'KnowledgeLab: Knowledge-First Social Epistemology' (grant agreement no. 948356). I'm extremely grateful to the European taxpayers, the ERC team, as well as their pool of reviewers for this fantastic level of support.

Many thanks to Sandy Goldberg and Hilary Gaskin at Cambridge University Press for all the excellent advice, continuous support, and efficiency.

Finally, many thanks to my partner Chris Kelp, my kids Max and Mia Kelp, and my grandparents Georgeta and Iordache Diaconita for all the extraordinary support.

Introduction

We have increasingly sophisticated ways of acquiring and communicating knowledge, but efforts to spread this knowledge often encounter resistance to evidence. Evidence resistance has dire practical consequences; recent examples include climate change denial and vaccine scepticism. The phenomenon of resistance to evidence, while subject to thorough investigation in social psychology, is acutely under-theorised in the philosophical literature. As a result, we are still to understand the normativity of this phenomenon: what is epistemically wrong with resistance to evidence? What are its triggers? How does resistance to evidence interact with norms of inquiry and the epistemic justification of belief? What are the best strategies for efficaciously addressing the phenomenon of resistance to evidence in policy and practice?

Traditionally, normative work in epistemology is, for the most part,[1] negative, in that it concerns itself with permissions: it deals with restricting what we are permitted to, for example, believe, assert, or use as a premise in reasoning. This book is concerned with positive epistemology: it argues that resistance to easily available evidence constitutes a breach of one's epistemic obligations. One useful way to think about this project is as the counterpart of the Cliffordian project. Whereas Clifford proposes that it is wrong everywhere for anyone to believe on the basis of insufficient evidence, this book investigates the other side of the evidentialist project: whether it wrong everywhere and for anyone to not believe when they have sufficient and undefeated evidence.

I develop and defend a full account of the nature and normativity of resistance to evidence, according to which resistance to evidence is an instance of input-level epistemic malfunctioning. The account is

---

[1] See Kornblith (2001), Fricker (2007), Chrisman (2008), Feldman (2008), Goldberg (2016, 2017), Jenkins-Ichikawa (2020), Lackey (2020), and Simion (2023a) for exceptions. In putting this distinction in terms of positive versus negative epistemology, I follow Jenkins-Ichikawa (2020).

naturalistically friendly and enjoys high normative prior plausibility in that it construes resistance to evidence as an instance of a more general type of malfunction often encountered in biological traits the proper function of which is input dependent. The account is developed in conjunction with novel views of evidence, defeat, permissible suspension, scepticism, epistemic dilemmas, and disinformation. At the core of this epistemic normative picture lies the notion of *p*-knowledge indicators as facts that one is in a position to know and that increase one's evidential probability that something is the case. Resistance to evidence is construed as a failure to uptake knowledge indicators.

0.1 Game Plan

0.1.1 Part I The Epistemology and Psychology of Resistance to Evidence

Chapter 1   Resistance to Evidence: Triggers and Epistemic Status
This chapter dwells at the intersection of the social psychology of knowledge resistance and epistemic normativity to offer the first full taxonomy of resistance to evidence. It first individuates the phenomenon via paradigmatic instances, and then it taxonomises it according to two parameters: (1) paradigmatic triggering conditions and (2) epistemic normative status. I argue that the phenomenon of resistance to evidence is epistemologically narrower but psychologically broader than is assumed in the extant literature in social psychology. This, in turn, gives us reason to believe that addressing this phenomenon in policy and practice will be a much more complex endeavour than is currently assumed. In the remainder of the book, I examine the extant literature on evidence, justification, defeat, permissible suspension, and epistemic responsibility in search of the normative resources required to fully accommodate the psychological breadth and epistemic normative status of the phenomenon of resistance to evidence.

Chapter 2   Evidence One Has and the Impermissibility of Resistance
This chapter argues that the main extant views on the nature of evidence one has lack the resources to account for the impermissibility of cases of resistance to evidence. I first examine classic internalist, seemings-based evidentialism and argue that it fails to account for evidence resistance. This, I argue, is an in-principle problem: internalist evidentialism cannot recover from this *because* it is internalist. I move on to externalist views of evidence, starting with factive externalism (i.e. Williamson's (2000) E = K), and I argue that, since resistant cognisers don't take up the relevant

facts in the world to begin with, the view fails to predict epistemic impermissibility in resistance cases. I also look at and dismiss several ways in which the champion of E = K might attempt to account for what's going wrong in resistance cases (i.e. via employing notions such as epistemic dispositions one should have had and epistemic blameworthiness), and I argue that the view faces insurmountable difficulties. Finally, I move on to less radical, non-factive externalisms and investigate the potential of prominent reliabilist views – indicator reliabilism (Comesaña 2020) and virtue reliabilism (Turri 2010, Sylvan and Sosa 2018, Sosa 2021) – to account for the phenomenon of resistance. I argue that these views are too agent-centric to successfully account for resistance cases.

Chapter 3   Evidence You Should Have Had and Resistance
This chapter considers one popular way to account for cases of resistance as cases of evidence one *should have had*, where the normative failure at stake is taken to be either (1) a breach of social normativity (Goldberg 2018) or (2) a breach of moral normativity (Feldman 2004). I argue that the social normative option is too weak, in that it allows problematic social norms to encroach on epistemic normativity, and that the appeal to moral oughts fails both on theoretical grounds – in that it cannot accommodate widely accepted epistemic conditions on moral blame – and on extensional adequacy.

Chapter 4   Permissible Suspension and Evidence Resistance
This chapter surveys recent accounts of the epistemic permissibility of suspended judgement in an attempt to thereby identify the normative resources required for explaining the epistemically problematic nature of evidence resistance. Since paradigmatic cases of evidence resistance involve belief suspension on propositions that are well supported by evidence, such as vaccine safety and climate change, the literature on permissible suspension seems to be a straightforward starting point for my investigation: after all, any plausible view of permissible suspension will have to predict epistemic impermissibility in these paradigmatic resistance cases. I look at three extant accounts of permissible suspension – a simple knowledge-based account, a virtue-based account, and a respect-based account – and argue that they fail to provide the needed resources for this project. Further on, the chapter identifies the source of the said difficulties and gestures towards a better way forward.

Chapter 5   Resistance to Evidence, Epistemic Responsibility, and Epistemic Vice
Available accounts of possessed evidence, evidence one should have possessed, and permissible suspension of judgement struggle to accommodate

the phenomenon of evidence resistance. Along the way, we have, in particular, seen that virtue reliabilist accounts of reasons to believe, permissible suspension, and propositional warrant don't do the needed work. At that point, some readers would have already thought that one straightforward explanation of the resistance data is afforded by the competing, virtue responsibilist camp: roughly, on this view, evidence resistance could be conceptualised as a failure to manifest epistemic responsibility in inquiry and/or as a manifestation/indication of epistemic vice. This chapter looks into the credentials of this move. I argue that once we distinguish epistemic virtues and vices proper from mere moral virtues and vices with epistemic content, it transpires that accounting for resistance cases, as well as accounting for epistemic virtue and vice, requires epistemic value-first unpacking.

0.1.2 Part II Resistance to Evidence and Epistemic Proper Function

Chapter 6 Resistance to Evidence as Epistemic Malfunction
This chapter argues that resistance to evidence is an instance of epistemic malfunction. It first puts forth a normative picture according to which the epistemic function of our cognitive systems is generating knowledge, and epistemic norms drop right out of this function. Second, it shows how this picture accommodates epistemic obligations, which, in turn, explain the normative failure instantiated in cases of resistance to evidence. According to this view, cognitive systems that fail to take up easily available evidence and defeat instantiate input-level malfunctioning. Input-level malfunctioning is a common phenomenon in traits the proper functioning of which is input dependent, such as our respiratory systems. Since our cognitive systems, I argue, are systems the proper functioning of which is input dependent, we should expect the failure at stake in resistance cases.

Chapter 7 Evidence as Knowledge Indicators
This chapter puts forth a novel view of evidence in terms of knowledge indicators, and it shows that it is superior to its competition in that it can account for the epistemic impermissibility of resistance cases, as well as for the effect that resistance to evidence has on doxastic justification. Very roughly, knowledge indicators are facts that enhance closeness to knowledge: a fact e is evidence for S that p is the case if and only if S is in a position to know e and e increases the evidential probability that p for S.

Chapter 8 Defeaters as Ignorance Indicators
This chapter puts forth and defends a novel view of defeat, and it shows that it is superior to its competition in that it can account for the epistemic

impermissibility of defeat resistance cases and normative defeat cases, as well as for the effect ignored defeat has on doxastic justification. On this account, defeaters are ignorance indicators: facts that one is in a position to know and that reduce one's evidential probability that p. Furthermore, I also put forth a novel account of the normativity at work in cases of normative defeat and negligent inquiry and evidence gathering.

Chapter 9   Inquiry and Permissible Suspension
This chapter develops an account of permissible suspension that builds on the views of justification, evidence, and defeat defended in the previous chapters. The view is superior to extant competitors in that it successfully predicts epistemic normative failure in cases of suspension generated by evidence and defeat resistance. On this view, doxastically justified suspension is suspension generated by properly functioning knowledge-generating processes. In turn, properly functioning knowledge-generating processes uptake knowledge and ignorance indicators.

0.1.3   Part III Theoretical Upshots

Chapter 10   Epistemic Oughts and Epistemic Dilemmas
The following chapters examine the theoretical upshots of the view proposed. The account developed so far delivers the result that epistemic justifiers constitute epistemic oughts. In this chapter, I discuss the worry that such accounts threaten to give rise to widely spread epistemic dilemmas between paradigmatic epistemic norms. I argue for a modest scepticism about epistemic dilemmas. In order to do that, I first point out that not all normative conflicts constitute dilemmas: more needs to be the case. Second, I look into the moral dilemmas literature and identify a set of conditions that need to be at work for a mere normative conflict to be a genuine normative dilemma. Last, I argue that while our epistemic life is peppered with epistemic normative conflict, epistemic dilemmas are much harder to find than we thought.

Chapter 11   Scepticism as Resistance to Evidence
The view of evidence, defeat, and suspension put forth here delivers the result that scepticism about knowledge and justification is an instance of resistance to evidence. This chapter argues that this result is correct. In order to do that, I look at extant neo-Moorean responses to purported instances of failure of knowledge closure (Pryor 2004, Williamson 2007) and warrant transmission and argue that they are either too weak – in that they concede too much to the sceptic – or too strong – in that they cannot

accommodate the intuition of reasonableness surrounding sceptical arguments. I propose a novel neo-Moorean explanation of the data, relying on my preferred account of defeat and permissible suspension, on which the sceptic is in impermissible suspension but in fulfilment of their contrary to duty epistemic obligations.

Chapter 12   Knowledge and Disinformation
Ideally, we want to resist mis/disinformation but not evidence. If this is so, we need accounts of misinformation and disinformation to match the epistemic normative picture developed so far. This chapter develops a full account of the nature of disinformation. The view, if correct, carries high-stakes upshots, both theoretically and practically. First, it challenges several widely spread theoretical assumptions about disinformation – such as that it is a species of information, a species of misinformation, essentially false or misleading, or essentially intended/aimed/having the function of generating false beliefs in/misleading hearers. Second, it shows that the challenges faced by disinformation tracking in practice go well beyond mere fact checking. I begin with an interdisciplinary scoping of the literature in information science, communication studies, computer science, and philosophy of information to identify several claims constituting disinformation orthodoxy. I then present counterexamples to these claims and motivate my alternative account. Finally, I put forth and develop my account: disinformation as ignorance-generating content.

PART I

The Epistemology and Psychology of Resistance to Evidence

CHAPTER I

Resistance to Evidence
Triggers and Epistemic Status

This chapter dwells at the intersection of the social psychology of knowledge resistance and epistemic normativity to offer the first full taxonomy of resistance to evidence. It first individuates the phenomenon via paradigmatic instances, and then it taxonomises it according to two parameters: (1) paradigmatic triggering conditions and (2) epistemic normative status. I argue that the phenomenon of resistance to evidence is epistemologically narrower but psychologically broader than is assumed in the extant literature in social psychology. This, in turn, gives us reason to believe that addressing this phenomenon in policy and practice will be a much more complex endeavour than is currently assumed. In the remainder of the book, I examine the extant literature on evidence, defeat, justification, permissible suspension, and epistemic responsibility in search of the normative resources required to fully accommodate the psychological breadth and epistemic normative status of the phenomenon of resistance to evidence.

1.1 Resistance to Evidence

The notion of resistance to evidence, while subject to thorough investigation in social psychology,[1] is acutely under-theorised in the philosophical literature. As a result, we are still to understand the normativity of the resistance phenomenon: What is (epistemically) wrong with resistance to evidence? What are its triggers? How does the normativity of resistance to evidence interact with norms of inquiry and the epistemic justification of belief?

Consider the following cases:

Case #1. **Testimonial Injustice:** Anna is an extremely reliable testifier and an expert in the geography of Glasgow. She tells George

---

[1] See, e.g., Kahan 2013, Klintman 2019. See also the 'Knowledge Resistance' multidisciplinary research project at Stockholm University: https://knowledge-resistance.com.

that Glasgow Central is to the right. George believes women are not to be trusted; therefore, he fails to form the corresponding belief.

Case #2. **Political Negligence:** Bill is a stubborn supporter of President Dump. In spite of all evidence that is readily available to him (via mainstream media, Dump's own actions and public statements, etc.) suggesting that Dump is a bad president, Bill stubbornly refuses to believe that Dump is a bad president.

Case #3. **Science Scepticism:** Neda is an anxious cogniser; in particular, she is very careful when it comes to accepting science communication: whenever well-recognised, reliable experts assert that anthropogenic climate change is occurring or that vaccines are safe, Neda suspends belief thinking, 'Well, scientists sometimes get it wrong! I'll do my own research.'

Case #4. **Perceptual Non-responsiveness:** Alice is looking straight at the table in front of her and fails to form the belief that there's a table in front of her.

Case #5. **Unwarranted Optimism:** Mary is an optimist. When her partner Dan spends more and more evening hours at the office, she's happy that his career is going so well. When he comes home smelling like floral perfume, she thinks to herself: 'Wow, excellent taste in fragrance!' Finally, when she repeatedly sees him having coffee in town with his colleague Alice, she is glad he's making new friends.

Case #6. **Misdirected Attention:** Professor Racist is teaching college-level maths. He believes people of colour are less intelligent than white people. As a result, whenever he asks a question, his attention automatically goes to the white students, such that he doesn't even notice the Black students who raise their hands. As a result, he believes Black students are not very active in class.

Case #7. **Friendly Detective:** Detective Dave is investigating a crime scene. Dave is extremely thorough but, at the same time, a close friend of the butler. Dave finds conclusive evidence that the butler did it – the butler's gloves covered in blood, his fingerprints on the murder weapon, a letter written by the butler confessing to the crime – but he fails to form the corresponding belief: Dave just can't get himself to believe that his friend would do such a thing.

What is going on in these cases? Note that they involve very different sources of knowledge (e.g. testimony, perception, inductive inference) and that the failures at stake come about for very different reasons (e.g. prejudice, motivated reasoning, epistemic anxiety, lack of attention, partisanship, bias, wishful thinking). All of these are bad things, epistemically, in their own right. At the same time, the cases also have one important feature in common: for all these subjects, there is excellent evidence easily available to them, which they fail to take up.

Several philosophers have offered source-bound diagnoses of particular incarnations of this phenomenon (in terms of, e.g., epistemic injustice (Fricker 2007), disregard for the nature and/or normativity of telling (Moran 2006, Hazlett 2017), breach of norms of attention (Siegel 2017)), but very few have tried to offer an overarching explanation of what they all have in common. However, once we look at these cases together, it becomes clear that, on top of the case-specific problems, they plausibly exhibit a common variety of epistemic failure: resistance to easily available evidence.

1.2 The Social Psychology of Evidence Resistance

1.2.1 Evidence Resistance and Motivated Reasoning

A predominant hypothesis in social psychology (e.g. Lord et al. 1979, Taber and Lodge 2006, Molden and Higgins 2012, Kahan 2013, Kahan et al. 2016) that seeks to explain 'knowledge resistance' (i.e. resistance to acquiring easily available knowledge) principally does so with reference to politically motivated reasoning. Under the banner of this wider hypothesis, we find various research results that have been taken, in various ways, to support the view that a thinker's prior political convictions (including politically directed desires and attitudes about political group membership) best explain why they are inclined to reject expert consensus when they do (Kahan et al. 2011, Kahan 2013).

Early studies in the psychological literature that set the groundwork for this explanatory thesis focused initially on how political ideology influences the evaluation of evidence. For example, Lord et al. (1979) report a study in which subjects were provided with the same set of arguments for and against capital punishment and were asked to assess the strength of these arguments. Subjects' assessment of the strength of the arguments then strongly correlated with their existing views about the rights and wrongs of capital punishment. In short, subjects *already disposed* to object to capital punishment were more persuaded by the arguments against it, and the opposite was the case for those initially predisposed to favour capital punishment. (See also Kunda 1987 for discussion of how political ideology seems to have a bearing on causal inference patterns.)

A second wave of research in this area, led largely by Dan Kahan and his colleagues, has suggested that political ideology not only influences how we think about the persuasiveness of arguments for and against those ideologies themselves but also that our inclination to accept (or reject) scientific consensus across a range of areas is highly sensitive to what political ideology we already accept. For example, Kahan and his collaborators present studies aimed at demonstrating that background political ideology impacts whether we align with or go against expert consensus on topics ranging from global warming to the safety of nuclear power (Kahan et al. 2011, Kahan 2014, Kahan et al. 2016; cf. Carter and McKenna 2020).

In light of this second wave of research, the received thinking about resistance to evidence takes such resistance to be principally a manifestation of politically motivated reasoning (Kahan 2013).

This position, while widely discussed in social psychology, has received comparably less attention in philosophy. Furthermore, typically, philosophers who have discussed it have explored the consequences of this empirical hypothesis while taking its merits at face value (e.g. Ancell 2019, Carter and McKenna 2020).

However, on closer and recent inspection, the hypothesis is both empirically and epistemically problematic. Empirically, there are worries that, in extant studies, political group identity is often confounded with prior beliefs about the issue in question; and, crucially, reasoning can be affected by such beliefs in the absence of any political group motivation. This renders much existing evidence for the hypothesis ambiguous (Tappin et al. 2021).

Epistemologically, the worry is that the hypothesis is ineffective for making crucial distinctions among a number of phenomena, such as (1) concerning epistemic status: between epistemically impermissible resistance to evidence, on the one hand, and justified evidence rejection, on the other – after all, if the extant priors that are correlated with political group identity are justified priors and if evidence resistance is sourced in these justified priors rather than in motivated reasoning, we will have failed to distinguish justified evidence rejection from unjustified evidence resistance; and (2) concerning triggers: between instances of motivated reasoning, on the one hand, and epistemically deficient reasoning featuring cognitive ('cold') biases and unjustified premise beliefs, on the other.

Furthermore, difficulties in answering the question as to what triggers resistance to evidence have very significant negative impacts on our prospects of identifying the best ways to address this phenomenon and to avoid its unfortunate practical consequences. If resistance to evidence has one main source – for instance, a particular type of mistake in reasoning, such as motivated reasoning – the strategy to address this problem will be unidirectional and targeted mostly at the individual level. In contrast, should we discover that a pluralistic picture is more plausible when it comes to what triggers resistance to evidence – whereby this phenomenon is, for example, the result of a complex interaction between social, emotive, and cognitive phenomena – we would have to develop much more complex interventions at both individual and societal levels.

1.2.2 Evidence Resistance and Epistemic Vigilance

One noteworthy way in which knowledge resistance manifests is in the context of a hearer's receipt of testimony from a speaker. Two kinds of examples which have received particular attention include cases of (1) resistance to expert testimony (e.g. widespread resistance to scientific evidence about climate change, as well as during the onset of the COVID-19 pandemic; Kearney et al. 2020), and (2) resistance to testimony from marginalised groups, which provides the central point of reference in the literature on testimonial injustice (Fricker 2007). In both kinds of cases, the hearer's response to testimony is epistemically defective.

An important strand in the social psychology of testimonial knowledge transmission suggests that the above phenomena could be explained via the misfiring of an otherwise beneficial epistemic vigilance mechanism. Research by Dan Sperber and colleagues (2010) and related work by Hugo Mercier (2020) suggest that the risks that we as testimonial recipients face in being accidentally or intentionally misinformed are ones that we are well positioned to navigate via a suite of cognitive mechanisms of epistemic vigilance for sorting, sifting, and discerning information coming from other human beings (whether immediately or mediately). It is this suite of mechanisms that is postulated, on the epistemic vigilance programme, as important in explaining both the honesty of speakers and the reliability of their testimony.

If Sperber et al. (2010) and Mercier (2020) are right and we do benefit from a suite of mechanisms that make us epistemically vigilant, the phenomenon of resistance to evidence may be explained as an instance of misfiring of our epistemic vigilance mechanisms. If these vigilance mechanisms are misfiring, they will lead us to respond with distrust and disbelief when trust and belief are the appropriate responses. In this way, epistemic vigilance may lead to resistance to evidence. One explanation for this might lie with the fact that we now inhabit a very different epistemic environment from the environment that our mechanisms for epistemic vigilance evolved in: recent technological advances have placed us in the midst of information (and misinformation) overload. Since our cognitive mechanisms of vigilance, the thought would go, have not evolved in such a heavyweight informational environment, they are misfiring in an attempt to cope.

Yet, a wave of research on deception recognition paints a mostly pessimistic picture about the plausibility of the very existence of vigilance mechanisms in us. A wide range of studies testing our capacities for deception recognition show that we are very bad at it: our prospects of getting it right barely surpass chance (e.g. Kraut 1980, Vrij 2000, Bond and DePaulo 2006). To see just how well established this result is in the relevant psychological literature, consider the following telling passage from Levine et al. (1999, 126): 'the belief that deception detection accuracy rates are only slightly better than fifty-fifty is among the most well documented and commonly held conclusions in deception research'.

Crucially, it is not hard to see that if these studies are right and we detect deception with an accuracy rate that is barely above chance, both the hypothesis that we have evolved cognitive mechanisms for epistemic vigilance to help us secure the reliability of testimonial exchanges and the idea that resistance to evidence is the result of our vigilance mechanisms misfiring become rather implausible.

More recently, though, some voices in the deception detection literature have grown disenchanted with the received view on the issue. In particular, J. Pete Blair et al. (2010) argue that the past forty years of research in deception detection have neglected the role of contextual clues. According to them, accuracies significantly higher than chance can be consistently achieved when hearers are given access to meaningful contextual information. On the face of it, this seems like it might be the sort of result vigilance champions need to establish that the vigilance mechanisms make the needed difference for testimonial entitlement (i.e. by increasing reliability). The vigilance mechanisms, the thought would go, have evolved to work in conjunction with the contextual information Blair et al. discuss.

Unfortunately, though, upon closer examination, these results will not do the trick for the epistemic vigilance champion. To see why, it is important to look more closely at the type of contextual information that has been given to the subjects for the purposes of this study and ask the question: 'How plausible is it that this kind of information (i.e. information that is shown to increase reliability in deception detection) is the kind of information that, when had, would still require us to have extra input from our vigilance mechanisms given the context?' After all, if the study gives information such as 'This is a reliable testifier', this is the kind of information that seems to justify testimonial belief on its own – it's simply evidence that the testifier is telling the truth. Conversely, if the study provides the subject with evidence that the testifier in question is unreliable, again, one need not host epistemic vigilance mechanisms in order to justifiably withhold belief.

The Blair et al. study identifies three types of what they dub 'contextual content' that raise the success rates for deception detection (2010, 424–425): (1) contradictory content – for example, a testifier claims to have been at home on a given night, but the hearer is told by a trusted source that she saw the testifier out at a restaurant on the night in question; it is likely that the testifier's statements will be flagged as deceptive; (2) statistically normal content – for example, knowledge about the testifier's normal activities; if the testifier's statements or performance are implausible given this statistically normal information, the statements are more likely to be flagged as potentially deceptive; and (3) information that increases the perceived probability of deceit – for example, a situation in which a number of shortages have occurred at a bank, but the shortages stop when one of the employees goes on vacation and begin again when the employee returns; this information may cause an interviewer to believe that the employee's statements are deceptive.

These results are, of course, hardly surprising, either empirically or epistemologically: it seems trivially true that, if given the right kind and amount of contextual information in advance, most of us should be and are able to go so far as to be impeccable deception detectors on mere garden-variety epistemic grounds – no extra mechanisms needed. As a limit case, if I know in advance that everybody is lying, for instance, I will likely be very good – indeed, infallible – at detecting deceit. What matters for us here, however, is whether the kind of information that does the trick in the study at hand is the kind of information that would plausibly increase the general reliability of our vigilance mechanisms rather than deliver sufficient evidence for/against a particular piece of testimony on its own. The plausible answer, however, I contend, is clearly the latter: no special vigilance-like psychological skills are required in these cases, as the evidence is enough to justify the response. Furthermore, and interestingly, one out of three Blair et al. experiments failed to confirm their hypothesis (2010, 427): this was the experiment that gave participants the most limited and subtle contextual information. Thus, the experiment that most closely resembled a garden-variety testimonial exchange, where the hearer does not have a whole lot of antecedent knowledge about the speaker, failed to deliver high rates of successful deceit detection. This, again, does no look very promising for the vigilance hypothesis.

If this is right – if the hypothesis that we host special epistemic vigilance mechanisms is implausible to begin with – then the hypothesis that instances of resistance to evidence are instances of our vigilance mechanisms misfiring remains unvindicated as well.

1.3 Rejecting Evidence: A Taxonomy

What we have seen so far is that the extant research on evidence resistance suffers from both empirical and epistemological shortcomings in identifying the triggers behind the target phenomenon: on the one hand, epistemologically, we need to distinguish between unjustified evidence resistance – sourced in all kinds of epistemically impermissible belief/suspension formation, such as motivated reasonings, biases, etc. – and epistemically justified evidence rejection – sourced in justified prior beliefs. On the other hand, even when zooming in on epistemically problematic instances of the phenomenon it is not clear how much evidence resistance is sourced in cold rather than hot biases or in updating on unjustified priors rather than biases.

These difficulties in answering the question as to what triggers resistance to evidence have, in turn, very significant negative impacts on our prospects of identifying the best ways to address resistance to evidence. If resistance to evidence has one main source – for instance, a particular type of mistake in reasoning, such as motivated reasoning – the strategy to address this problem will be targeted at the individual level. In contrast, should we discover that a pluralistic picture is more plausible when it comes to what triggers resistance to evidence, we would have to develop much more complex interventions at both individual and societal levels. Finally, if it turns out that the vast majority of instances of alleged evidence resistance are actually explained by epistemically justified evidence rejection – say, because cognisers find themselves in environments polluted with misleading defeaters for the evidence at stake – our interventions should only target the relevant epistemic environment rather than any particular cogniser or belief-formation mechanisms.

Of course, the question as to what is actually happening, on the ground, in evidence-resistant communities and individuals is to be answered by careful, epistemologically informed empirical studies. It is not my ambition to settle this question from the armchair – nor should any epistemologist attempt to do so.

The ambition of this book is to offer the first epistemology of evidence resistance that can inform future empirical studies on the topic. To this effect, I will start by putting forth in Table 1.1 a simple taxonomy of the phenomenon in order to isolate the epistemically problematic instances that we are interested in.

In theory and practice, it is crucial, before undergoing an epistemological analysis of problematic cases of evidence resistance and before testing an empirical hypothesis having to do with the instantiation of this problematic phenomenon in a particular community, to first distinguish evidence resistance from its epistemically benign cousin: justified evidence rejection. One reason why this is crucial has to do with addressing the phenomenon in policy and practice: depending on whether we are dealing with justified evidence rejection or epistemically impermissible evidence resistance, different interventions are warranted. For combatting epistemically justified evidence rejection, engineering enhanced social epistemic environments should do the trick: since we are dealing with reliably epistemically responsive agents, we can rely on them to update in line with a non-polluted epistemic environment. This will likely require combatting rebutting defeaters via evidence flooding: evidence-resistant communities, inhabiting polluted epistemic environments, cannot be reached via the average communication strategies designed to reach the mainstream population inhabiting a friendly epistemic environment (with little to no misleading evidence). What is required is quantitatively enhanced reliable evidence flow (more evidence in favour of the scientifically well-supported facts will, in rational agents, work to outweigh the misleading evidence they have against the facts), as well as qualitatively enhanced reliable evidence flow (evidence from sources that the agent trusts – that are trustworthy vis-à-vis the agent's environment). Furthermore, to combat mistrust in reliable sources, quantitatively and qualitatively enhanced evidence aimed at combatting undercutting defeat (misleading evidence against the trustworthiness of reliable sources) will be needed. One straightforward way to do this is by flooding evidence-resistant communities with evidence from sources they trust in favour of the trustworthiness of sources they fail to trust due to misleading undercutting defeaters.

Table 1.1 *Evidence rejection: a taxonomy*

Evidence rejection							
Epistemically justified				Epistemically unjustified (*evidence resistance*)			
Via rebutting epistemic defeat		Via undercutting epistemic defeat		Via unjustified doxastic defeat		Independent of doxastic defeat	
Misleading	Not misleading	Misleading	Not misleading	Via proper updating	Via improper updating	One-off/ isolated	Dispositional
							Sourced in cold bias / Sourced in hot bias

In contrast, for combatting cases of unjustified evidence resistance agent-based interventions will be needed: for example, increasing the availability of cognitive flexibility training (e.g. in workplaces and schools, alongside anti-bias training) will be among the more efficient interventions. Cognitive flexibility training helps with enhancing open-mindedness to evidence that runs against one's held beliefs and to alternative decision pathways (Garner 2009, Griffin et al. 2012).

1.3.1 Justified Evidence Rejection

Let's take the science sceptic case as our toy case to illustrate. In the original variation of the case, of course, Neda was evidence resistant *tout court* due to her epistemic anxiety. The point I am trying to impress on you, however, with the above taxonomy, is that not all science sceptics need be like Neda: they need not be unjustifiably nor irrationally rejecting scientific evidence. A science sceptic Neda* could be rejecting scientific testimony about, for example, the safety of vaccines because her environment is polluted with misleading defeaters: say, she lives in a community where an overwhelming majority of testimony that she gets suggests that vaccines are not safe. Say, also, that these testifiers are otherwise reliable testifiers, with an impeccable track record (who just happen to get things wrong on this particular occasion – after all, reliability does not imply infallibility): whenever, in the past, Neda* relied on their say-so, she was not disappointed. By any account of testimonial justification in the literature, in this variation of the case Neda is justified to believe vaccines are not safe: according to anti-reductionism, this is because she has no defeaters to this testimony; according to reductionists, this is because she has inductive evidence of the reliability of these testifiers (Leonard 2023).

If Neda* is justified to believe vaccines are not safe, then she has a (in this case misleading) rebutting defeater for the scientific testimony that vaccines are safe. The defeater need not be a full defeater: laymen testimony might not be heavy enough – epistemically – to outweigh expert testimony. But Neda* will have reason to lower her confidence in the safety of vaccines: her (partial) rejection of scientific evidence is epistemically justified.

This is a case of misleading defeat. Of course, defeat to scientific testimony, generating epistemically permissible evidence rejection, can also be non-misleading: consider a case in which vaccinating toddlers is recommended by the experts to the sole benefit of the population at large (for generating herd immunity), since toddlers are not vulnerable to the virus that the vaccine targets. At the same time, say that the vaccine is shown to have some side effects – albeit in very rare cases – the cause of which remains under-researched due to lack of funding: since these cases are rare, there is little incentive to invest in identifying the cause of the problem. Furthermore, say that Neda* is well aware of all of these facts, and thus she rejects scientific testimony that the vaccine is safe for her toddler and decides not to vaccinate him. This is a standard case of non-misleading rebutting defeat: Neda* is not only justified to reject the expert testimony that the vaccine is safe for her toddler; she is also, arguably, morally right to do so.

Justified evidence rejection need not only come through evidence against the proposition at stake (i.e. rebutting defeat). It can come about – and most often, I believe, it does come about – from undercutting defeat: reason to believe the expert source is not trustworthy. Consider again vaccine scepticism: sociological studies investigating vaccine hesitancy in Black and Caribbean communities in the UK, for instance, suggest that distrust in the safety of vaccines ultimately boils down to distrust of the National Health Service and medical science (Adekola et al. 2022). The thought is, in a nutshell, that a solid inductive basis suggests that the interests of these communities are not forefront concerns of these actors: historically, for instance, new medicines are not often tested on Black subjects before being commercialised. If so, this inductive evidence constitutes itself in undercutting defeat to the expert testimony in question. And, again, while undercutting defeat is often misleading when it comes to scientific expert testimony, it need not be such.

The above are ways in one can epistemically justifiably (partially or fully) reject evidence from highly reliable sources. These instances (i.e. instances of justified evidence rejection) will not make up the subject of this book. Likely, though, these will be the most ubiquitous instances on the ground: we are highly reliable cognitive machines. Bracketing very isolated cases of biased and heuristics-based cognition (which are often biological adaptations themselves), we are very good at responding to our epistemic environment: one can see this from the fantastic practical successes we enjoy as a species, which would not be possible without the associated epistemic high performance.

1.3.2 Evidence Resistance

Evidence resistance is an oddball in our species' cognitive life. As I will argue, it is an instance of epistemic malfunction of our cognitive system – similar to other input-level malfunctions occurring in other biological traits.

On a first approximation, evidence resistance can occur either in virtue of doxastic defeat or independently of it. Doxastic defeat (also sometimes referred to as psychological defeat in the literature) is defeat that lacks epistemic normative power but induces belief loss or downwards confidence adjustment nevertheless. The paradigmatic case of this has to do with proper updating on unjustified priors: I unjustifiably believe that all vaccines are unsafe and update accordingly to 'the COVID vaccine is not safe'. Some equate proper updating with rationality, in virtue of the epistemic value of coherence; most, however, shy away from offering such epistemic praise to cognisers who are fully coherent but completely disconnected from reality: take the perfectly coherent Nazi, for instance. Are we comfortable to call them perfectly rational? I would personally prefer to assign positive evaluative properties to a slightly incoherent version thereof – on both epistemic and moral grounds.

As the reader might have already guessed, my preference lies squarely with the second camp – the one that doesn't attribute much epistemic value to coherence alone and thus is sceptical about taking proper updating to be the mark of rationality. Not much will hinge on this for the rest of this book though. If impatient to read the relevant discussion, the reader can skip to Chapter 11.

Importantly, doxastic defeat need not occur via proper updating: improper updating is also an option (i.e. giving extant priors more evidential weight than they would deserve, even were they to be justified). Anchoring bias in all of its incarnations is a paradigmatic case.

Finally, evidence resistance need not be the result of updating at all – be it proper or improper. One such non-doxastically sourced, less common, and most simple variety can be an unexplained one-off instance of evidence resistance: maybe I'm looking straight at the table in front of me and, due to tiredness or lack of focus, I fail to notice the cup lying on it in plain view. Or say that I am very depressed and thus find it impossible to update on all of the evidence that my life is going really well.

Most commonly, though, non-doxastically sourced evidence resistance will be sourced in some variety of bias. Biases come in various shapes, and they can present as cognitive ('cold') biases (e.g. mental noise, heuristics) or motivational ('hot') biases (e.g. wishful thinking). To be clear, in many instances this variety of evidence resistance will be biologically beneficial, evolved in virtue of its biological benefits, and thus arguably practically rational. Compatibly, though, biased reasoning is epistemically deficient reasoning. Testimonial injustice is a paradigmatic case of evidence resistance due to bias: the hearer fails to give the testifier the level of credibility that she deserves in virtue of a sexist bias that leads them to downgrade them as a testifier.

1.4 Conclusion

This chapter has done two main things: first, I looked at some of the recent literature on evidence resistance in social psychology, and I have argued that it misses important epistemological distinctions – such as, crucially, the distinction between epistemically justified evidence rejection and epistemically impermissible evidence resistance. I have then put forth a taxonomy of evidence rejection to help with isolating the problematic instances thereof, which will be my concern in the remainder of this book. In the following chapters, I will zoom in on evidence resistance and investigate the epistemological resources we need in order to explain its epistemic impermissibility.

CHAPTER 2

Evidence One Has and the Impermissibility of Resistance

The chapter argues that the main extant views of the nature of evidence one has lack the resources to account for the impermissibility of cases of resistance to evidence. I first examine classic internalist, seemings-based evidentialism and argue that it fails to account for evidence resistance. This, I argue, is an in-principle problem: internalist evidentialism cannot recover from this *because* it is internalist.

I move on to externalist views of evidence, starting with factive externalism (i.e. Williamson's (2000) evidence is knowledge (E = K)), and I argue that, since resistant cognisers don't take up the relevant facts in the world to begin with, the view fails to predict epistemic impermissibility in resistance cases. I also look at and dismiss several ways in which the champion of E = K might attempt to account for what's going wrong in resistance cases (i.e. via employing notions such as epistemic dispositions one should have had and epistemic blameworthiness), and I argue that the view faces difficulties. Finally, I move on to less radical, non-factive externalisms and investigate the potential of prominent reliabilist views – indicator reliabilism (Comesaña 2020) and virtue reliabilism (Turri 2010, Sylvan and Sosa 2018, Sosa 2021) – to account for the phenomenon of resistance. I argue that these views are too agent-centric to successfully account for resistance cases.

2.1 Evidence Internalism

Evidence matters: the concept of evidence is central to epistemology, the philosophy of science, the philosophy of law, the ethics of responsibility. Outside philosophy, the concept of evidence is highly employed as well: lawyers, judges, historians, scientists, economists, investigative journalists, and reporters, as well as ordinary folk in the course of everyday life, talk and think about evidence a lot.

Both within and outside of philosophy, what we care most about is not just the nature of evidence alone, but rather what it is for a subject to *have* evidence. We care, as it were, about evidence had. That makes sense in philosophy because we are interested in the quality of our beliefs and our actions, and the latter will mostly be affected by the evidence we have. Outside of philosophy, evidence one has bears relevance to one's legal status, professional performance, decisions, policies, voting, plans, etc. Evidence one has, the thought goes, but less so evidence one does not have, will influence all of one's walks of life.

It is interesting to note – in line with the main scholarly source on the nature of evidence, the *Stanford Encyclopedia of Philosophy* article on the issue (Kelly 2016) – that the ways in which we think of evidence outside and within philosophy are strongly incompatible with each other. In philosophy, we disagree a lot about the nature of evidence, but one thing that the vast majority of theorists have always assumed is that the having relation is somehow related to the limits of one's skull: one has evidence, on this received view, when one uptakes it 'in one's head' – be it via seemings, beliefs, knowings, etc. In contrast, outside of philosophy, the having relation has never been about the skull: just try to tell a judge that you had no evidence that the butler did it, even though he did it right in front of you, because you couldn't believe your eyes; see how that goes down.

Of course, one might think, what's the surprise there? Experts know best in all domains – that's what semantic externalism teaches – and philosophy is not an exception. The way in which us laymen conceptualise 'depression' is likely different from the way in which psychiatrists do; that's fine, we're wrong, and the experts are right. The same goes for evidence one has.

In what follows, I will argue that this way of thinking about the issue at hand is mistaken: in particular, I will propose that the philosophical conception of the having relation – as having to do with the limits of one's skull – fails on extensional grounds – having to do with failing to account for the impermissibility of evidence resistance – and, as a result, it also fails to fulfil its central function in predicting accountability and legal responsibility.

Let's start with a classic: according to internalist evidentialist, phenomenal conceptions of evidence, a subject S's evidence consists (roughly) in what it seems to S to be the case. This view has a notable tradition: Russell, for instance, thought of evidence as *sense data*, mental items of one's present consciousness with which one is immediately acquainted. Similarly, Quine thought that evidence consisted of the stimulation of one's sensory receptors. Finally, and more recently, according to Connee and Feldman (2004), one's evidence consists exclusively of one's current mental states.

The view accommodates our intuition in New Evil Daemon cases: the recently envatted brain-in-a-vat version of myself, the thought goes, is, intuitively, just as justified as I am to believe that she's typing on her laptop right now. An evidentialist account of justification, in conjunction with a phenomenal view of evidence, vindicates this intuition.

A classic problem, however, for this way of thinking has to do with seemings with bad etiologies: sometimes, our seemings are based in wishful thinking and racial bias rather than proper cognitive mechanisms. When this happens, the phenomenal conception predicts – against intuition – that we have evidence for our corresponding beliefs. In turn, this problem renders the phenomenal conception of evidence incapable to distinguish between epistemically permissible evidence rejection and problematic evidence resistance. Take the science sceptic Neda again: in the good case, it seems to Neda that vaccines are unsafe because of reliable testimony that they are unsafe. In the bad case, her seemings are sourced in an irrational fear of needles. The phenomenal conception of evidence has trouble distinguishing between the good and the bad cases.

2.2 E = K

According to the prominent, knowledge-first view of having evidence (Williamson 2000), for any subject S, S's evidence is S's knowledge. Since knowledge implies belief, and since all of the protagonists in Cases 1–7 from Chapter 1 lack the relevant beliefs, E = K will predict that the subjects in question lack evidence: for example, Bill, the fervent supporter of President Dump, does not believe, and therefore does not know, that Dump is a bad president; furthermore, he does not believe, and therefore does not know, any of the statements by the media, etc., that suggest as much, and thus, on this view, he has no evidence that Dump is a bad president. And the same will hold for all of the protagonists of Cases 1–7. In this, E = K cannot make good on the resistance intuition – at least not when unpacked as resistance to evidence one has. Furthermore, several knowledge-first theorists explicitly embrace this result: according to people like Hawthorne and Srinivasan (2013), for instance, short of knowing, one should withhold belief.

One alternative way to account for our cases within an E = K framework would be by employing the notion of being in a position to know in order to account for evidence that is easily available but not possessed by the agent. Plausibly, the thought would go, the Dump supporter is in a position to know that Dump is a bad president: that's what explains our intuition that he's failing epistemically when he fails to form the corresponding belief.

Of course, a lot will hinge on how the relevant notion of 'being in a position to know' is spelled out: importantly, the relevant notion should be E = K-friendly (i.e. it should be compatible with the thought that evidence one has amounts to knowledge). Consider, first, a view on which I am in a position to know that p if and only if there is evidence for p available to me, and evidence is available to one just in case it consists of facts that follow from or are made probable by one's extant knowledge. On this view, Bill is in a position to know p: 'Dump is a bad president' in virtue of the fact that it follows from his other extant knowledge – such as his knowledge that presidents shouldn't lie, shouldn't make racist and sexist comments, etc., together with his knowledge that Dump engages often in all of the above.

Unfortunately, this view will not deliver the needed result if we describe the case as one in which Bill's system of (false) beliefs about Dump being a great president is perfectly coherent (in that Bill either doesn't believe that lying, etc., are bad or doesn't believe Dump lies, etc.), although unjustified: p will not follow from any piece of knowledge Bill has. To bring this point into even sharper relief, consider also the Perceptual Non-responsiveness case: what is the relevant piece of knowledge here?[1]

Here is one alternative E = K-friendly way to unpack being in a position to know: S is in a position to know that p if and only if, were S to believe that p, S would know that p. Bill, then, on this account, is in a position to know that Dump is a bad president if and only if, were he to form the relevant belief, he would come to know that Dump is a bad president.[2]

The problem with this account is that if, on the one hand, we keep Bill's psychology otherwise fixed, and all that changes is his forming the relevant belief, it will fail to constitute knowledge in virtue of its acute incoherence with the rest of his belief system. On the other hand, if, in order to assess Bill's actual epistemic situation, we go and look at the closest world where Bill's psychology is radically different, such that, indeed, were he to form

---

[1] The view should also be rejected on independent grounds for being too liberal about available evidence. The view predicts, for instance, that all arithmetical truths constitute evidence available to me, in virtue of the fact that they follow from Peano axioms, which I know. I find this flattering but highly implausible.
[2] Thanks to Carlotta Pavese for suggesting this route to me.

the belief that Dump is a bad president, it would constitute knowledge, our account of being in a position to know becomes too strong.[3] To see this, consider Alvin Goldman's (1988) benighted cogniser – let us call him Ben. This fellow lives on a secluded island where he's been taught that reading astrology is an excellent way to form beliefs and where he has no access to any clue to the contrary. Plausibly, there is no evidence available to Ben for *p*: 'astrology is an unreliable way to form beliefs', nor is he in a position to know it. However, at the closest world where things are different enough (say that Ben leaves his benighted community), such that now he believes the relevant proposition, he knows it. As such, the account construed along these lines will mistakenly place Ben in the same boat as the Case 1–7 protagonists, in spite of the fact that Ben has no way to access information of the unreliability of astrology.

One last move available to the defender of E = K is to argue that what is present in Cases 1–7 and explains resistance intuition is *potential* evidence: evidence that Bill, the Dump supporter, would have had, had he not had bad epistemic dispositions.[4] Since, plausibly, one should have good epistemic dispositions rather than bad epistemic dispositions, the view predicts that Bill is in breach of an epistemic 'should'. Williamson (2000, 95 and in conversation) gestures at a view like this.

One important problem with this move, however, is that it is both too weak and too strong.

To see why the view is too weak, note that a version of the E = K account thus construed will miss an important distinction between synchronic and diachronic epistemic shoulds: the distinction between the synchronic 'should' of epistemic justification and the diachronic 'should' of responsibility in inquiry.[5] Proceeding responsibly in inquiry (e.g. thoroughly searching for evidence diachronically) is one thing; synchronically responding well to available evidence is another. However, both are governed by epistemic shoulds.[6]

To see this, think back to the Friendly Detective case. Say that, this time around, Dave is investigating the crime scene with his colleague, Greg. Greg is rather lazy and distracted: he briefly looks around, fails to find any evidence at the crime scene, and concludes that there's no evidence to

---

[3] Thanks to Amia Srinivasan for suggesting this route to me.
[4] Thanks to Tim Williamson for suggesting this route to me.
[5] For excellent work on the nature and normativity of inquiry, see Friedman (2017) and Kelp (2021).
[6] Ernie Sosa (2021) helpfully distinguishes between *narrow-scope*: (forbearing from X'ing) in the endeavour to attain a given aim A; and *broad-scope*: forbearing from (X'ing in the endeavour to attain a given aim A).

suggest that the butler did it. In contrast, Dave is extremely thorough, but, at the same time, a close friend of the butler. Dave finds conclusive evidence that the butler did it at the crime scene but fails to form the corresponding belief.

I submit that both Dave and Greg are rather rubbish detectives, in that they fail to conduct their inquiry well – they are both in breach of the diachronic epistemic should of inquiry. Also, both Dave and Greg display pretty bad epistemic dispositions: Greg is a sloppy epistemic agent, while Dave fails to believe what the evidence supports. Compatibly, I submit, there is an important epistemic difference between Dave and Greg: Dave, but not Greg, is aware of all of the evidence in support of the hypothesis that the butler did it and fails to form the relevant belief nevertheless; Dave is resistant to available evidence.

The view, then, is too coarse grained to do the work needed to account for this datum. What is needed is a principled way to identify the epistemic dispositions and the corresponding epistemic should that matter in resistance cases.

To see why the view is also too strong, note that one need not have bad epistemic dispositions in order to fail, epistemically, in the way in which, for example, Bill, the Dump supporter, does: it can be a one-off affair. Maybe Bill is an excellent epistemic agent in all other walks of life: it's only this particular belief – that Dump is a bad president – that he refuses to form against all facts speaking in favour of it.[7]

2.3 Reliable Indicators

We have seen that strong, factive externalism struggles to accommodate the resistance data. In what follows, I will look at non-factive, reliabilist externalisms, in search for the normative resources we need to this effect. In this section, I take on Juan Comesaña's (2010, 2020) reliabilist view of evidence. In the next section, I will look at virtue reliabilist (e.g. Sylvan and Sosa 2018, Sosa 2021) account of reasons to believe and Turri's virtue reliabilist account of propositional warrant.

It is surprising to see just how very few fully fledged non-factive externalist accounts of the nature of evidence and defeat are available in

---

[7] One way for Williamson to escape this problem is by making the view one that asks for the relevant dispositions not only to be present, but also to be exercised. Note, however, that, on any plausible view, our good epistemic dispositions are fallible – albeit reliable. If that is the case, one-off failures are predicted by the model even in cases in which the dispositions are manifest. The account, furthermore, would remain problematic in virtue of being too weak.

the literature. Comesaña's account is one that supplies this lack. The view falls squarely in-between the main camps on the market when it comes to the study of evidence: it is less demanding than factive views of evidence à la Williamson, in that, on Comesaña's account, one can have evidence that is false. It is, however, more demanding than internalist views, in that experiences will only provide their content as a reason for belief when belief in the content is ultima facie justified. In this, Comesaña's account promises both to reap the benefits of the main competitors and to avoid all of their downsides. To see this, consider the following case:

> **CANDY:** Tomás wants a candy, and so he grabs the candy-looking thing Lucas is offering him and puts it in his mouth. Tomás has no reason to think that there is anything amiss with Lucas's offer; he thinks that Lucas is genuinely being generous and sharing his Halloween bounty with him. However, what Lucas gave Tomás was no candy but a marble. Lucas himself is unaware of the fact that there is a candy-looking marble among the candy.

Understandably, Tomás is disappointed – but was he irrational in acting as he did? Juan Comesaña's answer is: obviously not. According to Comesaña, Tomás's action was rational because it was based on the rational belief that the candy-looking object Lucas was offering him was a candy. Tomás's belief was rational because it was based on evidence that, in Comesaña's view, is constituted by those propositions that Tomás is basically justified in believing by his experiences.

According to this account, then, an experience provides its content as a reason when the subject is justified in believing its content. The justification in question in the account, importantly, (1) is non-factive and (2) must be ultima facie: if an experience of the subject S provides them with prima facie justification for believing its content but this justification is defeated by something else S is justified in believing, then S does not have the content of the experience as evidence (Comesaña 2020, 119).

(Early) Comesaña favours a reliabilist account of justification. If coupled with his view of evidence, this will render the latter stronger than internalism about evidence, in that only those contents of experience that are believed based on a reliable process will qualify as evidence.

In contrast to E = K, the view accounts for the intuition of rationality in CANDY: Tomás's belief that Lucas is offering him candy will come out as justified and thereby as a proper part of his body of evidence. The view, when coupled with reliabilism about justification, also scores points over the internalist, in that it nicely accounts for a normative difference that we want our view of evidence to predict between Tomás and, for example, a wishful thinker or a biased cogniser: after all, wishful thinking and forming beliefs based on biases are not reliable processes, therefore the contents of the thus generated experiences will not constitute evidence.

At first glance, the account also promises to deliver the result we want in several of the resistance cases. Take, for one, Testimonial Injustice:

> **Case #1. Testimonial Injustice**: Anna is an extremely reliable testifier and an expert in the geography of Glasgow. She tells George that Glasgow Central is to the right. George believes women are not to be trusted; therefore, he fails to form the corresponding belief.

Since on the view under consideration an experience provides its content as a reason just in case the subject is justified in believing its content, and since, by stipulation, Anna is an extremely reliable testifier, the content of George's experience of her telling him that Glasgow Central is to the right constitutes evidence. Anna's testimony provides George with a reason to believe Glasgow Central is to the right, which he fails to take up. Similarly, the account correctly predicts that the Dump supporter has evidence that Dump is a bad president, which he ignores, that Mary has evidence that her husband is cheating, that the detective has evidence that the butler did it, etc. All of these people have experiences with the relevant contents that are reliably generated, the contents of which thus count as evidence on Comesaña's view.

Unfortunately, on closer inspection, it turns out that granting the indicator reliabilist success on resistance cases is a bit premature. In particular, as I'm about to argue, the reliabilist treatment of the case of Professor Racist (and, relatedly, of any cases with a similar structure; i.e. cases where no experience of the facts at stake is present) is problematic at two crucial junctures. Here is the case again for convenience:

> **Case #6. Misdirected Attention**: Professor Racist is teaching college-level maths. He believes people of colour are less intelligent than white people. As a result, whenever he asks a question, his attention automatically goes to the white students, such that he doesn't even notice the Black students who raise their hands. As a result, he believes Black students are not very active in class.

First, note that, against intuition, indicator reliabilism will predict that there is no evidence for Professor Racist that the Black students are active in class. After all, he has no experience with this particular content; therefore, he has no reliably generated experience with this content either. I take it that this is not a great result in itself. More generally, I take it, if our epistemology predicts that, simply because they ignore the facts, there is no evidence for racists and sexists that, for example, Black people and women are to be trusted, that they are deserving of good treatment, etc., we should probably go back to the drawing board.

Furthermore, note that the case of Professor Racist is not unique in this respect: we can modify all of the other cases along the exact same lines (i.e. ramping up the epistemically bad features) to get the same wrong predictions. Here is how: first, we can make it such that our characters not only don't form the relevant beliefs because of sexism, politically motivated reasoning, etc., but they don't even host the corresponding experiences. Say that George, for instance, in Testimonial Injustice, not only doesn't believe what Anna says, but he doesn't even register that she said anything at all due to his sexist bias: he just zones out when women speak. In all cases like these, contra intuition, indicator reliabilism will predict absence of evidence. Furthermore, the view now has the unpalatable consequence that tuning up epistemically bad properties can lead to an improvement in an agent's epistemic position. Making sexist George more sexist such that he not only discounts the female passer-by's words, but he doesn't even listen to her when she kindly provides him with directions to the Glasgow Central will amount to an improvement in his overall epistemic state. I find this consequence highly problematic.

Second, consider a variation of the case in which sexist George systematically mishears what he is being told by female speakers in general, such that whenever he encounters disagreement, he hears agreement. It is perhaps even harder to believe that this trait should lead to an improvement in his epistemic position towards the relevant propositions.

Third, note that we can now even drop the gender-discriminatory component of the case. We may suppose that George simply mistakes disagreement *by anyone* for agreement. Again, it's implausible that, as a result, George should be insulated from epistemic normativity: clearly, George is not justified in his beliefs.

2.4 Virtuous Reasons

This section investigates whether virtue epistemology has the resources needed to account for what is going wrong in Cases 1–7. For the most part, virtue epistemologists distance themselves from talk of evidence. However, they have other resources that they could employ to explain what is going wrong in Cases 1–7: the market features well-developed virtue-theoretic views of reasons to believe (Burge 2013, Sylvan and Sosa 2018) and propositional warrant (Turri 2010). According to these authors, broadly speaking, competences come first in epistemic normativity. I will examine these accounts in turn.

According to Kurt Sylvan and Ernie Sosa (2018), a fact is an epistemic reason to believe for S just in case it is competently taken up and processed by S. At root, then, reliable epistemic competence is doing the epistemic warranting work, even when reasons are involved. The only way in which a reason can have any epistemic normative standing is if it is competently taken up and processed by the agent: "[We] think [...] claims [about reasons supporting a species of justified belief] could only be true if possession and proper basing are themselves grounded in a deeper normative property of competence" (Sylvan and Sosa 2018, p. 557).

In turn, epistemic competences are traditionally unpacked as dispositions to believe truly (Sosa 2016) or know (Miracchi 2015, Kelp 2018, Schellenberg 2018).

The view, whether construed along truth-first or knowledge-first lines, is too weak to account for what is going wrong in cases of resistance to evidence: Think back to the case of Bill, the Dump supporter; on this view, we get the result that there are no reasons for Bill to believe that Dump is a bad president, since he is not uptaking the relevant facts (i.e. media testimony, Dump's own actions, etc.) via his cognitive competences. The same will hold for all of Cases 1–7: there will be no epistemic reasons for sexist and racist subjects to believe women and Black people; there will be no reason for Alice to believe that there is a table right in front of her; there will be no reason for Mary to believe that her partner is cheating; and finally, there will be no reason for Detective Dave to believe that the butler did it. All of these facts fail to constitute epistemic reasons on this view, since they are not competently processed by the subjects.

But can't the virtue theorist appeal to these epistemic agents' lack of competence to explain the poor epistemic status of beliefs that they do hold and account thereby for the impermissibility intuition?[8] For instance, can't the virtue theorist argue that what is going on in cases like Political Negligence is that Bill is an epistemically incompetent believer, which results in him not being justified in his belief that Dump is a good president. This, the virtue theorist may argue, is enough to explain the intuition of epistemic impermissibility; we don't also need to predict that there are reasons for Bill to believe that Dump is a bad president.

Two things should be said about this: first, note that it need not be that Bill is a rubbish epistemic agent overall. Indeed, maybe Bill is actually an

---

[8] Many thanks to Ernie Sosa for suggesting this route to me.

extremely reliable believer, including about political matters. It's only on this particular instance that he gets it wrong (after all, competences need not be infallible but merely reliable; thereby, their presence and manifestation are compatible with occasional failures). If so, the virtue theorist cannot appeal to lack of competence to explain this datum.

Second, I take it that it is independently problematic if a view predicts that there are no reasons for Bill to believe that Dump is a bad president; that is, independently of the epistemic status of his belief that Dump is a good president. To see this, consider a variation of the case in which Bill just doesn't have any belief on the issue, in spite of all the media reports, Dump's own actions, etc. It still seems as though there is something epistemically impermissible about Bill's doxastic behaviour. However, since Bill is not forming any belief on the matter of Dump's fitness for office, he isn't forming any incompetent belief either.

One way to go for the virtue theorist here would be to blame the impermissibility on the availability of propositional warrant. The thought would go something along the following lines: what triggers the resistance intuition has to do with warrant that one has but that one fails to update on.

Unfortunately, resistance cases also generate problems for the virtue-theoretic view of propositional warrant, and for pretty much the same reason why they generate problems for virtue-theoretic accounts of reasons: because virtues come first in the relevant analysis. According to John Turri, for all p, p is propositionally warranted for a subject S iff S possesses at least one means to come to believe p such that, were S to form the relevant belief via one of these means, S's belief would be doxastically warranted. In turn, doxastic warrant is unpacked in terms of epistemic competence: S is doxastically warranted to believe p iff S's belief is the product of a reliable belief-formation competence of S's.

On this view, since sexists, racists, and wishful thinkers are, by definition, people who lack the dispositions to form true or knowledgeable beliefs on the relevant issues, we get the counterintuitive result that these subjects lack propositional warrant and thus are not doing anything wrong, epistemically, in not forming the relevant beliefs.[9]

---

[9] Turri sees the worry and proposes an error theory: according to him, there are times when we attribute propositional warrant based on what the agent themself has the ability to believe and times when we do so based on what the *type* of agent at stake has the ability to believe. I don't think an error theory will do the work here: on pain of prior implausibility, we don't want to say that, merely in virtue of the fact that you are a vicious or incompetent believer, you are exempt from the normative pressure of available evidence.

What are we to do? Here is one move the virtue theorist might want to make here: dispositions can fail to manifest themselves when 'masked.' Consider the fragility of a vase. When in a room filled with pillows, the vase is still fragile, although its disposition to break cannot manifest itself. Similarly, virtue theorists could argue, Bill has an epistemic ability to form the relevant true belief about Dump, but it's 'masked' by the presence of many incompatible – though false – beliefs about Dump. Similarly, sexist George's epistemic competences are masked by his sexism, Professor Racist's by his racism, and so on.

There are two problems with this move, however. First, the view thus construed overgeneralises, for it, once more, threatens to mistakenly place Goldman's benighted cogniser and the protagonists of Cases 1–7 in the same epistemic boat. After all, Ben the benighted cogniser is the straightforward epistemic counterpart of a vase in a room full of pillows: were he to move to a friendlier epistemic environment, he would employ the right kinds of methods of belief formation. In this, he has a masked disposition to do well, epistemically.

Second, factors that 'mask' dispositions are commonly believed to be environmental factors (Choi and Fara 2018) – recall again the vase in the room full of pillows – rather than factors somehow 'internal' to the item in question; indeed, when the problem lies within the object itself – say that we inject all of the pores of the vase with glue, for instance – the more plausible diagnosis is lack of disposition – no fragility – rather than masked disposition. However, in many of the Cases 1–7, it is the subject's own mental state (biases, wishful thinking, etc.) that interferes in the formation of the relevant beliefs.[10]

In a nutshell, then, since the virtue theorist conceives of epistemic normativity as sourced in an agent's competences, and since Cases 1–7 are cases of incompetent belief formation by stipulation, the virtue theorist has difficulties explaining the datum at hand.[11]

2.5 Conclusion

This chapter has examined the prospects of some of the most popular contemporary internalist and externalist theories of evidence, reasons to

---

[10] What the literature on dispositions dubs 'intrinsic finks' might deserve investigation as a better way to go here (see Choi and Fara 2018).
[11] But see Christoph Kelp (2022) for a virtue-theoretic account of normative defeat in terms of epistemic proficiencies that carries promise when it comes to dealing with resistance cases.

believe, and propositional warrant to account for what is going wrong in cases of resistance to evidence. I have first argued that evidence internalism suffers from in-principle difficulties. Further on, I have shown that the belief condition on evidence possession generates inescapable difficulties for the E = K view, according to which one's evidence is one's knowledge. Still further on, I looked into indicator reliabilism, and I found that it lacks the normative resources needed to explain resistance to evidence as it predicts – against intuition – that biased cognisers lack evidence speaking against their biased beliefs just in virtue of dogmatically ignoring it. Finally, I have examined virtue epistemological accounts of reasons and propositional warrant, and I found a common culprit that prevents these accounts from accommodating impermissible resistance to evidence: on these views, epistemic virtues constitute the bedrock of epistemic normativity. Unsurprisingly, when virtues are missing or inactive in the case at stake, there are no normative resources available to explain epistemic impermissibility. Since that is precisely what is the case in resistance cases, I have argued, virtue epistemology is too agent-centric to accommodate the phenomenon we are discussing.

CHAPTER 3

Evidence You Should Have Had and Resistance

This chapter considers one popular way to account for cases of resistance as cases of evidence one *should have had*, where the normative failure at stake is taken to be either (1) a breach of social normativity (Goldberg 2018) or (2) a breach of moral normativity (Feldman 2004). I argue that the social normative option is too weak, in that it allows problematic social norms to encroach on epistemic normativity, and that the appeal to moral oughts fails both on theoretical grounds – in that it cannot accommodate widely accepted epistemic conditions on moral blame – and on extensional adequacy.

3.1 The Social 'Should'

In recent work, Sandy Goldberg has taken up the task of developing an account of the normativity of evidence one should have had and normative defeat. One key thought that motivates Goldberg's project is that social roles – for instance, being a medical doctor – come with normative expectations. These normative expectations may be, and often enough are, epistemic. For instance, there is a social epistemic expectation that medical doctors are up to speed on the relevant literature in their field. Another key thought is that to believe that *p* justifiably one must live up to all of these legitimate expectations. Doctors who fail to be up to speed with the most recent research in their field are not justified in their corresponding beliefs, in virtue of being in breach of the social expectation associated with their role. For instance, a doctor who believes that stomach ulcers are caused by stress, in ignorance of the widely available evidence that suggests that they are caused by bacteria, is not justified to believe that ulcers are caused by stress. As such, Goldberg grounds the normativity of evidence one should have had in the social expectations associated with the believer in question's social role.

It is easy to see that Goldberg's key thoughts promise to give us the ideal resources to handle cases of resistance to evidence. Take, for instance, the case of Professor Racist from Chapter 1. Recall that this fellow is biased against people of colour, and, as a result, whenever he asks a question, his attention automatically goes to the white students, such that he doesn't even notice the Black students who raise their hands. In virtue of occupying his social role, by the first key thought, Professor Racist is subject to normative expectations that are associated with this social role. In particular, he is subject to the expectation to fairly distribute his care and attention in the student population. Since Professor Racist doesn't live up to this expectation, by the second key thought, he does not believe justifiably that the Black students are not active in his class.

This is a very rough description of how Goldberg aims to deal with the kind of cases of resistance to evidence that we are concerned with here. Even so, here is a worry that arises immediately: social expectations can be legitimate social expectations, but also illegitimate social expectations. Women, for instance, are often illegitimately expected to carry most of the household burden and to underperform in leadership roles. If so, it would seem as though social expectations cannot play the normative grounding role that Goldberg wants them to play, since they seem to require further normative unpacking themselves: we seem to need further normative notions to help distinguish between epistemically legitimate and epistemically illegitimate social expectations.

If so, the question that arises is: aren't the social epistemic expectations that Goldberg appeals to in order to explain intuitive epistemic failure grounded in epistemic norms? And if so, won't we have to invoke the relevant epistemic norms in the final analysis of what goes wrong in cases of resistance to evidence? As a result, doesn't Goldberg's story remain very much at the surface, too much so to offer a satisfactory account of resistance cases?

To see why one might think this, suppose that social epistemic expectations are grounded in epistemic norms. If so, the reason why there is a social epistemic expectation that doctors be up to speed with the literature is grounded in an epistemic norm that applies to doctors and that requires them to be up to speed with the literature. Crucially, however, it is precisely these epistemic norms that we need to explain if we are to give a satisfactory account of the epistemic impermissibility of resistance to evidence. It may appear, then, that Goldberg's treatment of evidence one should have had does little more than appeal to a symptom of the norms that need to be explained by an adequate account of what is wrong with resistance to evidence. As a result, it may also appear that Goldberg's treatment doesn't cut deep enough to offer a satisfactory account of evidence resistance.

While this worry seems prima facie legitimate, it is ultimately unfounded. The reason for this is that Goldberg develops a view that reverses the standard direction of explanation between norms and expectations. According to Goldberg, epistemic norms are explained in terms of social epistemic expectations rather than the other way around. If Goldberg is right about this, the above worry can be laid to rest. His account cuts exactly as deep as it needs to.

At the same time, a lot hinges on the credentials of Goldberg's account of epistemic norms. Goldberg defends a view he calls 'coherence-infused reliabilism'. According to this view, very roughly, one's belief that *p* is prima facie proper if and only if it is held by a process that one is permitted to rely on and that satisfies a reliability and a minimal coherence-checking condition.

Goldberg observes that we are deeply social creatures who are engaged in practices of information sharing and joint action. These practices are supported by a rationale in that opting out of them would be practically irrational for us. Crucially, these can only be supported by this kind of rationale if we are entitled to certain expectations. More specifically, Goldberg argues that we must be entitled to expect others to live up to the requirements of coherence-infused reliabilism. We must expect them not to form beliefs in unreliable ways, and we must expect them to ensure coherence. If we couldn't expect them to form their beliefs in these ways, it would not be rational for us to engage in the kind of cooperative ventures in which we rely on the truth of others' beliefs for success. For instance, suppose you and I wanted to move a sofa. If you couldn't expect me to reliably form beliefs about where the sofa is and not to have incoherent beliefs about the matter, it would not make sense for you to embark on this venture with me.

In this way, the fact that we are engaged in information sharing and joint practical ventures and the fact that there is a rationale for this presuppose that we are entitled to have certain expectations of one another. These expectations ground epistemic norms. In particular, one important norm that they ground is the norm that specifies the conditions for prima facie proper belief.

What about ultima facie proper belief and evidence one should have had? To explain cases like these, Goldberg appeals to general expectations that *go beyond* the *explicit* normative criteria at issue in prima facie proper belief and that may serve to disqualify a prima facie proper belief from being ultima facie proper.

Goldberg argues that there is independent reason for thinking that these general normative expectations do exist, and that they can and often do the work in the way that he needs them to do. By way of support, Goldberg considers a number of examples. Suppose your firm is hiring, and you are currently interviewing a number of applicants. The explicit criteria for the job provide one important standard for your evaluation, perhaps the most important one. However, beyond the explicitly stated criteria, there are also general expectations, including, for example, that candidates be appropriately dressed. Or suppose that you are on the committee that awards the Nobel Prize. Again, while the explicit criteria for your evaluation provide an important standard for your evaluation, there are general expectations, including that nominees mustn't be Nazis. Crucially, job applicants and Nobel Prize nominees who do not live up to these general expectations may be disqualified because they don't. If I show up in flip-flops, shorts, and a vest to your job interview, you may not give me the job even if I meet all of the criteria explicitly mentioned in the job description. Similarly, even if a certain person produced amazing science, if it transpires that they are an all-out Nazi, they should not be awarded a Nobel Prize.

Goldberg's thought is that we find these general normative expectations in cases of epistemic assessment, too. Most importantly for present purposes, one relevant expectation is that one play one's social epistemic roles properly. In the case of a medical doctor, to play this role properly is to remain up to speed with the relevant literature. As a result, while a doctor who fails to do so may satisfy the conditions for prima facie proper belief that p, they fail to live up to the general normative expectations that come with their role as a practicing doctor.

Similarly, the thought could go, there are social epistemic expectations on taking up easily available evidence that explain the impermissibility intuition in the resistance cases. The characters in Cases 1–7 fail to live up to these social expectations. In turn, this failure disqualifies their beliefs from being proper, just as the underdressed job applicant was disqualified from getting the job and the Nazi scientist was disqualified from winning the Nobel Prize.

3.2 Worries for Social Epistemic Normativity

While Goldberg's account may look promising at first glance, there is reason to think that it remains ultimately unsuccessful. I will argue that there are two main problems that Goldberg's view encounters due to the social grounding of epistemic normativity: the first has to do with the scope of epistemic normativity; the second is a normative strength problem.

3.2.1 The Scope Problem

To bring the scope problem with Goldberg's account into view, notice first that, since on this normative picture epistemic norms are grounded in social expectations, which, in turn, are grounded in reliability constraints that are cooperation-generated, the scope of epistemic normativity only reaches as far as our rationale-supported practices of information-sharing and joint action. This is a theoretically heavy burden to carry: it amounts to a claim that epistemic normativity strongly co-varies with a particular subset of practical normativity: since, plausibly, the rationality at stake in the information sharing and joint action that Goldberg appeals to is (or, at least, can be, and often will be) practical rationality, it will follow on Goldberg's view that, for all x epistemic practices, x is epistemically permissible insofar as it is practically rational to the aim of information sharing and joint action. This is an extremely strong normative co-variance proposal.

To see why this is a problem, consider a society that has practices of sharing information and acting jointly on a wide range of issues. Suppose, furthermore, that these practices are supported by a rationale in the way envisaged by Goldberg. The result that we get is that members of this society are entitled to expect others to form beliefs reliably and minimally coherently on this range of issues. But now suppose that this society also has a practice of *not* sharing information and acting jointly on certain issues. To take an example that is close to home, let's suppose that they don't have the practice of sharing information and acting jointly on cases of sexual assault. Since there is no practice of sharing information and engaging in joint action, members of this society cannot expect others to form beliefs reliably and minimally coherently on this issue, nor to be sensitive to the corresponding testimonial evidence, at least not if Goldberg is right and this expectation is grounded in our practices of sharing information and joint action. But if it is practice-generated expectations that explain epistemic normative standards, the result that we get is that whatever epistemic norm there may be that requires (or at least permits) members of this society to trust the word of others will not extend to the word of victims of sexual assault. As a result, in this society, the word of victims of sexual assault need not be uptaken, nor can it defeat beliefs in the innocence of sexual predators. And that, clearly, is the wrong result. It cannot be that we diminish the epistemic status of the testimony of victims of sexual abuse simply by tuning up the degree of sexism in a society (no matter how many practical benefits the sexist practices in question may generate).

The problem Goldberg encounters here is grounded in the absence of certain social practices. A similar problem arises from the presence of bad social practices. Consider a community of agents that have a social practice of actively distrusting the testimony of victims of sexual assault. This practice not only fails to give rise to epistemic expectations – it also gives rise to bad epistemic expectations. For instance, one expectation that this practice gives rise to is that those who claim to have suffered sexual assault are not to be believed. If it is practice-generated expectations that explain epistemic normative standards, the result that we threaten to end up with here is that the word of victims of sexual assault can permissibly be disregarded (in other words, members of this community threaten to end up having standing defeaters for the word of victims of sexual assault simply as a result of having a bad social practice). And, of course, this result is even worse for Goldberg's view.

Before moving on, I'd like to consider some rejoinders on behalf of Goldberg.

A first route of resisting this result that Goldberg might explore is that the practices of sharing information and acting jointly on a range of issues entitles you to have expectations that are universal rather than restricted to the range of issues in question.

Unfortunately, there is reason to think that this route is ultimately not viable. One reason for this is that legitimate social epistemic expectations of the kind Goldberg envisages will be environment dependent: it is legitimate for me to expect people to know a lot about the history of Eastern Europe if I'm in Eastern Europe, for instance, but less so if I'm in Canada. Since environments can restrict the issues on which one can have legitimate social epistemic expectations of others, it follows that our practices of sharing information and acting jointly only entitle one to expectations restricted to a range of issues rather than to universal expectations. And if Goldberg is right and it is certain expectations we are entitled to have that determine epistemic standards, then the reach of epistemic standards is limited also. By the same token, the prospects of resisting this problematic result by holding that the expectations have universal reach are not bright either.

One might wonder, secondly, whether Goldberg's reliability constraint cannot help with this problem. After all, testimony from sexual assault victims is notably highly reliable.

Unfortunately, on Goldberg's view, it cannot, for two reasons: first, because the reliability of a practice is not enough to warrant its existence on Goldberg's view – it also needs to be grounded in the cooperation rationale. Since we can easily imagine a world where this is not so, we get the result that the absence of the practice of trusting victims of sexual assault is unproblematic. How about the practice of actively distrusting them? Can't Goldberg insist that the practice of distrusting the word of victims of sexual assault is not reliable, nor supported by a rationale?

Again, the answer here is 'no'. First, this is because disbelieving is not plausibly subject to reliability constraints in the way believing is: I can unproblematically fail to believe a lot of propositions that are true, whereas I cannot unproblematically believe a lot of propositions that are false. Second, this is because normativity is modal: even if this practice is not, as a matter of fact, supported by a rationale, insofar as the practice *may* be supported by a rationale – in that it may be practically irrational to opt out of it – it may, on Goldberg's view, generate legitimate social expectations. Consider a world in which sexual assault is widespread in that most adult men engage in it. In that case, it may well be practically irrational for them to opt out of this practice. At the same time, it may also be practically irrational for women to opt out – say, because this opting out is punished severely. In addition, it may be that abandoning or changing the practice is practically catastrophic not just for each individual human, but for humanity as a whole. To take a particularly drastic illustration of this point, suppose there is a powerful evil demon who will extinguish all of humanity if they abandon the practice of distrusting the word of victims of sexual assault. It is easy to see, then, that even bad practices can be supported by a rationale in Goldberg's sense, in that opting out individually or abandoning or changing the practice as a whole is practically irrational. By the same token, Goldberg cannot hope to avoid the problem even in its second incarnation by appealing to the absence of a rationale.

Again, the underlying problem for Goldberg's view is the normative co-variance claim. On his account, epistemic normativity strongly co-varies with (a subset of) practical normativity: since, plausibly, the rationality at stake in information sharing and joint action that Goldberg appeals to is (or, at least, can be, and often will be) practical rationality, it will follow, on Goldberg's view, that epistemic permissibility will co-vary with practically rationality to the aim of information sharing and joint action. Since we can easily imagine cases in which what is beneficial for information sharing and joint action departs from what is epistemically permissible, the view is bound to get such cases wrong.

Furthermore, note that one does not even have to come up with very far-fetched examples to illustrate this point. We do, as a matter of fact, live in a world where many societies have a practice of disbelieving women and people of colour. We can imagine that one might even come up with a practical rationale for these practices – having to do, for example, with division of labour. Nevertheless, gender- and race-based epistemic injustice remains epistemically problematic.

Furthermore, research in cognitive psychology (e.g. Nisbett and Ross 1980, Kahneman et al. 1982, Gilovich et al. 2002) notably indicates that human beings tend to rely on heuristics when engaged in probabilistic reasoning, with these heuristics making people prone to commit elementary probabilistic fallacies. Also, according to error management theory (Haselton and Buss 2000, 2009, Haselton and Nettle 2006), the fallibility of human cognition, at least in many cases, is the result of natural selection. Evolutionary psychologists argue that, given the limited information and computational power with which organisms must contend, an inference mechanism can be advantageous if it often enough (for biological purposes, such as survival) draws accurate conclusions about real-world environments, and if it does so quickly and with little computational effort. The heuristics humans rely on in probabilistic reasoning, some of these psychologists maintain, are mechanisms of just that sort.

Note that it is plausible that these evolved epistemically deficient practices are beneficial for both biological and social evolution – otherwise, it seems implausible that they would have been selected to begin with. Indeed, it seems plausible that relying on heuristics like those discussed above will be beneficial to the aim of information sharing and joint action – due to limited information and computational power. If so, Goldberg's view will predict epistemic permissibility in all of these cases of intuitive epistemic failure.

To put the worry in more theoretical terms, here is the problem: if our model predicts that epistemic norms are grounded in the rationality of our practices of information sharing and joint action, and if the latter are (very plausibly) aimed at the survival of our species, then our model predicts that epistemic norms will track survival norms. Our belief-producing processes, for instance, will only be as reliable as needed for survival. However, there is nothing to ensure that the socially and biologically set reliability threshold will coincide with the epistemically needed reliability threshold. That is, the threshold of reliability required for epistemic purposes may well be higher than what is needed for our practices of information sharing and joint action, and in turn for biological benefit. Socially and biologically reliable enough need not coincide with epistemically reliable enough. Similarly, epistemic norms for sensitivity to evidence and for evidence gathering may set the threshold for epistemic permissibility differently than social and practical norms for joint action and survival.

3.2.2 The Strength Problem

A second problem for Goldberg's account concerns the strength of the resulting epistemic normative requirements. In particular, the fact that, on his account, epistemic normativity is sourced in social expectations generates failures of extensional adequacy due to it being too weak to capture the distinction between epistemic shoulds: that between the synchronic 'should' of epistemic justification and the diachronic 'should' of responsibility in inquiry.[1] Goldberg's view shares this important theoretical lacuna with Williamson's E = K. Again, proceeding responsibly in inquiry (e.g. pursuing worthwhile questions) is one thing; synchronically responding well to available evidence is another. However, plausibly, both are governed by epistemic shoulds and accompanied by the corresponding social expectations.

To see this, remember the slightly modified version of the Friendly Detective case from Chapter 2: this time around, Dave and his colleague, Greg, were sent to investigate the crime scene. Greg is rather lazy and distracted: he briefly looks around, fails to find any evidence at the crime scene, and concludes that there's no evidence to suggest that the butler did it. As a result, he does not believe that the butler did it. In contrast, as we've already seen, Dave is extremely thorough, but, at the same time, a close friend of the butler. Dave finds conclusive evidence that the butler did it at the crime scene but fails to form the corresponding belief.

Both Dave and Greg are rather rubbish detectives, in that they fail to conduct their inquiry well – they are both in breach of the diachronic epistemic should of inquiry, and they both fail to meet the social expectations associated with their roles. Compatibly, there is an important epistemic difference between Dave and Greg: Dave, but not Greg, is aware of all of the evidence in support of the hypothesis that the butler did it and fails to form the relevant belief nevertheless; Dave is resistant to available evidence.

This problem is a normative strength problem for Goldberg's view: an account in terms of social expectations is too weak to individuate the relevant epistemic normative demands, in that it overgeneralises. At the same time, this strength problem, coupled with the scope problem identified above, serves to further suggest that the main underlying issue is the normative co-variance claim between the social and the epistemic: we sometimes (practically rationally) socially expect people to *phi* when they

---

[1] For excellent work on the nature and normativity of inquiry, see e.g. Friedman (2017) and Kelp (2021).

epistemically shouldn't *phi*, and, conversely, other times we fail to expect people to *phi* when they epistemically should *phi*. By the same token, social normativity seems ill-suited to accommodate the epistemic impermissibility of resistance data that we want explained.[2]

3.3 Problems for the Moral 'Should'

We have seen that Goldberg's view, accounting for what is intuitively epistemically amiss in resistance cases in terms of evidence one (socially) should have had, runs into trouble due to its underlying strong normative co-variance claim for the epistemic and the practical.

One might wonder, alternatively, whether the resistance cases we have been worried about aren't really cases of moral failure rather than cases of genuine epistemic failure to begin with. On this account of the data, the intuition of impropriety in the resistance cases has a non-epistemic normative source: we think, for instance, that George is doing something wrong in the Testimonial Injustice case because he's doing something morally wrong in not listening to the female passer-by: epistemic injustice, the thought would go, is the stuff of intellectual ethics, not of theory of knowledge proper. However, our intuitions are not fine grained enough to see the difference: theory is needed. Indeed, here is Ernie Sosa on this topic:

> [T]he theory of *knowledge* [...] is the department wherein we find the core issues of knowledge [...] in the history of epistemology, by contrast with the wisdom of inquiry, and with the intellectual ethics wherein we find issues of epistemic justice and epistemic vice, broadly conceived. (2021, 71, emphasis in original)

Here also is Richard Feldman:

> It's surely true that there are times when one would be best off finding new evidence. But this always turns on what options one has, what one cares about, and other non-epistemic factors. As I see it, these are prudential or moral matters, not strictly epistemic matters. (2004, 190)

I don't find this move particularly plausible: the failure in question in Cases 1–7 is a genuinely epistemic failure. Here are a few reasons to think so: first, it is hard to see how, in the cases that exhibit morally problematic

---

[2] In more recent work, Goldberg (2022) gestures towards a moral source of epistemic normativity to account for some of the resistance cases.

features, these could be instantiated without bad epistemic underpinnings. After all, one thing that the vast majority of the theorists of blame[3] strongly agree with is that there is an epistemic condition on moral blame: very roughly, moral blameworthiness implies that one is not epistemically blamelessly ignorant that one is doing something wrong. But this suggests that in the morally pregnant cases above, for example, the sexist and the racist are doing something epistemically wrong as well. Otherwise, if they were epistemically blameless, they could not be morally blameworthy. But they are.

Second, and most crucially, while some of these cases exhibit ethically problematic features, others do not. To the contrary, some of these cases (e.g. the case of Mary the wishful thinker and that of the friendly detective) can be plausibly construed as cases of moral success while remaining intuitively problematic with regard to the lack of evidence uptake. This suggest that the source of the intuition is, indeed, epistemic failure (absent other normative constraints at the context). Take, for instance, the case of Mary, the optimistic spouse: when her partner, Dan, spends more and more evening hours at the office, she's happy that his career is going so well. When he comes home smelling like floral perfume, she compliments his taste in fragrance. Finally, when she repeatedly sees him having coffee in town with his colleague, Alice, she is glad he's making new friends. She never considers the question as to whether Dan is having an affair. Is Mary justified to believe as she does that Dan is a faithful, loving husband? Clearly not. Note, however, that it's hard to find moral flaws with Mary's epistemic ways: after all, many moral philosophers (and a good number of epistemologists, e.g. Stroud 2006) agree that we owe more trust to our friends and family than to people we have never met: if so, Mary's suspension is morally impeccable but epistemically problematic.

3.4 Conclusion

This chapter has looked into the option of explaining the impermissibility datum in resistance cases via appeal to social or moral normativity. I have argued that a social expectations-based account of the epistemic impermissibility of resistance is too weak to explain cases of epistemically bad social expectations, sourced in practical considerations pertaining to cooperation. Further on, I looked at the plausibility of explaining

---

[3] Indeed, there is an entire *Stanford Encyclopaedia* entry dedicated to '[t]he epistemic condition on moral responsibility' (Rudy-Hiller 2018).

resistance cases away as pertaining to the moral rather than the epistemic domain, and I argued this doesn't work on both theoretical and empirical grounds: first, a view like this fails to accommodate a widely accepted epistemic condition on moral responsibility. Second, since some of the resistance cases we have been looking at are cases of clear moral success, the view will be unsatisfactory on grounds of extensional adequacy.

CHAPTER 4

Permissible Suspension and Evidence Resistance

This chapter surveys recent accounts of the epistemic permissibility of suspended judgement in an attempt to thereby identify the normative resources required for explaining the epistemically problematic nature of evidence resistance. Since paradigmatic cases of evidence resistance involve belief suspension on propositions that are well supported by evidence, such as vaccine safety and climate change, the literature on permissible suspension seems to be a straightforward starting point for my investigation: after all, any plausible view of permissible suspension will have to predict epistemic impermissibility in these paradigmatic resistance cases. I look at three extant accounts of permissible suspension – a simple knowledge-based account, a virtue-based account, and a respect-based account – and argue that they fail to provide the needed resources for this project. Further on, the chapter identifies the source of the said difficulties and gestures towards a better way forward.

4.1 Proper Suspension: The Simple Knowledge-Based View

It is widely agreed that justification – be it moral, prudential, epistemic, etc. – is defeasible. For instance, suppose that you justifiably head towards High Street on a Sunday because you wish for a new pair of shoes, but as you're walking, I tell you that you left your wallet at home. In this case, you have a defeater for your (prudential) justification for going into town. Should you continue on your way, your action will no longer be (prudentially) justified. Similarly, suppose that you (epistemically) justifiably believe that the structure you are looking at is a barn. Suppose, further, that I tell you that most of the things that look like barns are actually fakes. In this case, you have a defeater for your belief that the structure you are looking at is a barn. If you continue to hold this belief, your belief is no longer justified.

While it is widely agreed that epistemic justification is defeasible, and much ink in epistemology has been spilled on the issue of the defeasibility of the justification of positive doxastic attitudes, such as beliefs and credences, very little has been said about the justification of suspension and about its defeasibility conditions. However, paradigmatic cases of evidence resistance involve epistemically unjustified belief suspension on propositions that are well supported by evidence. Of course, this need not be the case: one can be evidence resistant by simply not taking up evidence and not updating properly in the light thereof, without thereby being suspended on the issue: indeed, it may even be that one hosts a fairly high credence that p is the case while, at the same time, resisting genuine evidence for p due to, for instance, bias against a particular source.

However, given that paradigmatic cases of evidence resistance involve defeated suspension, work on permissible suspension seems like an excellent place to start an inquiry into resistance impermissibility. As such, the fact that the amount of work done to date on the justification and defeasibility of suspension is relatively minimal poses a problem.

I take the most notable views of permissible suspension on the market to be the following: (1) the simple knowledge-based account (e.g. often implied but not often explicitly defended in Williamson 2000, Sutton 2005, 2007, Hawthorne and Srinivasan 2013), (2) the virtue-based account (Sosa 2021), and (3) the respect-based account (Miracchi 2017, Sylvan and Lord 2021, 2022).

The knowledge-based account, while not being explicitly defended in many places, follows straightforwardly from endorsing a biconditional knowledge norm of belief (defended most notably in Williamson (2000), but also in, e.g., Sutton (2005, 2007), Hawthorne and Srinivasan (2013), and Littlejohn (2020)), according to which belief is epistemically permissible just in case it is knowledge. If non-knowledgeable belief is impermissible, it follows that one should suspend belief in cases in which one does not know.

To put my cards on the table from the very beginning: I take a simple knowledge-based account of permissible suspension to suffer from insurmountable in-principle difficulties in dealing with resistance cases. On a view like this, one is permissibly suspended on p just in case on does not know that p. The main trouble for any account along these lines comes from the sufficiency claim: since knowledge implies belief, the sufficiency of lack of knowledge for permissible suspension claim implies that suspension implies permissible suspension. After all, should one not know in virtue of refusing to believe, on a view that takes lack of knowledge to be enough for permissible suspension, one would thereby be diagnosed as permissibly suspended. '*x* implies permissible *x*' is not a great result for suspension or, more generally, for any *x*, subject to any sorts of normativity. Furthermore, and even more interestingly, upon closer scrutiny, the account has further problematic results: since belief is predicted to be impermissible in cases of lack of knowledge due to lack of belief, suspension of belief will not only be merely permissible, but even obligatory. To see this, take a paradigmatic case of evidence resistance. I falsely believe that not-*p*: it is not the case that climate change is happening. All experts in climate change come and tell me that *p*. In virtue of politically motivated bias, I refuse to believe them and suspend on the issue. At this stage, the simple knowledge account's diagnosis is that indeed I should suspend, since I don't know that climate change is happening – even though the reason why I don't know is because I refuse to believe it. As such, on the simple knowledge-based view, suspension implies obligatory suspension.

I take these considerations to signal insurmountable difficulties for a simple knowledge-based view of permissible suspension.

Williamson is sensitive to this problem when he writes:

> A Pyrrhonist sceptic may hope to comply vacuously with all three norms [(N) Believe only what you know, (DN) Be the sort of person who is disposed to believe only what one knows, (ODN) Do the thing that a person who is disposed to believe only what she knows would do] by having a general disposition never to believe anything. If one has no beliefs, then a fortiori one has no untrue beliefs, no beliefs that fail to constitute knowledge, no beliefs that are improbable on one's evidence, no inconsistent beliefs, and so on. The Pyrrhonist, if such a person is possible, complies with all three norms even in the sceptical scenario. [...] Non-sceptics may find little to admire in the Pyrrhonist's self-imposed ignorance, especially when that ignorance concerns the needs of others. There may be positive norms for knowledge, such as a norm enjoining knowledge-gathering in various circumstances, and so positive as well as negative norms for beliefs. (Williamson forthcominga)

I agree with Williamson that what is needed here is input from positive epistemology. This book attempts to do just this, and it does so in keeping with the knowledge-first picture – albeit not with a simple version thereof. Chapter 9 develops a view according to which proper suspension has to do with what one is in a position to know.

Before this, however, in what follows, I will look at a prominent recent defence of a virtue-theoretic account of permissible suspension from Ernie Sosa.

4.2 Sosa on Virtue, Telic Normativity, and Suspension

Very little has been said in the literature about the justification of suspension and about its defeasibility conditions. Ernie Sosa's most recent book (2021) supplies this lack: Sosa offers a comprehensive virtue-theoretic account of the nature and normativity of suspension in terms of the nature and telic normativity of agential attempts more generally.

In what follows, I first briefly outline the position and take issue with some details of its normative structure. In particular, I argue that Sosa's telic normativity is in need of normative expansion if it is to accommodate the defeasibility of justification to suspend. Further on, I consider several paths for developing Sosa's view to accommodate this datum and argue that we can find the needed resources in general telic normativity.

Sosa's virtue epistemology is a normative framework for the evaluation of attempts (henceforth also 'telic normativity'). Attempts have constitutive aims. As a result, we can ask whether or not a given attempt is successful. We can also ask whether a given attempt is competent (i.e. produced by an ability to attain the attempt's aim). Finally, we can ask whether a given attempt is apt (i.e. successful because competent).

Virtue epistemologists standardly take beliefs to be attempts that have truth and/or knowledge as their constitutive aims. Given that this is so, we can ask whether beliefs are successful (i.e. whether they are true). In addition, we can also ask whether they are competent (i.e. whether they are produced by an ability to believe truly) and whether they are apt (i.e. true because competent).

According to Sosa, the above gives us the basic account for first-order evaluations of attempts. Crucially, however, Sosa does not take this to be the whole story. Rather, he countenances two further types of aptness alongside first-order aptness, or 'animal' aptness as Sosa calls it. These additional types of aptness are 'reflective' and 'full' aptness. Attaining these further types of aptness requires accurate and indeed apt attempt at a higher order, in addition to animal aptness. In a nutshell, the thought is that attempts will rise to these higher levels of aptness only if, alongside animal aptness, one has aptly ascertained that one's attempt is free from any relevant risk that one may be running: one must have arrived at an apt awareness that one's attempt would be apt. While animal aptness in conjunction with apt risk assessment will be enough for reflective aptness, full aptness additionally requires that first- and second-order aptness are connected in the right way: one must be guided to animal aptness by one's reflectively apt risk assessment.

It comes to light that there are a number of normative properties that attempts can enjoy. Crucially, according to Sosa, full aptness enjoys special status among these properties. More specifically, according to Sosa, full aptness is the fully desirable status for attempts, and attempts fall short unless they attain full aptness. Moreover, he is also clear that this claim holds with full generality: any attempt attains fully desirable status qua attempt if and only if it is fully apt; and it falls short qua attempt if and only if it isn't.

According to Sosa, various psychological categories – most importantly, guessing, belief, and judgement – are species of affirmation and, as a result, attempts. (Sosa's main interest is with affirmations with a specifically epistemic aim that, at a minimum, involves truth.) While Sosa countenances a variety of psychological categories with epistemic aims, his main focus is on judgement (and judgemental belief). Judgement differs from other psychological categories in that it has a particularly robust epistemic aim: judgement aims not only at truth, but at aptness. To understand this normative requirement on judgement, Sosa asks us to consider Diana, the huntress: as Diana surveys a landscape in search of game, she may see prey in the distance (in good light and calm wind). If a shot is too risky, it is ill-advised. A shot, then, can attain quality in it being well rather than negligently selected. An aiming, then, is assessable by reference to how likely it is to succeed (relative to one's possession of the pertinent competence), so as to avoid recklessness, and it is also assessable by reference to how negligent (or not) it may be.

Similarly, according to Sosa, for a judgement to be apt, more is required than merely apt affirmation. What is needed for apt judgement is that one is guided to aptness by apt risk assessment. An apt judgement is a fully apt affirmation.

Where does suspension fit in this picture? After all, telic normativity is a normativity of attempts, but isn't suspension a paradigm of something that is not an attempt, but rather an instance of forbearing from attempting?

To answer this question, Sosa introduces a distinction between two varieties of intentional forbearing:

Narrow-scope: (Forbearing from X'ing) in the endeavour to attain a given aim A.
Broad-scope: Forbearing from (X'ing in the endeavour to attain a given aim A).

According to Sosa, the first, narrow-scope variety of forbearing pertains to telic normativity proper: the forbearing is done with the domain-internal aim in view. The second, in contrast, is domain-external forbearing, in that the agent who forbears in this sense does not attempt to reach the central aim of the domain in question to begin with: whether to engage in a domain is not a question within the domain itself. In that, broad-scope forbearing, according to Sosa, does not make the proper subject of telic normativity.

To see the place of forbearing in the normativity of attempts, consider Diana again. Diana's archery shots can be more or less well selected. When she spots some prey, Diana can properly aim as follows: to make an attempt on that target if and only if the attempt would succeed aptly. Accordingly, there are two ways in which Diana can fall short with regard to this aim: she could make an attempt on the target when she would not succeed aptly – because, maybe, the shot would be too risky, given the wind. But she could also fail in her attempt by failing to make an attempt (on the target) when one would succeed aptly.

So, in a nutshell, according to Sosa, narrow-scope forbearing is itself an attempt with an aim: that of attempting if and only if the attempt would succeed aptly. This is the place of forbearing in telic normativity.

How does this translate to epistemology? Again, just like with normativity in general, Sosa thinks that it is only narrow-scope forbearing that is of internal interest to the theory of knowledge proper in that it is aimed at the epistemic goal of attaining aptness. More specifically, Sosa thinks that epistemic narrow-scope forbearing is what constitutes deliberative suspension of judgement, which is an attempt in its own right, one that shares with judging an epistemically distinctive aim: the aim of affirming alethically (positively or negatively) if and only if that affirming would be apt (and otherwise suspend). Conversely, on Sosa's view, one properly suspends belief on a question if and only if one suspends based sufficiently on one's lack of the competence required in order to answer that question aptly (2021, 85).

In contrast, broad-scope forbearing, according to Sosa, is the stuff of intellectual ethics (i.e. it pertains to the question as to whether to engage in inquiry as to whether *p* to begin with). In this sense, it is external to the theory of knowledge proper. Here is Sosa:

> Whether to engage in a certain domain is not generally a question *within* that domain. Telic assessment within a domain assesses mainly the pursuit of aims proper to that domain. An exhausted tennis competitor *may* of course properly consider whether to default, but this is not a decision assessable *within* the sport. When you sense a heart attack in progress and quit for that reason, this is not a decision assessable by athletic criteria in the

domain of tennis. Whether to keep on playing is not a tennis decision; it is a life decision. (2021, 66, emphases in original)

Similarly, Sosa thinks that epistemic broad-scope forbearing is tantamount to non-deliberative suspension of judgement. It is also an intentional forbearing from alethic affirmation (both positive and negative), but it is not aimed at apt judgement as to whether p; it derives rather from omitting inquiry into the question as to whether p to begin with, whether the refusal is implicit or consciously explicit. As such, norms governing broad-scope forbearing will be norms of intellectual ethics, not epistemic norms proper:

> Broad-scope forbearing [i.e. not taking up a question] is not a standing *within* the domain of inquiry into a particular question, wherein it would be subject to the epistemic assessment of attempts that are potentially knowledge-constitutive. (2021, 70–71, emphasis in original)

To bring my first worry into clear view, I'd like to start with a particular case of evidence resistance involving ignored defeat. To take a variation on a famous example, consider the case of a scientist, Gabriel, who doesn't believe anything his female colleagues say, because he is a sexist (Lackey 2018). Now suppose Gabriel carries out two experiments to test his hypothesis that p. Experiment §1 strongly supports that p. Experiment §2 strongly supports that not-p. The scientist comes to suspend on p on this basis. Suppose, next, that a female colleague of his, Dana, discovers a serious flaw with experiment §2, which she points out to Gabriel. Due to sexist bias, Gabriel discounts Dana's word and maintains his suspension on p. This is a paradigm case of higher-order defeat: after Dana's testimony that q: 'there is a flaw in experiment §2', Gabriel's suspension on p is no longer justified.

What does Sosa's account have to say about this case? It would seem that, for all we have been told so far, telic normativity does not have the resources to accommodate the result that Gabriel is not justified to suspend. Rather, Gabriel's failure will, at best, be categorised as pertaining to intellectual ethics. To see this, note that Gabriel never takes up the question as to whether q to begin with due to his sexist bias. As such, since no attempt at apt judgement is made, the suspension at stake in the case of q will have to be classified as non-deliberative suspension. If that is so, however, its normative properties will not have the capacity to affect the normative properties of Gabriel's suspension on p either: after all, even if present, normative failure outside the domain of theory of knowledge proper need not affect domain-internal normative properties. Even if

Gabriel's suspension on *q* is impermissible on non-epistemic grounds, it cannot affect the epistemic permissibility of Gabriel's suspension on *p*.

Recall also that, on Sosa's view, suspension is permissible insofar as it is sufficiently based on one's lack of the competence required in order to answer that question aptly. It is easy to see that this account predicts, against intuition, that it is permissible for Gabriel to suspend based on his sexism-generated lack of competence to believe aptly what Dana tells him.

Now, it is worth mentioning that there may be an easy way for Sosa out of this case: one thing he could do is insist that Gabriel does, in fact – albeit implicitly – inquire into whether *q* by simply hearing the testimony from Dana. After all, Sosa's notion of inquiry is a very 'light' one, whereby the mere monitoring of one's environment counts as such. If so, Gabriel will count as having epistemically impermissibly suspended on *q*, since, in the course of his (implicit) inquiry into whether *q*, he missed the opportunity to affirm aptly that *q*.

That said, the route back to problems for Sosa's account is quite short from here. To see this, note that we can easily tweak the case following a recipe that will be familiar by now, such that Gabriel doesn't even hear that Dana told him that *q*. Once more, suppose that Gabriel simply zones out whenever a female colleague talks to him. As a result, Gabriel didn't even register that Dana told him that there is a problem with his experiment. In this case, Gabriel's epistemic behaviour is no better than in the original case. If anything, it's worse. Most importantly for present purposes, the case is equally one of testimonial injustice and one of defeat. Once Gabriel is told about the flaw in his experiment, Gabriel's suspension on *p* is no longer justified. The fact that Gabriel didn't bother to listen does not improve his situation vis-à-vis the original case on either count.

Sosa has not discussed the issue of normative defeat directly. However, in *Epistemic Explanations* (2021), he has started theorising about negligence within his virtue-epistemological framework. Most importantly for present purposes, he suggests that negligence may preclude competent performance. In particular, negligent failure to inquire may preclude competent judgement. If so, we could maybe avail ourselves of this normative resource to explain how negligent failure to inquire may preclude competent suspension as well.

Note, first, that cases of normative defeat do plausibly count as cases of negligent failure to inquire. Consider the case of Gabriel, the sexist scientist, once more. Gabriel is told by his female colleague, Dana, that there is a flaw in one of the experiments that led him to suspend on *p*, but

Gabriel doesn't even listen. Isn't this a prime example of a negligent failure to engage with the question as to what he was told? If Sosa is right and negligent failure to inquire precludes competent judgement, then presumably it also precludes competent suspension. Given that justified suspension is competent suspension, we get the desired result that Gabriel is not justified in his suspension.

Unfortunately, there remains a fly in the ointment: negligence is itself a normative property. If your failure to inquire into whether *p* is negligent, then you didn't inquire into whether *p*, although you *should* have. Crucially, while one may agree that we need to understand normative defeat in terms of violations of the norms requiring us inquire, the task Sosa faces is to offer an account of these norms within the scope of theory of knowledge proper – rather than intellectual ethics. For virtue epistemologists like Sosa, this means offering an account that is available to virtue epistemology. Since the kind of negligence that precludes justified suspension is a normative epistemic property, this means that what we need is a substantive account of the kind of negligence that precludes justified suspension in terms of the abilities or other resources available in the theoretical machinery of Sosa's framework. To say that cases of external defeat are cases in which competent suspension is precluded by negligent failures to inquire gives us a way of identifying the task that we are facing, but not yet a way of accomplishing it.

Unfortunately, there is an in-principle reason to worry that it will not be trivial to accomplish this task, given Sosa's framework. To see why, note again that Sosa conceives of telic normativity as the normativity of attempts: whether an attempt is successful, competent, or apt presupposes that an attempt was made. In this way, telic normativity presupposes that the agent has made an attempt. As a result, whether or not the agent *should* make an attempt is not assessable in terms of Sosa's telic normativity of attempts. Recall also that, to make sense of norms requiring us to inquire, Sosa distinguishes between the epistemic normativity of the theory of knowledge (i.e. telic normativity) and the broader normativity of inquiry. Obligations to inquire fall into the broader normativity of inquiry, which pertains to intellectual ethics.

The trouble is that Sosa's suggestion that negligence may preclude competent judgement is hard to square with the claims above. To see this, let's return to the case of the sexist scientist once more. Recall that the thought was that when Gabriel doesn't even listen to Dana, he falls foul of negligent failure to engage with the question of what Dana tells him. But negligence is normative: to be negligent is to fail to do certain things that one should have done. In particular, the way in which Gabriel is negligent here is that he fails to take up the question of what Dana tells him, even though he should have done so.

We are now in a position to see the in-principle problem for Sosa. If Gabriel's negligence consists in his failure to take up the question whether q, even though he should have done so, his failure does not fall within the normativity proper to the theory of knowledge, but into the broader epistemic normativity of inquiry. As a result, it is now hard to see how his negligence may preclude deliberative competent suspension on p. After all, deliberative competent suspension does fall within the normativity proper to the theory of knowledge. At the same time, this normativity is autonomous and protected from incursion of extraneous normativity, including that of the broader normativity of intellectual ethics. It looks as though accounting for cases of normative defeat in terms of negligence that we are envisaging is not available to Sosa after all, at least not provided that the rest of his theory stays put.

Sosa (2021) does offer an account of the kind of negligence that is at stake in the cases discussed. He considers a case in which you are adding numbers via mental arithmetic. If the set of numbers you are adding is sufficiently large, you will not be sufficiently reliable to arrive at a competent belief about the sum. Suppose you are still sufficiently reliable but barely so. At the same time, you have a calculator ready at hand, which would keep you safely above the relevant reliability threshold. If you insist on mental arithmetic here, Sosa argues, you fall foul of negligence.

With the case in play, let's move on to Sosa's view of negligence. Here is the crucial passage:

> I am suggesting that negligence is a failure of competence, that one proceeds inappropriately in performing as one does if one *should* have taken the steps by not taking which one is negligent. One is then to blame (in the negligence mode) for not having taken those steps. [...] *Competent attainment of aptness requires availing yourself of sufficiently available means that would enable a more reliable assessment of your first order aptness and competence.* If there are no such means, then there is no such negligence, and no such incompetence. In such a circumstance, the agent might then be able to determine with sufficient competence that they are in a position to proceed competently enough on the first order. (2021, 64, emphases in original)

Sosa's key idea is that if you can assess your first-order competence by more reliable means but fail to do so, then you are negligent. In particular, you fall foul of a kind of negligence that precludes what he calls the competent attainment of aptness.

Most importantly for present purposes, given that competent suspension requires that one suspends based sufficiently on one's lack of the competence required in order to answer the question aptly, negligence precludes competent suspension: sexist scientist Gabriel does have sufficiently available means that would enable a more reliable assessment of the aptness of his suspension – Dana's testimony. Since he ignores it, Gabriel will count as a negligent suspender.

The problem with this account of negligence, however, is that it is too strong: it makes negligence, and hence defeat, too easy to come by. To see this, consider a case in which I ask my flatmate, who is currently in the kitchen, whether we have any milk left. He tells me that we do. Now, I do have several more reliable means of assessing my first-order competence available to me. For instance, I could go to the kitchen and have a look myself. Crucially, however, failure to avail myself of these means doesn't make me negligent. And, most importantly for present purposes, it doesn't preclude my judgement that there is milk in the fridge from being competent.

Sosa's account of negligence is insufficiently normative. What matters, according to Sosa, is the *availability of alternative means* that would lead to a more reliable assessment of first-order aptness and competence. However, the difference maker is normative, not descriptive: what matters is not (only) whether one has alternative means available that would have led one to a more reliable assessment of first-order aptness and competence, but (also) whether one *should* have availed oneself of these means. In the case of the sexist scientist, he should have taken the woman's testimony into account in assessing the credentials of hypothesis *p*. Similarly, Mary should not have ignored all of the evidence suggesting that her husband is having an affair. In contrast, in the milk case, it is not the case that I should have had a look myself.

Sosa's account of the normativity of negligence in terms of available alternative means doesn't work unless we add that the available means are means one should have availed oneself of. Crucially, it is precisely this 'should' that we wanted to explain in virtue-epistemological terms. We are thus back to square one once more.

In more recent work (Sosa 2022), and in reply to my worries, Sosa goes into more detail about the normativity of negligence. On this novel view, availing oneself of more reliable alternative means is only normative in cases in which the initial performance was lacking to begin with. Looking left and right, for instance, is something you could easily enough have done and should have done before crossing the street. Omitting to do so is a case of negligence. This refurbished view straightforwardly takes care of the flatmate case, since that is a case of permissible belief formation.

The question that arises is: how does this account of negligence fit with Sosa's general normative picture?

According to Sosa, such lacks and omissions can diminish the agency of an agent and can thus be negatively assessable telically even though they are not attempts. Since they are attributable to the agent, they thereby speak to their skill. When you cross that London street without looking, the failure to look is presumably attributable to you – it speaks badly of your competence.

Here is, however, the worry I have for this reply: Sosa's telic epistemic normative picture is a reliabilist normative picture. As such, Sosa's competences admit for failure even when they are manifest – indeed, any reliabilism will predict this. Consider, now, one-off cases of suspension on *p* in spite of easily available evidence for *p*: say that Gabriel, the scientist, is not a sexist, and indeed he's a fantastically competent epistemic agent, but he simply fails this time around to give the weight it deserves to his colleague's testimony. This failure will not speak against his competence – indeed, it cannot: failures are predicted in a reliabilist picture about competence. If this failure does not speak to Gabriel's competence, however, Sosa's picture is left without resources to predict it as epistemically relevantly negligent – since, on his view, epistemically relevant negligence is competence-relevant negligence. As such, Sosa's picture will lack the needed resources to accommodate cases of one-off impermissible suspension by competence-manifesting epistemic agents.

One way around this problem[1] would be to derive the impermissibility of negligence straight from the success condition involved in Sosa's picture – in the case of judgement, from knowledge. I agree: this is exactly the route I will take in Chapter 9.

4.3 The Respect-Based View of Permissible Suspension

More recently, Lisa Miracchi (2017) and Kurt Sylvan and Errol Lord (2022) have proposed more nuanced virtue-theoretic views of permissible suspension. The views are more nuanced than their straightforward knowledge-based and virtue-based competition in the following ways: in contrast to the simple knowledge-based account, these views do not make

---

[1] Suggested by Ernie Sosa in conversation. Another route Ernie seemed partial to in conversation is to take some varieties of failure to imply lack of competence manifestation. The difficulty with this approach will be finding a principled way to distinguish between varieties of failure that are compatible with competence manifestation and varieties of failure that are not.

direct appeal to the absence of epistemic value to explain the permissibility of suspension. In contrast also to Sosa's classic virtue-theoretic approach, their accounts conceive of the permissibility of suspension in terms of manifesting *respect* for the epistemic value in question – be it truth or knowledge – rather than in terms of value-conduciveness.

Henceforth, I will run with Miracchi's view, due to hers being the first such proposal on the market. According to Miracchi, epistemic virtue not only involves aiming to get what is fundamentally valuable (knowledge, on her knowledge-first virtue epistemological picture), but also involves respecting the aim of getting what is fundamentally valuable. Respecting the aim of getting knowledge, she claims, is derivative from the fundamental aim. On Miracchi's view, suspension is permissible just in case it manifests respect for the aim of knowing. In this, the features that make epistemic rational assessment applicable to suspension are derivative from the features that make such assessment applicable to beliefs. Here is Miracchi:

> When an agent generally can be characterized as aiming to A (e.g. aiming to know), we can understand withholding from or omitting a performance of A-ing as manifesting a kind of practical respect for what it takes to A. The agent manifests this respect precisely by not endeavoring to A. (2017, 433)

This account is well equipped to deal nicely with many paradigmatic cases of evidence resistance: it seems right that, in not uptalking relevant, easily available evidence, our resistant agents in the cases under discussion fail to manifest respect for what it takes to know, which, indeed, casts doubt on their knowing competences. This suggests that the sufficiency direction of Miracchi's view holds.

I think Miracchi's derivative, respect-based account makes significant progress in understanding the paradigmatic virtue-theoretic flaws involved in impermissible suspension. Unfortunately, I don't think it will quite get us there as an *analysis* of permissible suspension due to considerations having to do with the strength of the respect condition. Here is why: one worry one might have for Miracchi's view follows the necessity direction – isn't a requirement of manifesting respect for knowledge going to be too strong for permissible suspension? After all, one might think, paradigmatically bad believers – conspiracy theorists, wishful thinkers, bullshitting politicians – can also, on occasion, suspend properly on everyday matters – for instance, on whether there is milk in the fridge. Think back also to the Pyrrhonist sceptic: this agent, one might think, is the paradigmatic example of a bad suspender, with little respect for knowledge.

Compatibly, should the Pyrrhonist (or conspiracy theorist, etc.) suspend on whether there's milk in the fridge based on, for example, conflicting testimony, their suspension would be justified.

Miracchi is aware that the respect condition needs to be fairly weak to do the job. She writes:

> In the case of knowledge, [respect] can be in the form of competently taking yourself not to have (or be able to have) sufficient evidence to settle p?, and so intentionally adopting a settled attitude of suspension on p?. But it can also be just a matter of having, on the first order, a competence to know. Having good dispositions to withhold is essential to possessing competences to know. (Otherwise, except in very special environments, the reliability condition would fail.) [...] When a person withholds in these ways, we can say that she demonstrates her competence to know without exercising it. (2017, 433)

As such, at least on the face of it, making the respect condition very weak may afford Miracchi the following way to accommodate one-off permissible suspension cases: paradigmatically bad believers can also, on occasion, manifest respect for knowledge simply in suspending in ways that demonstrate their having a competence to know – even if, in the vast majority of their epistemic walks of life, they fail to do so, and thus fail to either manifest or demonstrate their said competence. Systematic failure to manifest a competence need not imply one does not have the said competence. I can have a competence to play the piano fabulously and still fail to do so whenever I get to it because, say, I am distracted. Insofar as the competence exists, however, it allows for one-off manifestations of competence, as well as for one-off demonstrations of competence. I can still play the piano fabulously on the few occasions when I care to do so (and thereby manifest my competence); I can also abstain from playing when I ascertain, for instance, that the conditions are not favourable (too dark), and thus I demonstrate my competence in forbearing from playing. Similarly, one could argue, bad believers and the Pyrrhonist may still have a competence to know and thus both manifest and demonstrate it on occasion. So far, so good.

Unfortunately, upon closer inspection, this response is not available to Miracchi. Miracchi's view is a reliabilist one. This will present her account with a strength dilemma related to cases of bad believers and what is involved in having a competence to know: according to Miracchi, the having of the said competence has to do with it being sufficiently objectively likely that whenever the sub-personal cognitive mechanisms that constitute the basis of the competence are operative, the conditions constitutive of knowledge obtain. It is easy to see that the case of bad believers presents an account like this with a strength dilemma: make the sufficiency threshold for the objective likelihood at stake too high and bad believers don't count as having the competence; if so, the account cannot explain one-off cases in which these people suspend permissibly. Conversely, make the likelihood threshold too low and the view is not a plausible reliabilism anymore.

The second reason why a reliabilist view like Miracchi's will struggle with permissible suspension goes, to some extent, back to the discussion of Sosa's negligence condition in the following sense: at the core of any reliabilist account lies an allowance for fallibility. My competences to know can fail to generate knowledge even when exercised; these are what Miracchi (2015) calls degenerate exercises of competence. When this happens, on Miracchi's view, one forms justified beliefs. The question that arises now is: if competences to know can be manifest in belief-formation episodes that fail to result in knowledge, it seems plausible that we should take the corresponding competence-demonstrating respect for knowledge to be manifest even in instances in which there is failure of permissible suspension. After all, since the competence is fallible, it should also be possible for it to fail in this way: I am an excellent epistemic agent, I evaluate my evidence thoroughly, and I come to suspend on the issue; unfortunately, this is one of the (otherwise very few) instances in which I am wrong about what my evidence supports. My suspension, intuitively, demonstrates my (fallible) competence to know; nevertheless, my suspension is unjustified. Note that this is also plausible on general grounds having to do with how manifesting respect works more generally: it doesn't always lead to success in treating the respected party in the right way due to, for example, moral bad luck. But if manifesting respect for knowledge allows for instances that lead to improper suspension, we are left without resources to explain what exactly is going wrong in these cases.[2]

4.4 Gesturing towards a Better Way

I share with several of the people discussed so far a commitment to a telic normative structure. In what follows, I thus want to go back to Ernie

---

[2] Finally, a similar problem arises (even more straightforwardly) for the Sylvan and Lord (2022) Kantian incarnation of the view. According to them, what it is for A's doxastic reaction (be it belief, suspension, etc.) D to respect the truth is for D to be the output of an exercise of a competence to react for normative epistemic reasons. Since the only plausible way to conceive of the competence at stake in creatures like us is to allow for its fallibility, the view will have trouble explaining the impermissibility of suspension in one-off cases of failure to properly assess one's normative reasons.

Sosa's view, for illustrative purposes, and gesture at a different way to accommodate the normative defeasibility of suspension within general telic normativity. In particular, I will suggest that what is needed is to enlarge the normative remit of epistemic telic normativity in line with plausible normative facts about general telic normativity.

Recall that we have identified two in-principle problems with the virtue-theoretic account of epistemically permissible suspension under discussion. First, Sosa's epistemic telic normativity is the normativity of attempts, but in the cases under discussion no attempt is being made to begin with: the defeating evidence is totally ignored. As such, what we need is an account that accommodates attempts that *should* have been made.

Second, on Sosa's account of suspension, one properly suspends belief on a question if one suspends based sufficiently on one's lack of the competence required in order to judge aptly. However, many of the protagonists in the cases we have looked at do lack the relevant competences: the sexist scientist, for instance, is not a competent uptaker of testimony from women due to his sexist bias. He does suspend based on his (sexism-induced) lack of competence to judge aptly. What seems to matter, then, is not whether one misses a competence or not, but rather whether one *should* have had the competence to begin with.

Both of these points suggest that we need more normative resources than epistemic telic normativity, as put forth by Sosa, provides: for a correct account of justified suspension, we need to be able to also assess (at least some) attempts that *should* be made and competences one *should* have within theory of knowledge proper, rather than merely at the level of intellectual ethics.

At the same time, of course, some 'shoulds' governing attempts and competences will fall outside of theory of knowledge proper indeed, falling squarely within the remit of intellectual ethics. The question as to whether I should or should not know more about mathematics, the geography of oceans, and the workings of the human lungs than I presently do will not concern the theory of knowledge, and the corresponding normative failures – should I exhibit them – will not defeat my justification for my current beliefs and suspensions.[3]

If all of this is right, it would seem that what needs to be done is that we must move the border between the theory of knowledge proper and intellectual ethics, such that we allow some 'shoulds' governing attempts

---

[3] But see Chapters 8 and 9 for more discussion of epistemic obligations to inquire.

and competences to fall on the side of theory of knowledge while others remain squarely within intellectual ethics.

I will begin by discussing shoulds governing attempts. First, to see why it is independently plausible that attempts that should have been made can be domain-internal, let's go back to Diana, the huntress: Diana's archery shots can be more or less well selected. We have seen that Sosa agrees that there are two ways in which Diana can fall short with regard to her aim to succeed aptly: she could make an attempt on the target when she would not succeed aptly – because, maybe, the shot would be too risky, given the wind. But she could also fail in her attempt by failing to make an attempt (on the target) when one would succeed aptly. There are thus two types of meta-competence failure that Diana can display: failure to assess risk properly, but also failure to assess opportunity properly. When going back to epistemology, the latter failure is the stuff of unjustified suspension: a failure to judge (affirmatively or negatively) when one would have judged aptly (independently of whether one attempted to do so or not).

Now, here is one question: why think that Diana's failure of the second kind (opportunity assessment failure) is conditional upon her making any attempts (including attempting to shoot and including attempts to shoot if and only if the shot is apt) to begin with? Why think that this should pertain to the normativity of extant attempts rather than to the normativity of attempts that should have been made? After all, it is plausibly constitutive of the huntress's professional role that she should make hunting attempts, including attempting to shoot if and only if the shot is apt. A huntress that fails to make any hunting attempts is a rubbish huntress. The meta-competence to assess risks and opportunities in Diana's case is not attempt-conditional. It is also, at the same time, not domain-external: the question is not whether Diana should become a huntress to begin with – that's, of course, the stuff of professional ethics. Rather, what is going on is that, in her capacity as a huntress, Diana shoulders shoulds pertaining to attempts she should make, not just shoulds governing the ones she does make. Indeed, plausibly, these shoulds are constitutive of what it is to be a huntress to begin with.

If this is so, on pain of losing the analogy, we should expect that the normativity internal to the domain of the theory of knowledge proper follows suit: there will be attempts that the epistemic agent should make, given that the opportunity arises to judge or suspend aptly as a result of making said attempts. Epistemic agents who will ignore easy opportunities by not even attempting will be rubbish epistemic agents, just like huntresses who don't bother to take easy targets, or who don't even bother to assess shooting opportunities, are rubbish huntresses.

There is, of course, an important disanalogy between the two cases: one can choose not to be a huntress. It's harder for agents like us, with our cognitive capacities, to choose not to be epistemic agents. If so, the domain-external question – should I engage in epistemic endeavours? – does not even arise for us: we just can't help it. What room is there left, then, on this picture, for questions of intellectual ethics?

Note that Diana is not an ideal huntress: there are limits to the amount of opportunities she can take. Should she find herself in a forest filled with thousands of easily available targets, she can only reasonably be expected to make a limited number of attempts. Likely, she will be normatively constrained to shoot at the most readily available targets. For the rest, it's up to her: she can't attempt to shoot at all of them, so it's up to other normative considerations not pertaining to the domain of hunting to decide which to go for. Maybe Diana has moral concerns against shooting cubs; maybe she has prudential interests in favour of shooting valuable prey; in all of these cases, these domain-external normative considerations will guide her choices.

Our epistemic environment is a bit like the forest filled with too many shooting opportunities. We have plenty of opportunities to judge aptly about thousands of things just as we walk down the street. We can't take them all: we are psychologically limited creatures. Some we should (epistemically) take: I should form the belief that there's a building before me when it's in plain sight; I should believe the testimony of others, absent defeat; and so on.

For the rest, there will be many opportunities that I just can't take because of the limited kind of being that I am: there's a limited number of attempts at apt judgement I can make. That's why whether I decide to study maths is a question of intellectual ethics, guided by prudential, moral, and other non-epistemic normative constraints. Epistemology only asks that I take the easiest of opportunities that lie right in front of me, just like hunting only asks that Diana makes attempts at the easy targets.

This concludes my discussion of attempts one (epistemically) should make: they correspond to (easy) epistemic opportunities one should take because one would thereby aptly judge. The should at stake is internal to the epistemic domain because it pertains to what it is to be a good epistemic agent to begin with.

How about cases in which you lack the relevant competence to begin with, although you should have had it? Recall that the case of the sexist scientist is plausibly like that: he does suspend based on his lack of competence to judge aptly, which, in turn, is triggered by his sexism: he can't give the woman the credibility she deserves. Is this failure also going to be epistemic domain-internal? After all, by stipulation, the sexist scientist does not miss an opportunity to believe aptly, since he lacks the competence to properly assess the woman's credibility to begin with.

I suggest that we step away from epistemology once more, go back to cases of general telic normativity, and ask the question: is it plausible to think that there are norms internal to the domain of hunting that regulate what competences huntresses should have? I think the answer is clearly 'yes'. Indeed, it is arguable that these are norms that are constitutive of the domain: huntresses should, at a minimum, be able to spot her prey, shoot, and hit it with some degree of reliability in normal environmental conditions. Huntresses who lack these basic abilities are rubbish huntresses; indeed, if they lack them all, they may no longer count as huntresses to begin with. And this is not the stuff of professional ethics but rather is constitutively normative of the domain of hunting itself.

Similarly, I want to suggest that epistemic agents who lack competences that are constitutive of the kind of epistemic agents that we are rubbish epistemic agents by the light of normativity internal to the epistemic domain itself. Sexists, hallucinators, and wishful thinkers alike are in breach of epistemic norms proper. This explains why the normativity of competences one should (epistemically) have can affect the normative status of one's epistemic attempts.

This section did not have the ambition to develop a full account of permissible suspension within a more inclusive theory that takes competences to matter for justification, but rather to gesture towards the resources that are needed if we are to make progress on this front. Chapter 9 will develop an account along these lines of permissible suspension that places centre stage the notion of being in a position to know.

4.5 Conclusion

This chapter looked at what I take to be the three most prominent accounts of permissible suspension recently put forth in the literature: the simple knowledge-based account, the simple virtue-based account, and the respect-based account. I have argued that the simple knowledge-based view faces insurmountable difficulties, in that it implies a highly problematic claim: that suspension implies obligatory suspension. I have then argued that Sosa's epistemic telic normativity is in need of normative expansion or else it cannot deal with normative defeat. I have also looked at a respect-centric variety of virtue theory about permissible suspension from Miracchi and Sylvan and Lord, and I argued that, while the knowledge/truth respect condition on permissible suspension that they favour may deal exceptionally well with paradigmatic cases of impermissible suspension, it is both too strong and too weak to be useful for an analysis thereof. Finally, on a positive note, I have suggested that, in line with general telic normativity, we should conceive of epistemic telic normativity as also concerning attempts we should have made, as well as competences we should have had.

CHAPTER 5

Resistance to Evidence, Epistemic Responsibility, and Epistemic Vice

We have seen that available accounts of possessed evidence, evidence one should have possessed, and permissible suspension of judgement struggle to accommodate the phenomenon of evidence resistance. Along the way, we have, in particular, seen that virtue reliabilist accounts of reasons to believe, permissible suspension, and propositional warrant don't do the needed work. At that point, some readers would have already thought that one straightforward explanation of the resistance data is afforded by the competing, virtue responsibilist camp: roughly, on this view, evidence resistance could be conceptualised as a failure to manifest epistemic responsibility in inquiry and/or as a manifestation/indication of epistemic vice. This chapter looks into the credentials of this move. I argue that once we distinguish epistemic virtues and vices proper from mere moral virtues and vices with epistemic content, it transpires that accounting for resistance cases, as well as accounting for epistemic virtue and vice, requires epistemic value-first unpacking.

5.1 Responsible Inquiry and Epistemic Character Traits

A prominent project in responsibilist virtue epistemology (henceforth also VR for short) is to develop 'maps' or 'perspicuous representations' of intellectual virtues, such as intellectual humility, intellectual courage, open-mindedness, and curiosity. The basic idea is to develop empirically grounded characterisations of epistemically admirable or praiseworthy character traits and to use these characterisations as guidance in a kind of regulative epistemology, sometimes with the aim of informing education theory. To take a few examples, Jason Baehr characterises the 'open-minded' person as someone who is 'willing [...] to transcend a default cognitive standpoint in order to [...] take seriously a distinct cognitive standpoint' (2011, 152). Heather Battaly characterises the 'epistemically humble' person as someone who is 'disposed to recognize her own fallibility, and to recognize and value the epistemic abilities of others [...]'

(2014, 194). James Montmarquet characterises the 'epistemically courageous' person as someone who has the disposition to 'persevere in the face of opposition from others (until one is convinced that one is mistaken) [...]' (1993, 23). And Roberts and Wood characterise the 'epistemically autonomous' person as someone who has the 'proper ability to think for herself and not be [...] improperly dependent on or influenced by others' (2007, 259).

In many ways, this work is an exciting new development in epistemology. For example, it highlights possible avenues for widening the traditional epistemological project. In particular, and importantly for my purposes, it might be thought that intellectual virtue and vice bear in crucial ways on the phenomenon of evidence resistance. Look back at our toy cases of resistance: in many of them, one might think, plausible epistemic vices – sexism, racism, laziness, partiality, closed-mindedness, wishful thinking, etc. – are explicitly present and manifest. The particular resistant episode traces back to said vice.

Let me, however, get a few things out of the way: it is crucial to note that, whatever the virtue responsibilist account of the impermissibility of evidence resistance will turn out to be, it cannot be too straightforward a view; that is, it cannot account for said impermissibility simply in terms of the absence of virtue/presence of vice in the resistant cogniser, nor can evidence resistance be simply accounted for in terms of the manifestation of some bad character trait. Agents with excellent epistemic characters can undergo isolated episodes of evidence resistance, and their virtuousness does not make the latter any less epistemically bad. Whatever the view is, then, it needs to be more subtle than this.

Jason Baehr notably champions an early (2009) stance on the issue that treats the data and VR's theoretical resources with the necessary care. Baehr argues at length against traditional evidentialism by bringing forth two types of cases: cases of failure in inquiry – where S's body of evidence is problematically affected by lazy or biased inquiry – and cases of bad responses to available evidence due, again, to some variety of bias or wishful thinking. His diagnosis is that traditional evidentialism needs to be supplemented with a good epistemic character condition. In what follows, I will mostly focus my analysis on Baehr's account, but, since his account features a fairly minimal responsibilist condition, everything I say should apply, *mutatis mutandis*, to all accounts that want to explain cases of evidence resistance as, in one way or another, having to do with character failure. Here is Baehr's proposal for what it means for a subject S to be justified:

Responsible Evidentialism (RE): S is justified in believing *p* at *t* if and only if S's evidence at *t* *appears to* S to support *p*, *provided that* if S's agency makes a salient contribution to S's evidential situation with respect to *p*, S functions (qua agent) in a manner consistent with intellectual virtue. (2009, 16, emphases in original)

Note a few advantages of RE. First, while it does feature a good character requirement on top of traditional evidentialist necessary conditions for justification, is not a very strong character requirement: the justified subject need not manifest intellectual virtues, nor be a virtuous agent to begin with – the epistemically vicious among us can also form justified beliefs, insofar as either their agency is not munch involved in arriving at a particular body of evidence at work in a particular belief-formation episode (and here Baehr has in mind as paradigmatic garden-variety automatic perceptual belief formation) or else, should their agency be thus involved, their evidential situation will have been arrived at in a manner consistent with intellectual virtue. In a nutshell, the vicious can form justified beliefs either automatically or via virtuous-like agency. The fact that the account does not require virtue to be present or manifest is a great feat: it does not implausibly exclude the vicious from having a chance at justified beliefs, and, even more crucially, it can, at least at first glance, accommodate one-off cases of evidence resistance, in which the subject's bad epistemic character is not to blame – since the subject is a virtuous yet fallible believer.

I think Baehr's account, in not imposing a particularly demanding epistemic character condition on justification, is probably as good an account as possible for trying to explain the impermissibility of instances of evidence resistance within a virtue responsibilist framework: after all, again, clearly, episodes of resistance do not require vice, nor vice manifestation, but rather can be mere one-off failures of otherwise perfectly virtuous believers.

Nevertheless, in what follows I will argue that Baehr's account does not work for two main reasons, having to do with (1) difficulties in precisifying the character condition and (2) epistemic virtue individuation. If I am right, these two problems together will paint a pessimistic picture for the prospects of accounting for the impermissibility of evidence resistance for the champion of virtue responsibilism: since Baehr's character condition is a very non-demanding one, *mutatis mutandis*, all of Baehr's difficulties will translate to most virtue responsibilist attempts to accommodate these data. In what follows, I will take these worries in turn.

The crucial responsibility requirement in Baehr's account of justification, and the one that is designed to take care of resistance cases, requires there to be the case that, if S's agency makes a salient contribution to S's evidential situation with respect to p, S functions (qua agent) in a manner consistent with intellectual virtue. Two things require more spelling out: first, what it is for a virtue to be a genuine intellectual (rather than, for example, moral or prudential) virtue – this is the individuation issue that we will look at in the next section; and second, what it is for a believer to function qua agent in a manner that is consistent with such intellectual virtue.

I will start with the latter: my worry is that it will be difficult to spell out the virtue consistency relation in a manner that is permissive enough for allowing for ubiquity of epistemic justification but also efficient in dealing with resistance cases. To see why, note, once more, that we are fallible creatures: whatever virtues we may have, it will be consistent with them that we fail to manifest them on occasion, and also that we fail to do the right thing on occasion, in spite of manifesting them. No matter how courageous I might be, I may, on occasion, fail to be the first to reach the enemy's lines. I need not do the perfectly courageous thing all of the time in order for my actions to be consistent with having the relevant character virtue. Furthermore, even in manifesting courage, I may end up doing things that look cowardly due to misreading the facts on the ground. Again, we are fallible creatures: in us, virtues can be manifested in instances of failure. If so, however, one-off cases of evidence resistance will be consistent with both having and manifesting intellectual virtue. In what sense of consistency, then, are we to interpret Baehr's character constraint?

One option would be to follow Williamson (forthcominga) and go modal: maybe what it is for a believer to function qua agent in a manner that is consistent with intellectual virtue has to do with doing what the virtuous person would do in the situation at stake. Unfortunately, this will not work either, once more, in virtue of virtue fallibility: after all, the impeccably virtuous person involved in a one-off case of evidence resistance is doing what a virtuous person – namely, themselves – would do in that situation.

As far as I can tell, what the Baehr account requires to solve this problem is character virtue infallibilism: on a view like this, resistance cases are not consistent with epistemic virtue because the virtuous person just would not fail in this way. Unfortunately, though, as soon as we go down this route, we lose both general plausibility for our account of epistemic character traits (we are fallible creatures!) and, even more crucially for our purposes, Baehr's responsibilist evidentialism renders justification a rare commodity, to be held only by the flawless among us.

I started off by saying that I had two worries for Baehr's view, having to do with spelling out consistency with epistemic virtue and, respectively, with individuating epistemic virtue. The remainder of this chapter concerns itself with the latter.

5.2 Content-Individuating Responsibilist Virtues and Vices

Virtue responsibilist epistemologies reveal some of the complex ways in which the disciplines of epistemology and ethics seem to overlap: character matters for normativity, the thought goes – be it moral or epistemic. However, this raises an important question: that of whether, or to what extent, a given intellectual virtue counts as distinctively *epistemic* as opposed to moral or prudential; after all, as we have already seen in Chapter 3, we have strong reason to be sceptical of the possibility of explaining away resistance cases in terms of mere moral failures.

It is here that I think the virtue responsibilist project requires careful handling. After all, the notion of virtue (in the responsibilist sense of a character trait) is familiar first and foremost from ethics. Moreover, it's not clear what relation the virtues at stake stand in to more traditional moral virtues, for example. Indeed, it seems plausible that some of them *just are* paradigm cases of garden-variety moral virtues as opposed to some other kind of virtue. A fully worked out account of the intellectual virtues should be able to clearly address this issue. It seems central to our understanding of the relevance of an investigation into some virtue or another for epistemology. It also seems central to our understanding of the scope of epistemology itself.

In what follows, I do three things: first, I argue that two popular individuation recipes for epistemic virtues and vices don't work. Second, I defend a value-centric way of individuating virtues, including intellectual ones. Third, I argue that this way of individuating virtues gives us reason to be somewhat more cautious in our claims to make progress in the epistemology of evidence resistance (and, more generally, in the epistemology of justification) by investigating intellectual virtues.

How can we individuate distinctively epistemic character traits? In order to answer this question, I'd like to start by looking into the way in which philosophers in the epistemic norms literature individuate epistemic norms and take it from there. After all, virtues and vices are normative; if so, individuating epistemic virtues and vices will benefit from whatever the correct individuation recipe is for epistemic norms. Let's first consider the following proposal:

Content Individuation (CI)
If a norm N concerns epistemic features required for permissible phi-ing, then N is an epistemic norm.

It is safe to say that, if there is such a thing as a received view in the epistemic norms literature concerning what that literature is theorising about in the first place, it is CI.[1] Many philosophers, for instance, when they ask what the epistemic norm for phi-ing is, take themselves to be asking, roughly, how much epistemic warrant one needs for proper phi-ing. For example, here is Jennifer Lackey (arguing that cases of isolated second-hand knowledge show that knowledge is not the epistemic norm of assertion):

> It should be emphasized that it is clear that the problem with the agents in the above cases is that it is not *epistemically* appropriate for them to flat-out assert that *p* [...]. One reason this is clear is that the criticism of the agents concerns the *grounds* for their assertions [...]. (2014, 38, emphases in original)

Thus, according to Lackey, insofar as norms concern epistemic grounds, they will be genuine epistemic norms. On a similar note, here is Ishani Maitra (on a view about the nature of assertion that she takes to be widely endorsed):

> Assertions are governed by an alethic or an epistemic norm – that is, a norm that specifies that it is appropriate to assert something only if what is asserted is true, or justifiably believed, or certain or known. (2011, 277)

There is very good methodological reason to endorse CI: it is both simple and user-friendly. CI provides a neat and straightforward way to individuate epistemic norms, ensuring that the debate can be framed on common terminological ground.

Most importantly for present purposes, CI might help us to individuate distinctively epistemic virtues. After all, if epistemic norms are individuated by content, as CI has it, since virtues are normative, it is independently plausible that the same goes for epistemic virtues.

Virtue Content Individuation (VCI)
If a virtue V concerns epistemic features required for virtuous phi-ing, then V is an epistemic virtue.

---

[1] For explicit endorsements, see, for example, Lackey (2011), Maitra (2011), Brown (2012), and Benton (2014). For implicit assumptions to this effect, see Hawthorne (2004), Gerken (2011), and Littlejohn and Turri (2015).

Note that the sorts of virtues that the VR literature has focused on, including open-mindedness, intellectual humility, curiosity, epistemic courageousness, and temperance, clearly concern epistemic features. By VCI, these virtues are epistemic virtues.

In fact, there is yet another way of making the very same point. Once more, virtues are widely taken to be normative. The following is an attractive way of capturing this thought:

Normative Charge of Virtues (NCV)
One's actions and states ought to manifest virtuous character traits.[2]

By NCV, virtues are associated with oughts. Note also that the oughts they are associated with are typed by the type of virtue in question. For instance, if the virtue to be manifested is a moral virtue, the ought at issue in NCV is a moral ought; if the virtue to be manifested is an aesthetic virtue, the ought at issue in NCV is an aesthetic ought; and so on.

NCV gives us the result that virtues of a certain type are associated with oughts of the same type. Now we may expect to use our recipe for individuating epistemic norms to home in on distinctively epistemic virtues. After all, given that types of virtues are by NCV associated with the corresponding types of norms, if we have a recipe for individuating types of norms, we might be able to use it to individuate the associated virtues as well. In particular, should CI be the right way to individuate epistemic norms, we get the result that, if the virtuous character trait at issue in NCV concerns epistemic features, then the norm is epistemic. And since the sorts of virtues that the VR literature has focused on and that are at issue in the relevant instances of NCV do concern epistemic features, we once more get the result that these virtues are indeed epistemic virtues.

And while it might be thought that this is all entirely as it should be, on reflection, there is reason to think otherwise. To see why, note that both of the above arguments rely on CI for their motivation. The first uses CI to motivate VCI, which is key to that argument, and the second uses CI expressly in the relevant derivation. The trouble is that there is excellent reason to think that CI is false. More specifically, as I will argue

---

[2] NCV requires some noteworthy qualifications. First, it's quite plausible that it needs to be restricted to *relevant* actions (i.e. those that can be performed in a way that manifests the relevant virtue). For instance, while it is plausible that I ought to be generous in my dealings with my friends, it does not seem to be the case that I ought to be generous in sitting down. Second, the oughts at issue here are defeasible. For instance, if I have overriding reason not to be generous in my dealings with my friends (perhaps because someone threatens to kill me if I am), it is not the case that I ought to be thus generous, at least not all things considered. Since these qualifications are of little consequence for the purposes of this chapter, in what follows we will take them as read.

momentarily, first, CI does not generalise in the right way, and, second, it is extensionally inadequate.

To see this why CI doesn't generalise as it should, let's get the generalisation on the table. Here is what it looks like:

Generalised Content Individuation (GCI)
If a norm N concerns features of type T required for permissible phi-ing, then N is a norm of type T.³

Unfortunately, there is excellent reason to think that GCI is false. Consider, for instance, traffic norms: driving one's car within city bounds will surely be subject to whatever the local traffic regulations have to say about it. Say that the relevant traffic norm forbids one from driving faster than 30 miles per hour. However, imagine that a terrorist group has placed a bomb in the centre of town and you are the only one able to diffuse it. In order to get there in time, you must break the traffic norm and drive at 40 miles per hour. Clearly, the latter (moral, prudential) requirement overrides the traffic norm and renders driving at 40 miles per hour the all-things-considered proper thing to do. In this case, the bomb threat drives the all-things-considered proper speed up to 40 miles per hour. The moral requirement, in this case, has traffic-related content: it regulates the morally (and all-things-considered) appropriate speed. If that is the case, however, it looks as though, just because a norm has traffic-related content – just because it regulates the appropriate speed – it need not follow that it is a traffic norm. GCI fails for traffic norms.

What's more, the traffic case is hardly isolated. Similar examples can be construed for many types of normativity. It can be prudentially or morally appropriate to drive faster or slower, to have a better or a worse grade point average, to wear a lighter or a darker dress at a funeral, or to speak louder or more quietly. Just because a norm regulates the appropriate degree of a traffic-related feature (i.e. speed), it need not follow that it is a traffic norm. Just because a norm regulates a fashion-related feature (i.e. colour of dress), it need not follow that it is a fashion norm. And so on. GCI is false.

What about CI? Given that GCI does not hold, there is, of course, every reason to believe that the same goes for epistemic norms: just because a

---

³ There are many problems with CI that I will not discuss here. One such problem, for instance, is: how is the typing supposed to work for biconditional norms, such as 'hit the emergency brake if and only if you see someone stuck on the escalator'? Is this a norm for permissible brake-hitting? If so, it has features of accident-witnessing as permissibility requirement. Or is it a norm for permissible accident-witnessing? If so, it has features of brake-hitting as permissibility requirements. Is it both, and does it have both as permissibility requirements and would thus be classed as a norm of two types?

norm regulates the appropriate degree of an epistemic feature, it need not follow that it is an epistemic norm. It may indeed happen to be an epistemic norm; but it may also be the case that it is a norm of a different nature – say, a prudential or moral norm – with epistemic content. It may be a norm of some other kind that simply happens to regulate the (morally, prudentially, etc.) proper degree of an epistemic feature. To see this, consider the following examples:

> SING. One must sing only songs one knows.
> JUMP. One must not jump in lakes unless one knows how to swim.
> ASSERT. One must assert only what one knows.
> BELIEVE. One must believe only what one has sufficient evidence for.

All four norms have epistemic content. Accordingly, CI will predict that they are all distinctively epistemic norms. However, that is intuitively implausible; while ASSERT and BELIEVE are plausibly epistemic norms, SING and JUMP are not. Instead, SING is plausibly an aesthetic and/or prudential norm, and JUMP is plausibly a prudential norm, although both have epistemic content.

What transpires, then, is that just because a norm has epistemic content, it does not follow that it is an epistemic norm. Just because it concerns epistemic features (i.e. what epistemic position one needs to be in in order to permissibly phi), it does not follow that it concerns distinctively epistemic permissibility. It can also regulate an epistemic feature required for prudentially, morally, aesthetically, etc., permissible phi-ing. What CI allows us to home in on are norms with epistemic content rather than genuinely epistemic norms.

If all of this is right, however – that is, if CI fails as a criterion for individuating genuinely epistemic norms – we should also be suspicious of the ways of individuating epistemic virtues that it serves to motivate, since virtues are normative. For instance, since CI fails to distinguish between epistemic norms and mere (moral, prudential, aesthetic, etc.) norms with epistemic content, we may legitimately wonder whether VCI correspondingly fails to distinguish between genuinely epistemic virtues and virtues of different stripes (e.g. moral, prudential, etc.) with epistemic content. And, of course, this worry is only more pressing for the individuating recipe that relies on CI directly.

And, indeed, on closer inspection, one encounters such cases in the literature. Consider, for instance, Roberts and Wood's example of the intellectual virtue of epistemic temperance:

> In Toni Morrison's novel *Beloved*, the slave-narrator comments on a slave-owner who was a cut about the average that he looked away when the slave

women were nursing their infants. This intentional foregoing of acquaintance expresses respect for the women's privacy and a sense of the limits that human proprieties set to appropriate knowledge [...]. To be an indiscriminate ogler is a trait of bad intellectual character, a failure of discipline of the will to know. (2007, 175)

Although this virtue is associated with an epistemic feature, it is not at all clear that it qualifies as a genuinely epistemic virtue rather than a virtue of some other denomination that has epistemic content. After all, by the lights of the authors themselves, this particular virtue expresses '*respect for the women's privacy* and a sense of the limits that *human proprieties* set to appropriate knowledge' (Roberts and Wood 2007, 175, emphases added). As such, it is more natural to read it as a kind of moral virtue, albeit one that has something to do with the epistemic domain – a moral virtue with epistemic content. Indeed, epistemic temperance through the foregoing of acquaintance looks like a paradigmatic example of a moral virtue, the exercise of which *limits* the gathering of information and knowledge. And from a purely epistemic perspective, at any rate, this seems like precisely the opposite of what the exercise of an epistemic virtue would be apt to limit.

Let us take stock. The challenge we aim to meet on behalf of VR is to find a criterion for normative typing that will allow VR to remain within the boundaries of epistemology proper. This will help us determine whether and to what extent the intellectual virtues being mapped by VR theorists are genuinely epistemic virtues and thus to be usefully employed for an account of epistemic justification and, conversely, of the epistemic impermissibility of evidence resistance. On the first view we looked at, epistemic norms and, by extension, epistemic virtues are concerned with distinctively epistemic features; that is to say, epistemic norms and virtues, as such, are norms and virtues with epistemic content. We have seen, however, that CI for epistemic norms and virtues runs into trouble on at least two counts. First, it doesn't generalise to other normative domains in the way it ought to. And second, on reflection, there is reason to think that it even makes counterintuitive predictions in the epistemic domain.

In what follows, I will look at a different proposal for individuating epistemic virtues and vices: by the psychological reality that they describe.

5.3 Psychological Vice Individuation

In her recent book, Alessandra Tanesini (2021) offers a systematic, comprehensive, thoroughly empirically informed picture of the nature and normativity of epistemic vice. The book is also aiming to carve out new methodological space in the epistemology of vice beyond the reliabilist/responsibilist divide in virtue epistemology. Tanesini sees her project to be one of 'autonomous' epistemology. The ground of epistemic vice on this view is neither responsibility nor reliability: it lies with psychological reality. If successful, the view offers an alternative individuation recipe for epistemic virtues and vices and thereby an alternative, psychology-of-vice-based explanation of what is going on in resistance cases.

On Tanesini's account, epistemic vices are taken to be essentially sourced in attitudes towards the self: fatalism, self-satisfaction, narcissistic infatuation, and self-abasement. The thought, roughly, is that some people have a self-infatuated stance towards their intellectual qualities, which they therefore assess as superlative without pausing to consider their true epistemic worth. Others, in contrast, adopt a self-abasing and negative stance towards their intellectual abilities. Consequently, they become ashamed of their intellectual qualities, which they perceive to be extremely limited.

Fatalism, self-satisfaction, narcissistic infatuation, and self-abasement are attitudes towards the self that ground epistemic vices of self-assessment. These are exemplified by those who do not have the measure of their intellectual abilities because they assess their epistemic worth using the wrong unit of measurement:

> [F]or instance, those who are motivated to self-enhance tend to compare themselves for how they differ from less capable individuals so as to find further confirmation of their excellence. I use the metaphor of measuring oneself by the wrong unit to describe this phenomenon of biased selection of the yardstick (as represented by the relative ability of another person or group) by which to evaluate one's own performance. (Tanesini 2021, 15)

Since these evaluations are crucial in the setting of realistic epistemic goals, in the choices of methods and strategies to adopt in inquiry, and in the process of epistemic self-improvement, those whose self-assessments are thus misguided are unlikely in ordinary circumstances to excel in their epistemic pursuits.

That being said, on Tanesini's account, the presence of vice is essentially connected to its being sourced in self-assessments that employ the wrong unit of measurement and not to the falsity of its constitutive doxastic attitudes, nor its (likely) unfortunate epistemic consequences.

In what follows, I take issue with Tanesini's vice internalism: epistemic vices are vices, I argue, only if externalistically individuated. I'll focus on what Tanesini calls 'vices of self-satisfaction', like narcissism and superbia, because they are the ones that are most paradigmatically relevant to episodes of evidence resistance – although evidence resistance in virtue of unwarranted lack of trust in one's epistemic abilities is also perfectly possible, and likely often encountered in historically marginalised groups. Nothing hinges on this though – the worries I outline generalise neatly to the entire framework.

The presence of vice, on Tanesini's account, is independent of the accuracy of the vice-constitutive beliefs about oneself – I might be right that I am the smartest person in the world, but if this belief is sourced in bad self-assessment processes, it has the disposition to be vice-constitutive nevertheless. Furthermore, it may be that my narcissism is, de facto, extremely reliable, in that it mostly outputs true beliefs: it remains an epistemic vice on Tanesini's view nevertheless. For this, Tanesini takes vices to supervene on subjects' psychologies (i.e. on particular attitudes towards the self). Here is what Tanesini thinks about individuals who are in the grips of vices of self-satisfaction:

> [These] individuals adopt a self-satisfied stance towards what they regard as their intellectual strengths. They believe that a great number of their intellectual features are impressive. These individuals are also often averse to working towards improvement. They adopt this stance because they believe that they are already great and thus have no need to improve. Hence, their mindset is [...] fixed since they judge themselves to be naturally talented and thus capable of effortless success. (Tanesini 2021, 15)

Vices of self-satisfaction will be individuated by the corresponding attitude. Accuracy doesn't matter: my self-satisfied beliefs about myself may well be (luckily) true. What's crucial to vice presence is that they are not sourced in/based on evidence, but rather are sourced in/based on mistaken self-directed attitudes (self-admiration, self-defence, etc). Here is Tanesini:

> We should expect narcissistic and self-satisfied self-evaluations to be off the mark by underestimating shortcomings and overestimating strengths. However, in unusual circumstances, it is possible that such individuals may have impressive intellectual strengths and through sheer luck their self-assessments may prove to be largely accurate. [...] The person with narcissistic tendencies, for example, is disposed to bullshit even though he holds true beliefs about his capacities. What makes his claims about the self, among other things, bullshit is that he does not care whether they are true. (Tanesini 2021, 15)

One can distinguish between two truth-independence claims in Tanesini's view: first, the presence of the vice is compatible with it being (mostly) constituted by true beliefs about oneself. Second, the presence of the vice is also independent of its epistemic consequences: it might be that, in virtue of holding this attitude towards myself, I am highly successful in inquiry – in the sense that I am more likely to discover truths and avoid falsehoods. Here they are, just for simplicity of use:

Constitutive Truth Independence (CTI): epistemic vices are compatible with the truth of their constitutive beliefs.
Consequence Valence Independence (CVI): vices are compatible with a positive epistemic valence of their epistemic consequences.

Furthermore, Tanesini proposes that epistemic vice fully supervenes on one's psychology – both metaphysically and normatively. Let's formulate this claim for ease of use as well:

Tanesini's Vice Internalism (TVI): epistemic vices supervene on the subject's psychological attitudes.

In what follows, I argue for three claims: first, that CTI and CVI do not suffice to support TVI, nor any other internalism about vice. Rather, CTI and CVI merely reinforce the already popular view that a simple, de facto reliabilist view of epistemic normativity is wrong. Compatibly, I argue, epistemic vices might still require externalistic individuation of a different flavour.

Second, I argue that, indeed, epistemic vice will need a hook in the world outside of one's skull if it is to be plausibly epistemically normatively problematic.

Finally, I consider a comeback on behalf of vice internalism: even though, if I'm right, CTI and CVI do not do the analytic work that the vice internalist needs them to do, they might still be useful for doing the social psychological work – that is, while vice internalism need not follow from CTI and CVI, it might still be the case that, in the world we inhabit, and given the kinds of creatures that we are, it is paradigmatically the case that vices will survive truth and reliability. I will put forth some worries for this claim.

Here it goes: I think Tanesini is right about CTI and CVI. Plausibly, epistemic vice can survive accuracy of constitutive beliefs and de facto reliability. That's hardly surprising, one would think: we already know from research on externalist theories of justification and the norm of belief that (1) plausibly, there's more to attributively good belief than truth, and (2) blunt, de facto reliabilism just won't do as a theory of epistemic justification (e.g. Norman the Clairvoyant[4] has taught us as much). If so (i.e. if positive normative properties of beliefs don't supervene on either

---

[4] Here is the famous case by Laurence BonJour: "Norman, under certain conditions, which usually obtain, is a completely reliable clairvoyant with respect to certain kinds of subject matter.

truth or de facto reliability), we should also expect that negative epistemic dispositional properties need not imply the lack thereof.

Luckily true beliefs based on, for example, coin tosses don't make for (attributively) good beliefs: they don't make for good tokens of their type. If so, the fact that a particular attitude towards the self is grounded in true beliefs need not suggest it's not an (attributively) bad attitude. Vices can be grounded in true beliefs.

Wishful thinking is not a proper way to form beliefs, nor does it lead to good beliefs, even if it's reliable. If so, just because a way to form beliefs reliably results in true beliefs, it does not follow that it is not a bad way to form beliefs. Vices can be reliable.

That being said, CTI and CVI do not imply vice internalism, more than, for example, the knowledge norm of belief is an internalist norm or normal worlds reliabilism is an internalist view of justification. Champions of both of these views agree, respectively, that true beliefs are not good tokens of their type, and that de facto reliability need not imply that a method of belief formation is a good way to form beliefs. Indeed, any externalism about epistemic normativity in general that denies these two claims will be perfectly compatible with CTI and CVI, while, at the same time, denying that epistemic normative categories are internalistically individuated. Knowledge normers, for instance, are free to claim that non-knowledgeable (albeit true) beliefs can constitute vice, and that dispositions or attitudes that reliably lead to truths – but not knowledge – can be epistemic vices. Non-de-facto reliabilists will agree that vices can be de facto reliable: they will just hold that they are incompatible with normal worlds reliability, or proper function, and so on.

CTI and CVI do not imply vice internalism and thereby fail to offer support to TVI. But is TVI independently plausibly true? If yes, maybe CTI and CVI are mere symptoms of this reality.

I don't think so: vice internalism is false. To see this, let's ask the following question: what is it that makes, for example, narcissism and superbia into vices? On Tanesini's view, recall, it is the biased selection of the measuring unit used to measure oneself that explains the problematic nature of vices of self-assessment. But what is wrong with biased selection? What explains its negative epistemic valence, in virtue of which it grounds

He possesses no evidence or reasons of any kind for or against the general possibility of such a cognitive power or for or against the thesis that he possesses it. One day Norman comes to believe that the President is in New York City, though he has no evidence either for or against this belief. In fact the belief is true and results from his clairvoyant power under circumstances in which it is completely reliable" (BonJour 1985, 41).

vice? Here are a few answers that are not available to internalism: self-measurements involving biased unit selection are epistemically problematic because they cannot lead to knowledge, because they don't have a tendency to get it right in normal conditions, or in normal worlds, because they were selected for biological rather than epistemic success, etc. All of these normative grounds are not available to the vice internalist because they lie outside of the skull's limits. In a nutshell, then, when Tanesini talks of vice being grounded in self-measurements that employ the wrong measuring unit, what is it that explains the relevant wrongness? More precisely, what is it, within the subject's skull, that explains it?

I conjecture that vice internalism will have just as hard a time answering this question as general internalism about epistemic normativity has historically had: what is wrong with beliefs based on wishful thinking? Well, they are formed via a bad belief-forming process. Why is wishful thinking bad? Because it's not the right kind of process for forming beliefs. What is the right kind of process? Short of offering an ad hoc list, notoriously the answer will have to appeal to something outside the believer's skull.[5]

Maybe TVI was never intended as a dismantling analysis of epistemic vice (i.e. as offering necessary and sufficient conditions for its instantiation) but rather as a paradigm case analysis thereof: maybe, that is, the claim is rather that, paradigmatically, vices are independent of the truth of their constitutive beliefs, as well as of the valence of their epistemic consequences.

I worry about the plausibility of this take on the view: first, it seems to me as though it is both psychologically and epistemologically implausible that the exercise of epistemic vice will often and easily co-exist with accuracy. Consider: I believe I'm very good at maths due to self-admiration alone. Next, I do some maths. As it turns out, I'm getting things right all of the time. I find it implausible, at this juncture, to think that the inductive evidence is not (at least part) of the basis of my belief. Implausibility is not impossibility, of course: it may be that I totally ignore this inductive evidence. I submit, however, that it is psychologically implausible, so it will not serve as a paradigm case analysis of the phenomenon we are looking at.

Second, the problem generalises: if, whenever I believe (from self-mismeasuring) that I am good at phi-ing, I phi and get inductive evidence

---

[5] In recent work in reply to my worries, Tanesini concedes that the way forward for vice individuation will have to appeal to truth – in particular, that what makes epistemic vices into epistemic vices regards, roughly, their being sourced in a non-truth-orientated psychological tendency.

that I am good at phi-ing, it will be hard to see how it is that I am still instantiating narcissism or superbia rather than a merely justified belief that I'm great, sourced in a solid inductive basis.

In sum, Tanesini's rich account teaches us a lot about the psychology and epistemology of vice: de facto lack of reliability does not matter, and false constitutive beliefs are not needed for vice. Compatibly, though, I have argued, Tanesini's self-mismeasuring attitudes need externalist normative grounding: the 'mis' in the 'mismeasure of the self' can't be restricted to the limits of the skull. Epistemic normativity – be it of virtue or of vice – is externalist normativity: it has to do with epistemic values that lie outside our skulls, such as truth and knowledge.

In what follows, I will look at a competing proposal for individuating genuinely epistemic normative notions: by the values they are associated with. This option, I argue, is not only theoretically superior, but it is also extensionally adequate. However, alas, with this improved method to hand, many of the virtues discussed in the VR literature will fail to qualify as genuinely epistemic virtues. Rather, as ever, they are moral virtues with epistemic content. If so, the prospects of employing them in unpacking the epistemic impermissibility of resistance to evidence are dim.

5.4 Value-Based Vice Individuation

This section looks at a theory-neutral individuation recipe for epistemic virtues and vices based on a widely accepted claim concerning the relation between the axiological and the deontic.

The theory of normativity has a theory-neutral answer to the question of normative individuation ready to hand: norms can be typed by the type of *good* they are associated with.

> *Value Individuation (VI)*
> A norm N is of type T if and only if N is associated with goods of type T.

According to VI, prudential norms are associated with prudential goods, moral norms are associated with moral goods, and so on. All normative domains have goods (values) that are central to them, in virtue of the kind of normative domains they are: survival is a prudential good; promise-keeping is a moral good; politeness is a social good; beauty is an aesthetic good; money is a financial good. Similarly, if etymology is any guide to what normative domain 'the epistemic' is supposed to refer to, knowledge is an epistemic good. But given that this is so, philosophers cannot just stipulate that, starting tomorrow, they will use 'moral' to refer to a type of normative domain that does not care about promise-keeping but does care about money, or 'financial' to refer to a domain of which the chief good is safe driving. Similarly, it would be odd to count wealth and having short nails amongst epistemic goods. We have some independent hold on the relevant types of goods. Given that this is so, VI holds out the hope of offering a helpful way of typing norms by the goods associated with them.

This is, of course, still rather vague, and in particular the association relation at issue requires spelling out. After all, one way in which a norm can be associated with a particular good is by requiring more or less of that good. This, however, will put us back in the same trouble we faced with CI: just because a norm requires me to know how to swim before jumping into lakes and is thereby associated with an epistemic good (i.e. knowledge), it does not follow that it is an epistemic norm.

On the view I favour, the association relation stands for one or another direction of explanation: either the goods explain the norm or the other way around. To see how this goes, it may be worth noting that VI is value-theoretically neutral in the sense that it does not come with any substantive commitments about the relation between the axiological and the deontic. That is because the association claim between norms and goals of the same type does not *imply* any particular direction of explanation. As a result, it is compatible with both of the two leading views about the relationship between the axiological and the deontic. Teleologists (e.g. Sidgwick 1907, Slote 1989, Moore 1993) explain the 'ought' in terms of the 'good'; they claim that the norm of type X is there to guide us in reaching the good of type X. In contrast, deontologists (e.g. Ewing 1947, Scanlon 1998, Rabinowicz and Rönnow-Rasmussen 2004) reverse the order of explanation: according to 'fitting attitude' accounts of value, for example, the goods of type X are only valuable to begin with because the norm of type X gives us reasons to favour them. Crucially, in either case, the mere *association* claim at issue in VI holds.[6]

Since we are interested specifically in the epistemic domain, I want to take a moment to take a quick look at how the association claim may be unpacked for distinctively epistemic norms within both a teleological and a deontological framework. Here is Peter Graham for an explicit statement of the teleological direction of explanation:

> Epistemic norms in this sense govern what we ought to say, do or think from an epistemic point of view, from the point of view of promoting true belief and avoiding error. (Graham 2015, 247)

---

[6] For a good general overview of the relevant literature in value theory, see, for instance, Schroeder (2012).

Here is Kurt Sylvan for a statement of the deontological direction of VI:

> [C]entral epistemic properties like justification, coherence, and substantive rationality derive non-instrumental epistemic value in virtue of the fact that they manifest different *epistemically fitting ways of valuing accuracy*. (Sylvan 2018, 389, emphasis in original)

Note also that VI makes plausible predictions about epistemic norms and norms with epistemic content. For instance, BELIEVE is correctly characterised as an epistemic norm. After all, it is a norm that is associated with the epistemic good of true belief. The easiest way to see this is by looking at the teleological direction of the association claim. Believing what one has good evidence for believing is a good means to true belief; it promotes true belief. Consider, by way of contrast, SING. Rather than being associated with distinctively epistemic goods (e.g. promoting true belief), it is associated with an aesthetic good. Again, in a teleological framework, singing only songs one knows is a way of promoting beauty. As a result, VI classifies it, again correctly, as an aesthetic norm, albeit one with epistemic content.

Now, just as we took CI to motivate the parallel content-based recipe for individuating epistemic virtues (due to the normativity of virtues), we may take VI to motivate the obvious value-based recipe for so doing. Here it goes:

Virtue Value Individuation (VVI)
A virtue V is a distinctively epistemic virtue if and only if V is associated with epistemic goods.

One might initially worry whether VVI preserves VI's value-theoretic neutrality. After all, given that virtues are associated with epistemic goods, one may get the impression that VVI commits me to a distinctively teleological value theory. Fortunately, the answer to this question is 'no'. After all, it may be that, in accordance with VI, the axiological is analysed in terms of the deontic. If so, it may still be that norms explain both goods and virtues. By the same token, VVI does preserve the value-theoretic neutrality after all.[7]

Importantly, there is reason to believe that several virtue responsibilists are attracted to VVI. In several places, leading VR theorists hint at something along VVI lines. Let's start with what Roberts and Wood themselves say about this issue:

---

[7] Again, we can also individuate epistemic virtues by VI and NCV. Since it's easy enough to see that the results will be the same, I will not go into detail about this here.

The difference between our study and a study in virtue ethics is simply that we are interested in the relations between the virtues and the intellectual goods. (Roberts and Wood 2007, 60)

Here is Montmarquet on epistemic virtues:

What I want to suggest, then, as a first approximation, is that the epistemic virtues are those personal qualities (or qualities of character) that are conducive to the discovery of truth and the avoidance of error. (Montmarquet 1993, 20)

Also, Jason Baehr's view about what distinguishes epistemic virtues from other types of virtues seems very similar to VVI;

While structurally similar to moral virtues, they are also distinct from what we ordinarily think of as moral virtues on account of aiming at distinctively epistemic goods like truth, knowledge, and understanding. (Baehr 2017, 96)

Last but not least, here is Linda Zagzebski:

I will argue that truth conduciveness is an essential component of intellectual virtues and I will attempt to ground these virtues in the motivation for knowledge. (Zagzebski 1996, 13)

Unfortunately, if VVI is correct, many of the purportedly epistemic virtues discussed in the literature turn out to be moral virtues with epistemic content rather than genuinely epistemic virtues. By the same token, these virtues will not be relevant to epistemic justification, nor will they be helpful in accounting for the *epistemic* impermissibility of resistance cases.

Let us start with an easy case. Consider, again, the virtue of epistemic temperance discussed by Roberts and Wood. Intuitively, Roberts and Wood are right: the slave-owner who looked away when the slave women were nursing their infants was, to this extent, manifesting virtue.[8] As Roberts and Wood well put it, 'To be an indiscriminate ogler is a trait of bad intellectual character, a failure of discipline of the will to know' (2007, 175). However, since we have seen that typing norms and virtues by content will not do, the question is: when Roberts and Wood talk about 'bad intellectual character', what type of badness is that? Is it genuinely epistemic (i.e. associated in the relevant way with epistemic goods) or rather badness of a different sort (i.e. associated with different types of goods), albeit badness that has epistemic content? It is hard to

---

[8] To be sure, the claim here is that the slave-owner manifests virtue *in this specific regard*, and not, of course, that the slave-owner in any way manifests virtue by being a slave-owner.

deny that it must be the latter. After all, what seems to be going on here is that a properly epistemic virtue, 'the love of knowledge' (which is, in the relevant way – either teleologically or deontologically – associated with an epistemic good, in this case knowledge), is being overridden ('disciplined') by another virtue, namely the virtue of 'epistemic temperance'. Plausibly, though, the latter is precisely not associated with epistemic goods in the relevant sense. After all, on neither direction of explanation does it plausibly stand in an association relation with epistemic goods. Neither is it is conducive to their acquisition, nor does it give one reasons to favour them. Rather, what seems to be the case is that epistemic temperance stands in the relevant relation with moral goods, such as respect for privacy or discretion. Indeed, depending on the details, one might conceive of the Roberts and Wood case as a case of all-things-considered permissible evidence resistance due to moral considerations overriding epistemic considerations.

If all this is so, then, the Roberts and Wood account is guilty of normative ambiguation: it is not the case that the slave-owner is an epistemically virtuous person in virtue of tempering his will to know in the relevant case; rather, the slave-owner manifests a moral virtue with epistemic content by tempering his will to know.

On a similar note, consider Heather Battaly's discussion of epistemic temperance as well as the corresponding vice that she calls 'epistemic self-indulgence':

> [T]he passions and actions associated with these traits are epistemic rather than physical, and include wanting, consuming, and enjoying beliefs, knowledge, and belief-forming practices. I argue that the epistemically temperate person desires, consumes, and enjoys only appropriate epistemic objects, only at appropriate times, and only in appropriate amounts. The epistemically self-indulgent person, however, [...] desires, consumes, and enjoys epistemic objects at inappropriate times (e.g., while having sex with his partner); or desires, consumes, and enjoys epistemic objects too much (thus preventing him from pursuing other things of value). (Battaly 2010, 232)

Note that the goods secured by 'epistemic temperance' are again social or prudential, precisely at the *expense* of epistemic goods. According to Battaly herself, the epistemically temperate person sacrifices the consumption of epistemic goods for the sake of 'pursuing other things of value'. Conversely, it is not clear why 'epistemic self-indulgence' should be considered an epistemic vice. After all, on both directions of explanation it is strongly associated with epistemic goods rather than bads. Thus, by the lights of VVI, it seems that Battaly's discussion also manifests the familiar mistake.

Importantly, this is not to say that a case cannot be made for the claim that epistemic temperance, in a particular context, can be an epistemic virtue proper, or that epistemic self-indulgence could be an epistemic vice – again, depending on context (i.e. depending on whether the relevant context associates these virtues with epistemic goods). Here is, very roughly, how an argument to this effect might go: consider someone who spends all of their epistemic resources on acquisitioning disparate items of knowledge about completely unrelated topics. Perhaps this person should temper their will for a high quantity of epistemic goods in favour of the quality of the epistemic goods. That is, perhaps a project of diving more deeply into a particular domain, in order to achieve understanding thereof, would be more *epistemically* worthwhile than one of simply acquisitioning disparate items of knowledge. At the very least, this question is well worth investigating.

Nenad Miscevic's (2016) discussion of curiosity (which he takes to be the basic epistemic virtue) raises similar concerns. Miscevic carefully draws our attention to the fact that what he means by the 'virtue of curiosity' is something that excludes *nosiness*. Indeed, he stipulates the term 'curiosity+' to pick out a kind of curiosity that is not too strong. Curiosity+ is just strong enough to secure some epistemic goods without thereby giving rise to bad moral side effects. Here is Miscevic:

> Curiosity, when a virtue, call it curiosity+ includes knowledge of appropriateness, and motivation for appropriate exercise. Curiosity−, the vicious inquisitiveness, is not really curiosity. [...] We would then in general have two sub-species of cognitive intrinsic desire to know, intrinsic curiosity+, and curiosity−, the bad intrinsic curiosity, The first is truly a virtue, the second is not [...]. Typical [...] cases of low-level object curiosity [are] aiming at private and intimate matters of others (nosiness), or [are] connected to morally problematic goals or consequences. (Miscevic 2016, 150–152)

Conduciveness to moral goods, though, does not bear on whether or to what extent a particular character trait is an epistemic virtue or not. Indeed, it is unclear why nosiness is not legitimately understood as an epistemic virtue, precisely insofar as it is associated with epistemic goods, and despite the fact that it plausibly fails to qualify as a moral virtue. Consider a teleological direction of explanation: nosiness, as morally indecent as it might be, will definitely be one good character trait to have for securing epistemic goods, such as knowledge or true beliefs. It is, then, unclear why we should endorse Miscevic's distinction between good curiosity (curiosity+) and bad curiosity (curiosity−) rather than allowing that curiosity simpliciter is an epistemic virtue, albeit one that may or may not also count as a moral virtue depending on whether or not it brings about bad moral consequences.

One question that the VR champion might rightly ask at this point is the following: is it not the case that, on the Aristotelian model, only *proper* exercise of a 'virtue' counts as an instance of genuine virtue, whereas *improper* exercise does not really count as an instance of virtue? Here is Miscevic on this issue, referencing a discussion by Philippa Foot:

> The courage of a whistleblower is courage, the bravery of an SS-officer is not. [...] Similarly, nosiness is not really curiosity, at best it is pseudo-curiosity [...]. Curiosity, when a virtue, [...], includes knowledge of appropriateness, and motivation for appropriate exercise. Curiosity−, the vicious inquisitiveness, is not really curiosity. (Miscevic 2016, 152)

The problem with this way to go is that 'proper exercise' is a normative notion. As such, it requires typing itself. There is such a thing as the epistemically proper exercise of a virtue, the morally proper exercise of a virtue, and so on. If VVI is right, epistemically proper exercise of curiosity will represent an epistemically virtuous exercise. Once again, though, it is not clear why episodes of nosiness will not count as epistemically proper exercises of curiosity – after all, they are apt to secure epistemic goods.

Instances of normative ambiguation resulting from a lack of a clear individuation recipe for virtues are ubiquitous in the VR literature and beyond. It would take too much space to point them all out in this chapter. However, I need not do so for present purposes. Rather, the ambition here is to draw attention to a potential problem sourced in this lack for the project at hand: that of explaining the impermissibility of evidence resistance by reference to genuinely epistemic character traits.

Importantly for our project, by the lights of VVI, even virtues that have been at the very heart of the VR literature, and that might be taken to paradigmatically explain the impermissibility of resistance to evidence – such as open-mindedness or intellectual humility – deserve closer scrutiny.

To see why this is the case, let's close with a brief examination of open-mindedness. Of course, at least at first glance, open-mindedness comes across as a paradigmatic epistemic virtue, and one that is paradigmatically missing in cases of evidence resistance: being open-minded opens one towards properly appreciating the views of others and thus properly assessing available evidence. Note, however, that whether a given case really qualifies as *proper* appreciation may depend on (1) the direction of explanation for unpacking VVI and (2) contextual features. To see this, consider open-mindedness in a teleological framework according to which virtues count as genuinely epistemic only insofar as they are conducive to epistemic goods. Now, plausibly, for most people of average epistemic endowment and living in an average epistemic environment, being open-minded is indeed conducive to epistemic goods. After all, when undertaking intellectual projects most of us are likely to encounter better (as in epistemically better) ideas/views, etc., than our own. Being receptive to these other ideas/views, etc., will thus be conducive to epistemic improvement.

In contrast, however, it is not clear that the same is the case when we move further up the scale of epistemic endowment. For a being that is well above average in cognitive ability, open-mindedness will often be conducive to epistemic loss. After all, it may be conducive to abandoning perfectly fine beliefs in the light of misleading evidence. An open-minded mathematical genius shouldn't abandon worthwhile beliefs in the light of less qualified testimony. Similarly, an expert in vaccines or climate change should not update on layman sceptical testimony. And so on.

If this is the case, whether open-mindedness is an epistemic virtue is a highly contextual matter.

Jeremy Fantl (2018) makes a similar point against the *tout court* epistemic goodness of open-mindedness, but in a more interesting way. He starts off with a fairly minimal account of open-mindedness, on which you are open-minded towards an argument if and only if (1) affective factors do not dispose you against being persuaded by the argument, (2) you are not disposed to unreasonably violate any procedural norms in your response to the argument, and (3) you are willing to be significantly persuaded conditional on spending significant time with the argument, finding the steps compelling, and being unable to locate a flaw. He then goes on to argue that open-mindedness is not always a good thing: in particular, he argues, there are many situations in which you know that a relevant counterargument is misleading whether or not you have spent significant time with the argument, found each step compelling, and been unable to expose a flaw. In cases like these, he argues, you should not let yourself be convinced by the argument. Such a dogmatism can be rational, according to Fantl, since often the best explanation of your situation is that your well-supported belief is correct and a clever individual has simply come up with a misleading counterargument (2018, 34). Furthermore, Fantl argues, such closed-minded dogmatism is a manifestation of intellectual humility – since you know of yourself to be fallible at identifying flaws in misleading arguments. This is why, according to Fantl, your knowledge can survive coming across an apparently flawless counterargument.

Of course, independently of its reliability in generating epistemic goods, open-mindedness is plausibly accurately characterised as a moral virtue with epistemic content. After all, being an open-minded person quite plausibly means treating other human beings as worthwhile epistemic sources, independently of whether they actually are reliable sources. This, arguably, is an instance of acting in accordance with a more general moral law requiring us to respect humanity.

Similarly, and for similar reasons, intellectual humility is more properly thought of as a moral virtue with epistemic content that, contextually, may become an epistemic virtue proper in cases where the context is such that it is associated with epistemic goods. In other contexts, to the contrary, epistemic courage will be the genuinely epistemically virtuous character trait to have and manifest (see Ichikawa (forthcoming) for an excellent book-length treatment of epistemic courage in relation to evidence resistance and positive epistemology more broadly).

Virtue responsibilist character traits are epistemic virtues only insofar as they are associated with epistemic goods. If this is so, however, appealing to character traits cannot constitute the normative bedrock for any account that tries to explain the epistemic impermissibility of evidence resistance: epistemic values will do the work. Values will come before virtues in explaining resistance data (as well as in accounting for other interesting epistemic notions and phenomena). The view developed in this book will do just that: explain the impermissibility of evidence resistance by appeal to knowledge and its availability.

5.5 Conclusion

This chapter investigated the virtue responsibilist camp for resources to explain the epistemic impermissibility of evidence resistance. I have argued that, if plausible at all, a responsibilist account of these cases better not be too strong (i.e. had better not explain resistance as absence/lack of manifestation of virtue or presence/manifestation of vice) since, in slogan form, good people can also believe bad things (Levy 2021): the epistemically virtuous are fallible, as they can be involved in one-off resistance cases. I have then looked at what I take to be the most successful account on the market in keeping the character condition permissive: Jason Baehr's responsibilist evidentialism. I have argued that the notion of virtue consistency in the account does not afford plausible unpackings that explain evidence resistance. Furthermore, I have shown that individuating epistemic character traits requires an appeal to epistemic values. If this is so, intellectual character traits don't do the grounding normative work in explaining what goes wrong in resistance cases: epistemic values do.

PART II

Resistance to Evidence and Epistemic Proper Function

CHAPTER 6

Resistance to Evidence as Epistemic Malfunction

This part of the book develops a full positive epistemology: an account of the epistemic normativity of evidence resistance, in conjunction with novel accounts of epistemic oughts, evidence, defeat, and permissible suspension. This first chapter argues that resistance to evidence is an instance of epistemic malfunction. It first puts forth a normative picture according to which the epistemic function of our cognitive systems is generating knowledge, and epistemic norms drop right out of this function. Second, it shows how this picture accommodates epistemic obligations, which, in turn, explain the normative failure instantiated in cases of resistance to evidence. According to this view, cognitive systems that fail to take up easily available evidence and defeat instantiate input-level malfunctioning. Input-level malfunctioning is a common phenomenon in traits the proper functioning of which is input dependent, such as our respiratory systems. Since our cognitive systems, I argue, are systems the proper functioning of which is input dependent, we should expect the failure at stake in resistance cases.

6.1 Epistemic Oughts

Let us start with the elephant in the room: the epistemic impermissibility of evidence resistance implies that there are such things as epistemic oughts to govern our practices of belief forming, updating, and maintaining. As such, any epistemology that is able to predict epistemic impermissibility in resistance cases will be an epistemology that is able to incorporate epistemic oughts.

This is not trivial. It is not trivial, first and foremost, methodologically: until very recently, normative work in epistemology has, for the most part, been negative, in that it has concerned itself with restricting what we are permitted to, for example, believe, assert, or use as a premise in reasoning. Investigations into epistemic oughts are thin on the ground.[1]

It is also not trivial normatively: permissions are not easily turned into obligations (henceforth I am following the literature in deontic logic[2] in using 'oughts' and 'obligations' interchangeably: nothing hinges on it – I am employing a notion of obligation that merely maps onto an ought). Just because I'm permitted to believe things about objects located towards the periphery of my visual field, it does not follow that I ought to do so – after all, a lot of things are happening in my visual field; I cannot possibly be expected to form beliefs about all of them. Furthermore – and going back to methodological difficulties – some permissions endorsed by traditional epistemological frameworks simply don't speak at all towards the kind of obligation I'm breaching when I'm evidence resistant. We have seen this problem surface clearly with permissions to believe in virtue of knowing: this permission is silent when it comes to obligations to update. Similarly, think of classical process reliabilism: even if we grant its champions that we are permitted to believe the outputs of our reliable belief-formation processes, the view remains silent on the norms I'm breaking when my processes fail to deliver outputs that they should deliver.

What we need is an epistemological framework that has the resources to be naturally extended to incorporate obligations to update.

Another, more well-known difficulty has to do with the nature of these epistemic oughts: most people think voluntarism about belief is false. Even bold voluntarists would likely accept that voluntarism is false about the vast majority of doxastic phenomena. Notably, people have worried about non-voluntarism being incompatible with epistemic oughts for belief: if ought implies can, the thought goes, and since I cannot believe at will, I cannot be subject to norms obliging me to do so either.

Now, a lot of ink has been spilled on the implausibility of an unrestricted 'ought-implies-can' principle for normativity in general, and on putting forth more or less successful restrictions thereof (e.g. see Ryan 2003 for excellent work on this topic). One thing that has become clear in recent years in epistemology is that, while we don't want an individual-based 'ought-implies-can' to constrain our normativity – after all, we don't want the sexist cogniser to come out as justified in his sexist beliefs just

---

[1] See Kornblith (2001), Fricker (2007), Chrisman (2008), Feldman (2008), Goldberg (2016, 2017), Lackey (2019), Jenkins-Ichikawa (2020, forthcoming), Kelp (2022), and Simion (2023a) for exceptions. In putting this distinction in terms of positive versus negative epistemology, I follow Jenkins-Ichikawa (2020).

[2] See, for example, McNamara and Van De Putte (2022).

because he can't believe otherwise due to his sexism – we do want general facts about limitations pertaining to adult human cognitive architecture to play a role in restricting our normative claims. Norms governing ideal epistemic agents are just not very informative, nor is there a straightforward way to go from ideal to non-ideal epistemological theorising: for instance, it's not clear what the obligations of an ideal agent who knows that they know for all of their pieces of knowledge imply for people like me, who can hardly come anywhere close to such achievements (nor do we particularly want to).

Keeping all of this in mind, several views in the literature attempt to offer accounts of epistemic ought that bypass the voluntarism objection; I will not run through all of them in great detail here. However, one thing that transpires from even a brief sketch of the literature is that the endeavour of incorporating epistemic oughts in one's epistemology is faced by a strength dilemma: make the source of the ought too thick, normatively, and it seems incompatible with non-voluntarism. Make it too thin and it seems to fail to capture intuitions of 'normative oomph' when it comes to the epistemic (i.e. that epistemic norms are, in a significant way, *'heavier'* than mere conventions). To see the dilemma, let's look at a couple of classic proposals.

According to Richard Feldman, epistemic obligations are what he calls 'role oughts':

> There are oughts that result from one's playing a certain role or having a certain position. Teachers ought to explain things clearly. Parents ought to take care of their kids [...]. Incompetent teachers, incapable parents [...] may be unable to do what they ought to do. Similarly, I'd say, forming beliefs is something people do. That is, we form beliefs in response to our experiences of the world. Anyone engaged in this activity ought to do it right. In my view, what they ought to do is to follow their evidence (rather than their wishes or fears). I suggest that epistemic oughts are of this sort – they describe the right way to play a certain role. (Feldman 2000, 677)

Feldman's account is the paradigmatic case of a theory that is affected by the lack of 'normative oomph' worry: after all, role oughts can – and often are – in an important sense uninteresting, or even bad oughts. Role oughts generated by the role of mafia boss, for instance, seem too normatively thin to constitute the right kind of model for epistemic normativity.

A similar worry affects Hilary Kornblith's view: according to Kornblith, a desire for truth, together with the corresponding hypothetical imperatives it generates, is all we need for explaining epistemic oughts. That's all there is to epistemic normativity: not much more 'normative oomph' than this is needed to explain the data we need to explain.

I share Kornblith's naturalism as well as, to a large extent, his 'normative oomph' scepticism. I think, however, that a desire-based picture remains unsatisfactory on precisely the desiderata Kornblith and I both endorse: naturalistic friendliness. To see why, note that desire is also, plausibly, normatively constrained: there are such things as more and less fitting desires. In turn, hypothetical imperatives are only as thick, normatively, as the desire triggering them is fitting. Ideally, we want to explain this datum in a naturalistically friendly fashion: we want to be able to predict – in a naturalistic normative framework – why some norms are thicker than others, and we want, ideally, to get the result that the epistemic is on the thicker side of things than, again, norms generated by mafia-boss-characteristic desires. In other words, we should be able to predict that nature cares more about the epistemic than about the mafia. Kornblith's response is that, as opposed to other desires, a desire for truth is pretty much implied by a desire for anything else, since whatever else one might be trying to achieve, truth will be needed in order to make the right decisions to the aim of getting it. This instrumental way of looking at things doesn't help much with a mafia boss-type issue, though: after all, on this instrumental picture, a desire for truth will be just as fitting as the desires it is instrumental to fulfilling; in this, the view fails to beef up the normative oomph-ness of truth-generated norms.

Finally, Matthew Chrisman ventures to explain belief oughts in a non-voluntarist-friendly fashion by pointing out a classic distinction between norms governing actions, or 'ought-to-dos' – which may be subject to some variety of the ought-implies-can principle – and 'rules of criticism', governing states, or 'ought-to-bes', which, Chrisman thinks, are not thus constrained. Here is Chrisman:

> In developing an account of robustly normative claims about what someone ought to believe, my strategy is to treat these as adverting to a species of state norms. For instance, the claim, 'You ought to believe you are reading this text right now' could be understood to be an instance of the general form, 'S ought to be in doxastic attitude A towards proposition p under conditions C'. Then, the crucial observation is that some such normative claims seem to be true, just like 'Clock chimes ought to be disposed to strike on the quarter hour', 'The beds ought to be made by 8am every morning', 'A child ought to be able to tie their shoes by age seven' [...]. Yet these true normative claims don't presuppose that their subjects be capable of voluntarily following the rule. (Chrisman 2008, 362)

The worry for Chrisman's account is, once more, one having to do with 'normative oomph': state norms are clearly not always normatively thick – indeed, several of the examples given are paradigmatic examples of social standards of correctness. Is there any interestingly thick normative sense in which beds that are unmade by 8 a.m. are defective? Not really. If so, we need to find extra normative resources to account for the epistemic.

The general lesson to be learnt, I think, is that we need a model for epistemic normativity that, at the same time, circumvents voluntarism worries and is normatively thick enough to account for the intuitively non-conventional nature of the epistemic. Otherwise, if the model put forth is too normatively thin, the suspicion will be that it only circumvents voluntarist worries *in virtue* of its normative thinness – and thus that an extensionally more adequate, normatively thicker incarnation thereof will fail to do so.

I think that the view we are after should be naturalistic, exhibit prior normative plausibility, and be generalisable to other normative domains but also, at the same time, have enough 'normative oomph' to explain the intuitive categoricity of epistemic normative constraints. In the next sections, I will develop a view that purports to meet all of these desiderata: on this account, epistemic normativity is etiological functionalist normativity.

6.2 Functions and Norms

In traits, artefacts, and practices alike, functions generate norms.[3] There is such a thing as a properly functioning heart, a properly functioning can opener, and a proper way to make coffee. If that is so, when we are interested in a particular type of norm governing a particular type of trait, it is helpful to first identify its function.[4]

On the etiological theory of functions,[5] functions turn on histories that explain why the item exists or operates in the way it does. Take my heart;

---

[3] See also, for example, Millikan (1984), Graham (2012), and Sullivan-Bisset (2017).
[4] I am not arguing for the functionalist picture here (I have done so many times (e.g. Simion 2019a, 2020, 2021a) and at considerable length); I assume it, develop the corresponding views, and show that they nicely explain the data that competing views have been struggling with. I also do not make the corresponding descriptive claim: the claim that reasoning is a functional kind (i.e. a kind that only affords a functionalist analysis and not a dismantling analysis). In a nutshell: for my purposes here, I only subscribe to normative functionalism, not metaphysical functionalism.
[5] Defended by people like Ruth Millikan (1984), Karen Neander (1991), and David J. Buller (1998). The etiological theory of functions is, by far, the most widely endorsed view in the literature. Its main competitor is the 'systemic' theory of functions, notably defended in Cummins (1975). Systemic functions describe how something works or operates – what it does – as a part of a larger system. Functions, in this sense, are the causal role capacities of parts that contribute to some capacity of the containing system. Systemic functions are widely believed to lack normative import, which is what explains, to a large extent, both the popularity of the competing, etiological account and why the latter is thought to be much better suited for applications to normative domains like epistemology.

plausibly, tokens of the type pumped blood in my ancestors. This was beneficial for my ancestors' survival, which explains why tokens of the type 'heart' continue to exist. As a result, my heart acquired the etiological function (henceforth also e-function) of pumping blood. Acquiring an etiological function is a success story: traits, artefacts, and actions get etiological functions of a particular type by producing the relevant type of benefit. My heart acquired a biological etiological function by generating biological benefit. Through a positive-feedback mechanism – the heart pumped blood, which kept the organism alive, which, in turn, ensured the continuous existence of the heart – our hearts acquired the etiological function of pumping blood.

Importantly, while aetiology does require some history of beneficial effects, it does not require an awful lot of it; what it all amounts to is explaining the existence/continuous existence of a trait through a longer or shorter history of positive feedback:

> Functions arise from consequence etiologies, etiologies that explain why something exists or continues to exist in terms of its consequences, because of a feedback mechanism that takes consequences as input and causes or sustains the item as output. (Graham 2014, 35)

Functions can be of different sorts: there are biological functions, aesthetic functions, social functions, etc. In contrast to the Graham/Millikan view, my account takes functions to be typed by the corresponding benefit. As such, if a trait produces a benefit of type B in a system, the function thereby acquired will be a function of type B. The heart's function to pump blood is a biological function in virtue of the fact that the produced benefit is also biological (i.e. survival). The function of art is an aesthetic function in virtue of the fact that the produced benefit is an aesthetic benefit. Now, of course, aesthetic benefit might, and often will, also result in biological benefit. This, however, in no way renders the function at stake a biological function. What is important to keep in mind is that the benefit that is *essential* to aesthetic function acquisition is the aesthetic one. The fact that biological benefit is also associated with the latter is a mere contingent matter of fact. Here is, then, the full etiological account to be employed here:

> **E-function:** A token of type T has the e-function of type B of producing effect E in system S iff (1) tokens of T produced E in the past, (2) producing E resulted in benefit of type B in S/S's ancestors, and (3) producing E's having B-benefitted S's ancestors contributes to the explanation of why T exists in S.

Note that etiological functions are successes. They explain the continuous existence of the trait that bears them because that is so. The etiological economic function of knife-producing economic systems is not just that of producing knives; it's to produce good, sharp knives. To see this, note that the positive-feedback loop that is presupposed by etiological function acquisition – the trait produces the effect and the effect benefits the system and thereby contributes to the explanation of the continuous existence of the trait – presupposes a history of success. What contributes to the explanation of the continuous existence of knife-producing economic systems is their producing good, sharp knives. Blunt ones would plausibly not have done the trick.

Just as the economic function of knife-producing economic systems is to produce good, sharp knives, the epistemic function of our belief-forming systems is to produce good beliefs. Mere belief, then, is a failure on the part of our cognitive system to fulfil its epistemic function just as blunt knives are failures on the part of knife producers to fulfil their economic function.

Note that functions will also come with associated norms: these prescribe the right way to proceed in order to reliably enough[6] fulfil the function in question under normal conditions. Because its function contributes to the explanation of its very existence, the trait in question *ought* to perform in a way that is associated with likely enough function fulfilment. Your heart will be properly functioning when it functions in the way that reliably enough delivers function fulfilment under normal conditions: it will beat at a rate between 40 and 100 beats/minute, which, under normal conditions (i.e. conditions similar to those present at the moment of function acquisition), reliably leads to pumping blood in your circulatory system.

In my view, generating knowledge is the function of our epistemic practice of inquiry; in turn, cognitive processes, in virtue of their being the central mechanisms engaged in our practice of inquiry, inherit this function of generating knowledge. Further, norms governing moves in inquiry – such as beliefs, suspensions, withholdings, credences, assertions, or pieces of reasoning – will drop out of this knowledge-generating function.

Moves in practices generally aim – either directly or indirectly – to fulfil the function of the practice. The difference between direct and indirect aiming lies with achievability: for some moves in practices, the function of

---

[6] How reliable is reliably enough? The threshold varies with the type of normativity, the type of trait, and evolutionary needs. The heart (biologically) ought to be very reliable for a species' continuous existence; in contrast, sperm cells only need to fulfil their function very rarely.

the practice is only indirectly rather than directly reachable. Cardiological consults are moves in the practice of medicine, and they aim directly at fulfilling the goal of the practice of medicine: curing diseases. In turn, some moves aim at this final practice goal only indirectly while aiming directly at intermediate goals: performing electrocardiogram (ECG) tests aims (directly) at informing the cardiologist as to how well the patient is doing, which, in turn, aims directly at their diagnosing the patient correctly and, further, at curing their disease. In this, ECG tests aim indirectly at the function of the practice of medicine: curing diseases. They aim at making progress towards it. Similarly, baking cakes is a move in the practice of cooking, and it aims directly at fulfilling the function of the practice: producing tasty, nourishing food. My getting the flour off the shelf aims indirectly at the general function of the practice by aiming directly at adding flour to the cake mix. It aims at making progress towards producing tasty, nourishing food. And so on.

Similarly, on the epistemic normative picture I favour, moves in the practice of inquiry – that is, all epistemically significant states and actions – will be governed by norms borne out by this central knowledge function of the practice. Moves in inquiry, that is, will aim either directly (plausibly: beliefs, assertions, reasonings) or indirectly (credences, suspensions, withholdings) at the aim of the practice of inquiry. The difference, once more, will lie with goal achievability: beliefs, assertions, and conclusions of reasonings can be knowledgeable in a way in which things like credences, suspensions, and withholdings cannot. Belief formation aims directly at the aim of the practice of inquiry (knowledge), whereas, at the same time, credence, withholding, and suspension aim at knowledge indirectly: they are transitional attitudes, in the sense in which these are attitudes held en route to knowledge but are not in the running for knowledge.

Just like the biological functions of our hearts generate etiological biological norms, the epistemic functions of our cognitive systems generate etiological epistemic norms governing our belief formation.

In previous work (e.g. Simion 2019a, 2021a), I have argued extensively that knowledge is the etiological function of our cognitive systems. This makes my epistemological approach, in a crucial sense, a knowledge-first epistemological approach: epistemic normative constraints, on this view, drop out of the knowledge function of our cognitive systems.

A few things by way of clarification are in order: in the more than twenty years since Timothy Williamson's (2000) seminal work putting forth the first defence of a full knowledge-first epistemological framework, the knowledge-first research programme has generated an impressive amount of high-quality work and very promising results across epistemological subfields (e.g. epistemic justification, defeat, evidence, epistemic normativity, social epistemology, know-how, the nature and normativity of inquiry) and also at the intersection of epistemology with philosophy of language (e.g. the nature of speech acts, contextualism), mind (e.g. the nature of mental states), and moral and political philosophy (e.g. blame, trust, responsibility, political discourse).

Against this backdrop, however, this book zooms in *only* on what I take to be the core normative claims of the knowledge-first programme: that knowledge is the central epistemic value, and that thereby central normative notions in epistemology – such as justification, evidence, and defeat – are to be analysed in terms of knowledge. This view, in contrast to its extant knowledge-first competition, analyses epistemic normative categories in terms of knowledge without requiring further theoretical commitments (e.g. to the non-analysability of knowledge or to knowledge being a mental state in its own right). These questions remain open.

The key claim that I endorse is that generating knowledge is the function of our cognitive systems. To see why this is plausible, very briefly, note that knowledge meets the conditions for an e-function: it is plausible that it has been generated by our cognitive systems and those of our ancestors in the past (after all, knowledge is readily available in our environment), that this benefitted our organisms (e.g. by informing us about the presence of predators and the whereabouts of food), and that the fact that knowledge benefitted us in this way contributes to the explanation of why cognitive systems continue to exist in individuals like us. So generating knowledge is at the very least *one* function of our cognitive processes. Is it the main function? Note that what determines the proper level of generality for main function individuation is the T-value of the relevant T-function. The main biological function of the heart, for instance, maps onto its most valuable biological contribution: its main function is not 'pumping blood and making a ticking sound', but neither is it merely 'pumping', for instance. Plausibly, that is because if the heart pumps orange juice in our circulatory system, that's not very valuable for our survival. I submit that knowledge is more valuable than any lesser epistemic standing[7]: that much is very widely accepted in the literature. It is easy to see that, if I am right about main function individuation, the distinctive value of knowledge thesis together with e-function deliver the

---

[7] See Kelp and Simion (2017) for an account of the value of knowledge as commodity.

result that the main epistemic function of our cognitive processes is generating knowledge.

Functions provide us with a straightforward way to identify the norms governing a particular trait or activity: first, if we are interested in identifying a norm of type T of the relevant trait, we start of by identifying its type T function. Once that is done, we look at the way in which it is reliably fulfilled under normal conditions. That will give us its conditions for proper function and, correspondingly, the content of the norm of type T we were looking for (Simion 2019a).

In what follows, I employ the functionalist machinery in investigating the epistemic normativity of belief. Before we move on, however, let us go back to the strength dilemma generated by voluntarist worry and the question of 'normative oomph': the good news is that, clearly, norms of proper function do not imply any voluntarist claim: just like my heart is governed by norms of proper function about blood pumping, my cognitive capacities are governed by norms of proper function about belief forming.

Is functionalist normativity going to generate a normatively thick enough model for epistemic normativity? Let's go back to norms and practices in the domain of mafia. Here is a worry one might have: mafia practices may well continue to exist because they achieve the corresponding 'values' internal to the domain of mafia. If so, on a functionalist picture, we can get norms out of these functions: norms that regulate proper ways of going about achieving the domain-specific values that the domain of mafia is organised around. But do the resultant 'norms' have any normative *oomph* at all?

One would think that the case of epistemic norms is different. For instance, the fact that S said that *p* and that S is very reliable on *p*-related matters seems like a reason to believe that *p* has normative force – I can't just set it aside in the way I can set aside the orders from my crime boss (e.g. Fricker 2007). These cases case *feel* different in a way that needs to be explained.

On functionalism, indeed, it can be the case that, for example, efficient killing is a domain-specific value in the domain of mafia, which, in turn, generates corresponding (domain-internal) functionalist norms. It's a completely different question, however, if the domain itself is, for example, valuable *simpliciter* to begin with – and I take it that the domain of mafia is not. If so, the normative force of its norms will be restricted to the domain of mafia.

I take it to be empirically plausible that doing well epistemically is, at least for the most part, good for us biologically. If so, the domain of the epistemic, in contrast to the domain of mafia, will itself be valuable; if so, its internal functional norms will bear 'normative oomph' in a way in which norms of the domain of mafia do not. Importantly, though, I can afford to stay neutral on *the extent* to which the epistemic is good or bad: for 'normative oomph', I just need the fairly weak claim that it is generally good for us. This is important because it gives my view the flexibility to adapt to empirical results that purport to show that, at times, epistemic unreliability co-varies with biological benefits.

Compatibly, though, and plausibly, the domain of epistemology is valuable for our survival in a way that generates thick normative constraints. My functionalism thus does have the capacity to distinguish different kinds and strengths of normative force. On my view, epistemic norms have (1) domain-bound normative force, in that they promote knowledge, which is the value around which the domain is organised, and (2) non-domain-bound normative force, in that 'the epistemic' is a domain that is (empirically plausibly) valuable for our survival.[8]

6.3 Resistance to Evidence as Epistemic Malfunction

On my account, the main function of our belief-formation systems is to generate knowledge. In turn, they are properly functioning just in case they work in a way that is normally conducive to generating knowledge. When that happens, the beliefs they generate are justified.

I dub my view of justification 'knowledge-first functionalism': the account is functionalist in that it follows Millikan (1984), Burge (2010), and Graham (2012) in taking the epistemic normativity of belief to drop out of the epistemic function of our cognitive capacities. It is knowledge-first epistemological in that, unlike traditional, truth-first functionalism, it unpacks the function at stake in terms of knowledge. Here is a more precise formulation of the view:

---

[8] Is it really knowledge, though, that is good for our survival rather than simply true beliefs? I have argued extensively in previous work (e.g. Simion 2016, 2020, Kelp and Simion 2017) for the distinctive value of knowledge over and above true beliefs that fall short of knowledge. In my view, knowledge as a commodity is distinctively valuable in that it is *our way* of correctly representing the world around us in virtue of its ready availability, just like water is our way of quenching our thirst in virtue of its ready availability: in a wide range of areas, knowledge is widely and readily available, just like water is widely and readily available. If so, just like water is a valuable commodity to us because it is our way of quenching our thirst, knowledge is valuable to us because it is our way of representing the world.

> **Knowledge-first functionalism (KFF)**: A belief is prima facie justified if and only if it is generated by a properly functioning cognitive capacity that has the etiological function of generating knowledge.

On this knowledge-centric picture, good belief is knowledgeable belief, while justified belief – belief that is permissible by the epistemic norm of belief – is belief generated by a properly functioning cognitive capacity that has the etiological function of generating knowledge. The standards for proper functioning are thus natural normative standards, and they are constitutively associated with promoting knowledgeable beliefs.

So far, we have been solely talking in moderate normative terms: we have taken justification of belief to supervene on epistemic permissibility and, in turn, epistemic permissibility to have to do with the proper function of our knowledge-generating belief-formation systems. How does resistance to evidence fit in this picture? After all, an epistemic subject being resistant to evidence seems to be a matter of obligation breach rather than permissibility breach: one is resistant to evidence insofar as there is evidence one should take up but one fails to do so.

I would like to propose an account of epistemic obligation according to which what all of subjects in Cases 1–7 from Chapter 1 have in common, epistemically, is that they are in breach of their epistemic ought to believe in virtue of resistance to available evidence. Here it is:

> **The ought to believe (OTB)**: A subject S has an *epistemic*[9] obligation to form a belief that p if there is sufficient and undefeated evidence for S supporting p.

Once more, importantly: when I talk of obligation, I am following the literature in deontic logic[10] in using oughts and obligations interchangeably (i.e. I am employing a notion of obligation that merely maps onto an ought). Now, note that OTB, together with a moderate evidentialist assumption that one's belief that p is epistemically justified only if there is sufficient and undefeated evidence for S supporting p, straightforwardly implies that epistemic justification is epistemic obligation (and, more generally, that justifiers are obligations). One might wonder, at this stage: is that right? After all, the vast majority of the literature assumes that epistemic justification is mere epistemic permission.

---

[9] Crucially, the obligation at stake is merely epistemic. Compatibly, prudential obligations, for example, might override the epistemic obligation and render it all-things-considered permissible to dismiss information that we are not interested in.

[10] See, for example, McNamara and Van De Putte (2022).

A few things about this: first, I take it that what resistance cases show is that this assumption was wrong all along. Mere epistemic permissions cannot, in virtue of their weak normative force, explain why the main characters in these cases (epistemically) *ought* to take up some evidence that they fail to take up.

Second, as I'm about to argue, there are in-principle theoretical reasons for which we should be suspicious of the thought that epistemic justification is mere epistemic permission. Here it goes: note that defeaters are obligations – when our justification is defeated, by definition, it is impermissible to ignore defeat and hold on to the corresponding doxastic attitude. Since it is impermissible to ignore defeaters, it follows that they constitute epistemic obligations (since it is always permissible to ignore mere permissions). Note, also, that there is such a thing as merely partial defeat: these are garden variety cases in which the epistemic agent needs to weigh their evidence in favour of p against their evidence against p. If Mary tells me that the train comes at 8 a.m. and you tell me that the train comes at 7 a.m., and Mary and you are, for all I know, equally reliable testifiers, my justification to believe that the train comes at 8 a.m. is partially defeated – I should lower my confidence in this being the case, but I don't have sufficient epistemic support to move to outright believing that the train doesn't come at 8 a.m. Similarly, I don't have enough epistemic support to believe or disbelieve what you said either: it is impermissible both to form an outright belief that the train comes at 7 a.m. and to form an outright belief that it does not. Justifiers and defeaters can outweigh each other.

However, if defeaters constitute epistemic obligations, and if defeaters and justifiers can outweigh each other, it follows that justifiers constitute epistemic obligations as well: otherwise, if they constituted mere permissions, they would be normatively inert against defeaters, since permissions are normatively inert against obligations. As such, it seems as though the mere possibility of partial defeat implies that justification maps on to epistemic obligation. Here is the argument unpacked for the reader's convenience:

(1) Defeaters affect what one is justified to believe.
(2) If defeaters affect what one is justified to believe, then it is epistemically impermissible to fail to adjust one's doxastic attitudes in light of defeaters.
(3) It is epistemically impermissible to fail to adjust one's doxastic attitudes in light of defeaters (from (1) and (2)).

(4) If it is epistemically impermissible to fail to adjust one's doxastic attitude in light of a normative consideration x, then x constitutes an epistemic obligation.
(5) Defeaters constitute epistemic obligations (from (3) and (4)).
(6) Defeat can be partial defeat.
(7) If defeat can be partial defeat, then justifiers can carry normative weight against defeaters.
(8) Justifiers can carry normative weight against defeaters (from (6) and (7)).
(9) Justifiers constitute either epistemic permissions or epistemic obligations.
(10) Permissions cannot carry normative weight against obligations.
(11) Epistemic justifiers constitute obligations (from (5), (8), (9), and (10)).

What is the source of epistemic obligation? What grounds the epistemic OTB, in my view, is proper epistemic functioning. Pieces of evidence are pro tanto, prima facie justification-makers: they are the proper inputs to our processes of belief formation, and when we have enough evidence and the processes in question are otherwise properly functioning, the resulting belief is epistemically justified. In turn, when our belief-formation processes either fail to take up justifiers that they could have easily taken up or they take them up but fail to output the corresponding belief, they are malfunctioning:

Resistance to evidence as epistemic malfunction (REEM): A subject S's belief-formation capacity C is malfunctioning epistemically if there is sufficient evidence supporting p that is easily available to be taken up via C and C fails to output a belief that p.

The proper function of belief-formation capacities, then, on my view, is input dependent: failing to take up the right inputs – whether this occurs by taking up the wrong inputs or by failing to take up the right inputs – is an instance of malfunctioning.

One illuminating analogy here is the proper functioning of the lungs: as opposed to functional traits whose proper function is not input dependent (e.g. hearts), what it is for our lungs to function properly is, partly, for them to take up the right amount of the right stuff (i.e. oxygen) from the environment. Lungs that fail to do so, in environments where oxygen is easily available, are improperly functioning – whether they fail via taking up carbon dioxide or by just failing to take up easily available oxygen.

In contrast, hearts can take up and circulate whatever liquid they are fed, while, at the same time, remaining properly functional. Take your heart and place it in a vat with orange juice: insofar as it continues to pump at the normal rate, your heart is normally functioning – in spite of the fact that now it's pumping orange juice rather than blood. The proper functioning of the heart is not input dependent.

Our cognitive systems do not work like hearts, they work like our respiratory systems; inputs matter for proper function. Our belief-formation capacities can't take up wishes and form beliefs based on them whilst at the same time remaining properly functional. A cognitive system that processes wishes into beliefs is malfunctioning. If this is so, it follows that the proper functioning of our cognitive systems is input dependent.

Similarly, then, just like in the case of our respiratory systems, we should expect our cognitive systems and belief-formation capacities to malfunction in at least two input-dependent ways: via taking up the wrong kind of inputs (e.g. wishes), but also, and crucially for my purposes here, via *failing to take up easily available good inputs (i.e. easily available evidence)*.

It is important to note that empirical results also overwhelmingly confirm the hypothesis that the proper functioning of our cognitive systems is input dependent (i.e. that our cognitive systems are malfunctioning if they fail to respond to environmental stimuli). Our levels of neuroplasticity[11] – the brain's disposition for neuron-level changes in response to the environment – predict the brain's capacity to take up information from the environment: when a cognitive system displays abnormally low levels of structural neuroplasticity,[12] learning in response to novel stimuli from the environment fails to occur at a normal rate. In turn, abnormally low levels of neuroplasticity, generating low responses to environmental stimuli, predict improper cognitive functioning. But if this is so, the proper functioning of our cognitive systems is input dependent: one way in which they can malfunction is by failing to respond to easily available environmental stimuli.

We now have a straightforward explanation of what goes wrong in cases of resistance to evidence: it is an epistemic incarnation of input-level malfunction. Our cognitive systems fail to take up easily available evidence from the environment. Just like respiratory failure is an instance of our

---

[11] For recent work on neuroplasticity in adults, see, for example, Lovden et al. (2010).
[12] Structural neuroplasticity, very roughly, has to do with the brain's capacity to change its physical structure as we learn new things or form new memories. Functional plasticity is the brain's ability to move functions from a damaged area of the brain to other undamaged areas.

respiratory systems failing to take up normal levels of oxygen from the environment, resistance to evidence is an instance of our cognitive systems failing to respond normally to stimuli from the environment.

6.4 Conclusion

The function of our cognitive systems is to generate knowledge, and justification turns on this function: we are justified to believe just in case our cognitive systems work in the way in which they generate knowledge reliably under normal conditions. This is not the full story, though: the proper functioning of our cognitive systems is not limited to the fair treatment of evidence that we pick up from the world – it extends to picking up the relevant evidence when easily available. When our cognitive systems fail to do so, they are malfunctioning and are in breach of epistemic norms.

In the next chapter, I further unpack REEM. I will not take a stance on what the sufficiency threshold stands for. Views will differ on this, and they will also differ on what fixes the threshold in question – whether it's a purely epistemic affair or whether practical and moral considerations may play a role.[13] My focus from here onwards will be on how to understand evidence, defeat, and permissible suspension in order to make good on REEM and, in turn, on OTB and the resistance intuition.

---

[13] I have done extensive previous work on this issue (e.g. see Simion 2021a).

CHAPTER 7

Evidence as Knowledge Indicators

This chapter puts forth a novel view of evidence in terms of knowledge indicators, and it shows that it is superior to its competition in that it can account for the epistemic impermissibility of resistance cases, as well as for the effect that resistance to evidence has on doxastic justification. Very roughly, knowledge indicators are facts that enhance closeness to knowledge: a fact e is evidence for S that p is the case if and only if S is in a position to know e and e increases the evidential probability that p for S.

7.1 Knowledge Indicators

In the previous chapter, I have argued that evidence resistance is an instance of input-level epistemic malfunctioning of our cognitive systems. Input-level malfunctioning is a common phenomenon in traits the proper functioning of which is input dependent, such as our respiratory systems. Since our cognitive systems, I have argued, are systems the proper functioning of which is input dependent, we should expect the failure at stake in resistance cases. I have also argued that, since pieces of evidence are pro tanto, prima facie justification-makers, they are the proper inputs to our processes of belief formation. When we have enough evidence and our belief-formation cognitive capacities are otherwise properly functioning, the resulting belief is epistemically justified. In turn, when our belief-formation capacities either fail to take up justification-makers that they could have easily taken up or they take them up but fail to output the relevant belief, they are malfunctioning.

The question that this chapter purports to answer is: how should we understand one's evidence such that we predict its normative impact on our properly functioning cognitive systems? Or, in other words, how should we understand one's evidence such that our account thereof predicts the epistemic impermissibility of resistance to evidence for cognitive systems that have generating knowledge as their epistemic function?

To lay my cards right on the table, the answer I will offer will make use of the notion of a knowledge indicator: on my view, evidence consists of knowledge indicators, which enhance closeness to knowledge by enhancing evidential probability. In turn, for any system S with a function F, since S ought to fulfil F, it is plausible that S ought to enhance closeness to F fulfilment. If so, our cognitive systems should take up pieces of evidence because they enhance closeness to function fulfilment (i.e. they enhance evidential probability and thereby closeness to knowledge).

Here is, in more detail, how I think about these things: evidence consists of facts. They can be facts about the world around us or mere facts about a subject's psychology. My having a perception as of a table in front of me is a psychological fact; it (pro tanto, prima facie) supports the belief that there is a table in front of me. So does the fact that there is a table in plain view in front of me.

In my view, evidence consists of facts that are knowledge indicators: facts that one is in a position to know and that increase one's evidential probability (i.e. the probability on one's total body of evidence) of p being the case. The fact that I see that there is a table in front of me is a piece of evidence for me that there is a table in front of me. It is a knowledge indicator, in that it raises the probability on my evidence that there is a table in front of me, and I'm in a position to know it.

Not just any psychological facts will constitute evidence that there is a table in front of me: my having a perception as of a table will fit the bill in virtue of having the relevant indicator property. Perceptions are knowledge indicators; the fact that I have a perception as of p is a fact that I am in a position to know, and that increases my evidential probability that p is the case. The fact that I wish that there was a table in front of me will not fit the bill, even if, unbeknownst to me, my table wishes are strongly correlated with the presence of tables: wishes are not knowledge indicators, for they don't raise my evidential probability of p being the case (although they may, of course, raise the objective probability thereof). For the same reason, mere beliefs, as opposed to justified and knowledgeable beliefs, will not be evidence material; they lack the relevant indicator property.

Here is the view in full:

> **Evidence as knowledge indicators:** A fact e is evidence for one for a proposition p if and only if one is in a position to know e and one's evidential probability that p is the case conditional on e is higher than one's unconditional evidential probability that p is the case.

Or, slightly more formally, and where P stands for the probability on one's total body of evidence:

Evidence as knowledge indicators: A fact e is evidence for p for S iff S is in a position to know e and $P(p/e) > P(p)$.

Let's unpack the view further. What is it for me to be in a position to know e? Plausibly, a certain availability relation needs to be instantiated. On my view, availability has little to do with the limits of my skull. Evidence may consist of facts 'in the head' or facts in the world. Some facts – whether they are in the head or in the world, it does not matter – are available to me; they are, as it were, 'at hand' in my (internal or external) epistemic environment. Some – whether in the head (think of justified implicit beliefs, for instance) or in the world, it does not matter – are not thus available to me.

Here are, for starters, some paradigmatic cases that illustrate what I'm talking about: if there is a table right in front of me, but I'm not paying attention to it, there is evidence for me that there is a table in front of me. If, unbeknownst to me, you put a new table in the other room, the fact that you put it there is *not available* to me: it is not evidence *for me*. Similarly, if I have some mental state that is so deeply buried in my psychology that I can't access it, it is not evidence for me.

As a first approximation, my notion of availability will track a 'can' for an average cogniser of the sort exemplified (e.g. with the relevant kind of cognitive architecture, social and physical limitations, etc.).

Here is some theory about this. First, there are *qualitative* limitations on availability: we are cognitively limited creatures. There are of *types* information that we just cannot access or process: the fact that there is a table in front of me is something that I can easily enough access. Your secret decision to put the table in the other room is not something I can easily access. There are also types of support relations that we cannot process: the fact that your car is in the driveway is evidence *for me* that you're home. But it's not evidence for my three-year-old son, Max, to believe that you're home. Max belongs to a variety of epistemic agents that are not sophisticated enough to process[1] the support relation into a belief that you are home. Evidence is not available to you if the kind of epistemic

---

[1] What is the relation between processing the support relation and knowledge indicators as probability enhancers? Is one supposed to be able to form probability beliefs in order to count as being able to process the support relation? The answer is 'no': merely treating an indicator as such is enough; awareness of its being one is not needed, nor is awareness of what makes a fact into an indicator. 'Treating' is a lowbrow affair: I can treat my cat as a friend without believing that she is.

agent that you are cannot access or process the particular variety thereof at stake (henceforth also *qualitative availability*).

There are also *quantitative* limitations on my information accessing and processing. The fact that there's a table somewhere towards the periphery of my visual field – in contrast of it being right in front of me, in plain view – is not something I can easily process: I lack the power to process everything in my visual field: it is too much information (henceforth also *quantitative availability*). My cognitive limitations make it such that the facts available to me are only a subset of what is going on in my visual field. More on this later.

The 'can' at stake here will be further restricted by features of the social and physical environment: we are supposed to read the newspaper on the table in front of us, but not the letter under the doormat. That's because we can't read everything, and our social environment is such that written testimony is more likely to be present in the newspaper on the table than under the doormat (henceforth also *environmental availability*).

In sum, for a fact to be such that I am in a position to know it, it needs to be at hand for me in my epistemic environment: at hand qualitatively (it needs to be the *type* of thing a creature like me can access and process), quantitatively (it needs to belong to the quantitatively limited subset of facts that a creature like me can access and process at one particular time), and environmentally (it needs to be easily *available* in my – internal or external – epistemic environment; i.e. in my mind or in my physical and social surroundings).

I take this availability relation to have to do with a fact being within the easy reach of my knowledge-generating cognitive capacities. A fact *e* being such that I am in a position to know it has to do with my having a properly functioning knowledge-generating cognitive capacity that can take up *e*:

> **Being in a position to know (BPK):** S is in a position to know a fact *e* if S has a cognitive capacity with the function of generating knowledge that can (qualitatively, quantitatively, and environmentally) easily uptake *e* in cognisers of S's type.

A few crucial clarifications about this account: first, note that BPK is a sufficiency claim. It is not necessary that *e* is available to me in order for me to be in a position to know *e*: I can also come to know *e* via taking up facts that increase my probability for *e*.

Second, note that BPK is a restricted ought-implies-can: agent obligations imply capacities in the kind of cogniser that they are. This opens the account to a mild generality problem, of course: how to individuate the relevant type of cogniser? Stable, constitutive features will matter: cognitive architecture, inherent social and physical limitations. Fleeting, contingent features will not (i.e. mere cognitive 'furniture'): biases, previously held beliefs, wishes, among others. The advantage of the view is that, in restricting 'ought implies can' to types of cognisers, the account will predict that biased cognisers are in breach of their epistemic obligations: they may be unable to, for example, believe women because of bias, but cognisers with their cognitive architecture can, and therefore they should too.

Third, it is important to distinguish between being in a position to know and being in a position to *come* to know[2]: I am in a position to know that there is a computer in front of me; I am not in a position to know what is happening in the other room. I am, however, in a position to come to know the latter. Roughly, then, the distinction will, once more, have to do with epistemic availability: if all that needs to happen for me to come to know *e* is that my relevant cognitive capacities take up *e* and process it accordingly, then I am in a position to know *e*. If more needs to be the case – I need to open my eyes, or turn around, or go to the other room, or give you a call – I am in a position to come to know *e* but not in a position to know it. For now, I have not made any claim about the epistemic import of being in a position to come to know. Compatibly, being in a position to come to know might also, in some cases, deliver epistemic oughts: some cases of normative defeat and failure of evidence gathering are cases in point (e.g. see Lackey 2008, Goldberg 2016, 2017) See the next chapter for a discussion of this phenomenon.

Finally, and crucially, note that quantitative limitations on being in a position to know will make it so that I can only take up a limited number of the $e_1, e_2, e_3 \ldots e_n$ facts that lie within reach with my knowledge-generating capacities. What facts go in my body of evidence in these cases? Which are the ones I am in a position to know, and which are the ones I am merely in a position to come to know (by changing focus, etc.)? On the account defended, in these cases, I will shoulder an epistemic obligation to take up a subset of $e_1, e_2, e_3 \ldots e_n$ that is as large as my quantitative take-up limitations. Therefore, my body of evidence will only include the relevant subset that a creature with my cognitive architecture can (quantitatively) take up at one time. When looking straight at my computer, my visual field is populated with very numerous facts, such that taking them all up exceeds my quantitative take-up limitations. I am only under an obligation to take up a quantitatively manageable subset of facts.

The crucial question that arises is: which is the set that takes normative primacy and thereby delivers my body of evidence? *Availability rankings* will

---

[2] Many thanks to Ernie Sosa and Matt McGrath for pressing me on this.

deliver the relevant set, on my view: the most easily available subset of facts that I can take up delivers the set of evidence I have. In the case of visual perception, for instance, these are the facts located right in front of me, in the centre of my visual field, which are the brightest, clearest, etc. – in general, those facts that are most easily available to the cognitive capacities of a creature like me.

Tim Williamson (in conversation) worries that there will be cases in which too many facts (too many for my quantitative limitations) will have the same availability ranking. I see the worry (although I suspect it can be alleviated for most cases by our relation to space, time, complexity, brightness, etc.). Maybe the easiest case to imagine along these lines is the case of very simple arithmetical truths. In these cases, other normative constraints will have to decide the relevant set: I will have an all-things-considered obligation to attend to a particular range of simple arithmetical truths, and, among these, the most easily available will constitute my evidence, in virtue of them delivering the corresponding epistemic obligation to take them up.[3]

With the account fully unpacked, let's move on to checking how it fares on accommodating the resistance data.

7.2 Evidence and the Impermissibility of Resistance

Here are, first and foremost, a few theoretical virtues of this view of evidence. First, it is naturalistically friendly, in that it situates the epistemic normativity of epistemic oughts to believe within an etiological functionalist picture of normativity: epistemic oughts to believe have to do with the proper function of our cognitive capacities, just like biological oughts to take up oxygen have to do with the proper function of our respiratory systems.

Second, the view enjoys high extensional adequacy. In line with intuition, it predicts that there is evidence for the Gettierised victim that there is a sheep in the field: the fact that they have a perception as of a sheep is a fact that they are in a position to know and that raises their evidential probability that there is a sheep in the field.

Also, there is evidence for the (recently envatted)[4] brain in the vat (BIV) for p: 'there is a tree in front of me' when they have a perceptual experience as of a tree, since that is a fact that they are in a position to know and that raises their evidential probability that there is a tree in front of them.

---

[3] Thanks also to Matt McGrath for many discussions on this topic.
[4] In line with content externalism, I take the BIV that has been envatted from birth to not have Earth contents and thereby no beliefs about Earth entities. Compatibly, my view predicts that they are justified to believe whatever they believe about vat entities.

There is no evidence for Norman the clairvoyant that the President is in New York: clairvoyant experiences are not evidential probability raisers when one is ignorant of the reliability of clairvoyance.

Finally, and most importantly for our purposes, it is easy to see that, when plugged into REEM, this view of evidence delivers the straightforward resistance intuition and thus explains that subjects in Cases 1–7 from Chapter 1 are in breach of their obligation to believe for failing to take up available evidence. Recall REEM:

Resistance to evidence as epistemic malfunction (REEM): A subject S's belief-formation capacity C is malfunctioning epistemically if there is sufficient evidence supporting p that is easily available to be taken up via C and C fails to output a belief that p.

Anna's testimony in Case 1; media testimony, Dump's statements, etc., in Case 2; the scientific testimony in Case 3; the perceptual experience as of a table in Case 4; the partner's behavioural changes in Case 5; the fact that the Black students raise their hands in Case 6; and the incriminating fingerprints, etc., in Case 7 all constitute facts that are indicators of knowledge in virtue of being evidential probability enhancers that the subjects in these cases are in a position to know. These indicators of knowledge are easily available to creatures such as our protagonists: the subjects in Case 1–7 are members of a type of cogniser that hosts cognitive capacities with the function of generating knowledge that can easily take up these facts. Since they fail to do so, their cognitive capacities are malfunctioning, just like their lungs would be were they to be disinclined to take up the right amount of easily available oxygen. The account predicts that these subjects are all exhibiting resistance to evidence (by REEM) and are in breach of their obligation to believe (by OTB).

To see just how efficacious a view like mine is in accounting for evidence resistance and obligations to update, it will be useful to compare my account to E = K once more. In *Knowledge and Its Limits*, Williamson considers an account of evidence in terms of being in a position to know, and he dismisses it based on the following rationale:

> [...] suppose that I am in a position to know any one of the propositions $p_1, \ldots, p_n$ without being in a position to know all of them; there is a limit to how many things I can attend to at once. Suppose that in fact I know p_1 and do not know $p_2, \ldots, p_n$. According to E = K, my evidence includes only p_1; according to the critic, it includes $p_1, \ldots, p_n$. Let q be a proposition which is highly probable given $p_1, \ldots, p_n$ together, but highly improbable given any proper subset of them; the rest of my evidence is irrelevant to q.

> According to E = K, q is highly improbable on my evidence. According to the critic, q is highly probable on my evidence. E = K gives the more plausible verdict, because the high probability of q depends on an evidence set to which as a whole I have no access. (Williamson 2000, 189)

Two things about this: first, note that, in virtue of the quantitative limitations that my account imposes on being in a position to know, the view does not suffer from the problem Williamson points to here. Indeed, given that there is a limit to how many things I can attend to at once, it is only the most available subset that I can attend to that is part of my body of evidence.

Even more importantly, I submit that once we put flesh on the bones of Williamson's case, my view, and not E = K, gives the intuitively right prediction. Here it goes:

> FRIENDLY DETECTIVE 2: It's highly probable that John killed the victim given that (p_1) John is a butler, (p_2) John is a very nice guy with an impeccable record, and (p_3) the only butler who's a very nice guy with an impeccable record was seen stabbing the victim. Friendly Detective is told p_1, p_2, and p_3 but can't get himself to believe p_3 because of wishful thinking, and he believes John didn't do it based on p_1 and p_2.

FRIENDLY DETECTIVE 2 is an instance of Williamson's case. It is easy to see, however, that it is E = K that delivers the counterintuitive result here: according to E = K, the detective is justified to believe John didn't do it. My view disagrees, and it scores on extensional adequacy.

Going back to the high societal stakes of evidence resistance: crucially, real-world, high-stakes cases of climate change denial and vaccine scepticism will sometimes be diagnosed by this account of evidence as evidence resistance. This will happen in cases of cognisers who have easily available evidence that climate change is happening and that vaccines are safe but fail to take it up and update their beliefs accordingly. It is compatible with this account, however, that this is not always the case: not all evidence rejection is evidence resistance. Sometimes, cognisers inhabit an epistemic environment heavily polluted with misleading evidence against the reliability of scientific testimony and public policy: if reliable testifiers in one's community testify that not-p: 'climate change is not happening', and one has every reason to trust them (say, because they have an exceptional track record of reliability as testifiers – although they get it wrong on this particular occasion), it can happen that one justifiably rejects evidence for p due to being in a position to know 'heavier' (albeit misleading) evidence against p. Note, however, that these cases – cases of justified evidence rejection – will be fairly specific cases epistemically that, while they may happen in fairly isolated communities, the more one has access to evidence for *p*, the less justified their evidence rejection will be.

Now, all of this tells us that the account put forth is extensionally adequate: the view gets the resistance cases right. That is an important theoretical virtue of the view, and, as we have seen, it singles it out in the epistemic normative landscape.

That being said, extensional adequacy is not explanatory adequacy: even if thinking of evidence in terms of evidential probability increasers that one is in a position to know delivers the result that there is evidence for the subjects in Cases 1–7 that they fail to take up, the question as to why they should have done so remains open. One task remains, then, for the theorist of evidence resistance: explaining the normative force exercised by available evidence on our properly functioning cognitive systems. Or, in other words, explaining why, given the account of evidence proposed, it is epistemically impermissible for cognitive systems that have generating knowledge as their epistemic function not to take up easily available evidence.

Here it goes: some evidence I take up with my belief-formation machinery, whereas some I fail to take up, although I should. What grounds this 'should', in my view, is proper epistemic functioning.[5] Because they are knowledge indicators, pieces of evidence are justification-makers: they are the proper inputs to our processes of belief formation that have generating knowledge as their function, and when we have enough thereof, and the processes in question are properly functioning in all other ways, the resulting belief is epistemically justified

Since evidence for S that *p*, on my account, consists of facts that enhance closeness to knowledge that *p* for S by enhancing S's evidential probability for *p*, our cognitive systems are malfunctioning if they fail to take up easily available evidence, in virtue of thereby failing to take up opportunities for enhancing closeness to knowledge. Since for any system S with a function F, S should fulfil F, and it is plausible that S should enhance closeness to F fulfilment, and since the function of our cognitive systems is to generate knowledge, our cognitive system should take up enhancers of closeness to knowledge. Our cognitive systems should take up pieces of evidence because they enhance closeness to function fulfilment (i.e. they enhance evidential probability and thereby closeness to knowledge).

In turn, when our belief-formation capacities either fail to take up knowledge indicators that they could have easily taken up or they take

---

[5] See, for example, Millikan (1984), Graham (2012), and Simion (2019a, 2023a).

them up but fail to output the corresponding belief, they are malfunctioning. A subject S's belief-formation capacity C is malfunctioning epistemically if S has sufficient evidence supporting *p* that is available to be taken up via C and C fails to output a belief that *p*.

7.3 Infallibilism: Evidence and Knowledge

Before moving on, I would like to address an important worry that has been put forth in recent literature for views of evidence like the one defended in this chapter (i.e. knowledge-centric views of evidence).

Most contemporary epistemologists are fallibilists: they think that you can know a proposition *p*, even if your evidence does not entail that *p*. In recent work, Jessica Brown (2018) offers a thorough defence of fallibilism against knowledge-centric views of evidence, or what I will dub 'new infallibilism'. More specifically, her central aim is to show that epistemologists who also want to be non-sceptics and want to endorse a non-shifty view of knowledge attributions should be fallibilists rather than new infallibilists. To this end, Brown argues that there is reason to think that fallibilism compares favourably with new infallibilism when it comes to evidence and evidential support. Perhaps most importantly, Brown identifies and takes issue with three key commitments of the new infallibilist's view of evidence, to wit:

> **The factivity of evidence:** If *p* is part of one's evidence, then *p* is true.
> **The sufficiency of knowledge for evidence:** If one knows that *p*, then *p* is part of one's evidence.
> **The sufficiency of knowledge for self-support:** If one knows that *p*, then *p* is evidence for *p*.

Brown argues against all three of these claims. Since fallibilists can avoid these commitments, the thought goes, fallibilism scores points against new infallibilism.

The account of evidence I defended in this chapter implies all of the claims above. As such, if Brown is right, my account is in trouble, alongside its E = K Williamsonian cousin.

However, I think that there are ways to be an infallibilist that survive Brown's excellent arguments. Thus, in what follows, I will explore ways in which new infallibilism can resist both Brown's case against infallibilism and her fallibilist response to at least some of the data points that have been thought to favour the new infallibilism.

Let's start by looking at Brown's argument against the sufficiency of knowledge for evidence (i.e. the claim that if one knows that p, then p is part of one's evidence). Brown's key idea is to appeal to citable evidence. She points out that one cannot felicitously cite p when queried about one's evidence for p, not even if one knows that p (Brown 2018, 49–50). But given that knowledge is sufficient for evidence, it is hard to see why this should be the case.

Note, however, that fallibilists, too, will need an account of when p is part of one's evidence. I can think of a few options here: if p is justified for one/if one believes that p/if one justifiably believes that p, then p is part of one's evidence. Crucially, since knowledge entails justified belief, their view entails the sufficiency of knowledge for evidence, no matter which of these options the fallibilist goes for. This means that in cases in which one knows that p, it is equally hard for fallibilists to explain why one cannot cite p when queried about one's evidence for p. In this way, there is no reason to think that new infallibilism is at a disadvantage here.

Let's move on to another of the claims above: the sufficiency of knowledge for self-support (i.e. that if one knows that p, then p is evidence for p). Why think that new infallibilists are committed to this claim in the first place? Here is Brown:

> To see why the infallibilist should embrace the *Sufficiency of knowledge for self-support*, consider [...] knowledge by testimony, inference to the best explanation and enumerative induction. It's hard to see how one has evidence for what's known in these ways which entails what's known without allowing that if one knows that p, then p is part of one's evidence for p. [...] So, it seems that embracing the *Sufficiency of knowledge for self-support* is the best way for the infallibilist to avoid scepticism. (Brown 2018, 43)

I agree that it may be hard for fallibilists to see how one can have the evidence for what is known here unless one subscribes to the sufficiency of knowledge for self-support. However, the same is not true of new infallibilists. Note that, according to new infallibilism, what one's evidence is will turn on worldly states (e.g. on the friendliness of the epistemic environment one finds oneself in). For instance, what is one's evidence for the claim that there is a barn before one may vary depending on whether one is in Normal Barn County or in Fake Barn County. But once this point is properly appreciated, there is little reason to think that testimony, inference to the best explanation, and enumerative induction pose a particularly difficult problem. While data from testimony, inference to the best explanation, and enumerative induction may not entail what is known, they may do so when conjoined with a sufficiently friendly epistemic environment.

This leaves the factivity of evidence (i.e. p is part of one's evidence only if p is true). Brown relies on a familiar line of objection to this claim. Here is Brown:

> As is well-known, this conception of evidence [which combines the factivity of evidence with the sufficiency of knowledge for evidence] is open to the objection that it holds that certain pairs of subjects who are intuitively equally justified in some claim (e.g. a person and her BIV twin), are not equally justified. (Brown 2018, 22)

Brown considers a response on behalf of new infallibilists in terms of blamelessness.[6] They key idea is that while BIVs don't believe justifiably, they are nonetheless blameless for their beliefs. At the same time, there is empirical evidence that suggests that we are prone to mistaking cases of unjustified but blameless belief for cases of justified belief, which is why intuition leads us astray in these cases.

According to Brown, this move remains unsuccessful. Her strategy is to look at a number of ways of analysing what blamelessness amounts to and to argue that none of these ways will do the trick for new infallibilists.

Note, though, that while it is true that the particular infallibilists (e.g. Williamson, Littlejohn) that Brown discusses have historically held a view that equates justification and knowledge, this is optional to new infallibilisms. There has been a surge of views in the literature that explain justified belief in terms of knowledge without identifying justified belief and knowledge (e.g. Bird 2007, Ichikawa 2014, Miracchi 2015, Kelp 2018, Schellenberg 2018, Simion 2019a). Champions of these views have argued at great length that these views can allow for agents in bad cases (e.g. BIVs) to be justified. If so, they can successfully explain the intuition at issue here. Crucially, the view of justification defended here is precisely one such view: on this account, BIVs believe justifiably insofar as they employ properly functioning cognitive capacities with the function of generating knowledge – which, by stipulation in the justification-intuition-triggering cases (paradigmatically, of recently envatted BIVs) they do. At the same time, and crucially, this view of justification is entirely compatible with new infallibilism. After all, what is key to new infallibilism is a view about the relation between knowledge and one's evidence.

---

[6] See Brown (2018, 70–73).

7.4 Conclusion

On the account defended here, one's evidence consists in facts that one is in a position to know and that increase one's evidential probability that something is the case. In turn, being in a position to know has to do with the variety of cogniser at stake: should one be the kind of cogniser that hosts cognitive processes that are able to pick up the relevant facts from the world, the facts at stake will belong in one's body of evidence.

CHAPTER 8

Defeaters as Ignorance Indicators

This chapter puts forth and defends a novel view of defeat, and it shows that it is superior to its competition in that it can account for the epistemic impermissibility of defeat resistance cases and normative defeat cases, as well as for the effect ignored defeat has on doxastic justification. On this account, defeaters are ignorance indicators[1]: facts that one is in a position to know and that reduce one's evidential probability that p. Furthermore, I also put forth a novel account of the normativity at work in cases of normative defeat and negligent inquiry and evidence gathering.

8.1 The Nature and Theoretical Importance of Defeat

The notion of defeat is central to epistemology, practical reasoning, and ethics. Within epistemology, it is standardly assumed that a subject who knows that p or justifiably believes that p can lose this knowledge or justified belief by acquiring a so-called defeater, whether this is evidence

---

[1] I have developed, defended, and presented my account of epistemic reasons, evidence, and defeat as knowledge/ignorance indicators starting back in 2018. Dutant and Littlejohn (2021) also call defeaters 'ignorance indicators', but their account is spelled out in very different terms, so any affinity is merely terminological. On their account, defeaters consist in evidence that one is not in a position to know. Gibbons (2013) and Kelp (2023) also develop and defend accounts along these lines. There are two main problems for accounts like these. The first is structural: these accounts are epistemically second order, in that defeaters are evidence that some epistemic status is missing. But for an agent to have this evidence, they need to be able to process the relevant content; many agents that can undergo defeat are not sophisticated enough to have the relevant contents, however. The second problem parallels a wrong-kind-of-reasons problem: matters that are intuitively irrelevant to justification and defeat can be evidence for or against one being in a position to know. Here is a case from Jonathan Jenkins-Ichikawa (personal conversation): say that your grandfather is not feeling well and you are searching for the thermometer to check whether he has a fever. Now, finding the thermometer is evidence that you are in a position to know that your grandfather has a fever, and, indeed, it is evidence that you will come to know that he does. However, clearly, it does not affect the justification of your corresponding belief. Conversely, not finding the thermometer is evidence that you are not in a position to know that he does have a fever, but it surely does not defeat whatever justification you might have had to believe that he does have a fever.

that not-*p*, evidence that the process which produced their belief is unreliable, or evidence that they have probably misevaluated their evidence. Within ethics and practical reasoning, it is widely accepted that a subject may initially have a reason to do something, although this reason is later defeated by their acquisition of further information.

Investigations into the nature and normativity of defeat come with high theoretical stakes. The notion of defeat has been central to a wide range of different philosophical debates, including, but not limited to:

(1) The nature of justification and knowledge: since knowledge and justification are taken by many to be defeasible, the extent to which one account or another of the nature of knowledge/justification is able to account for/accommodate defeat constitutes an important ground for assessing its theoretical credentials.

(2) Internalism versus externalism: several epistemologists worry that epistemic externalism has a hard time accommodating psychological defeat; at the same time, conversely, if justification supervenes on mental states alone, as per internalism, it seems mysterious that it could be defeated by normative defeaters lying outside of the cogniser's ken.

(3) Epistemic norms and reasons: for accommodating the phenomenon of defeat, debates on epistemic norms and epistemic reasons owe us, at a minimum, an account of epistemic normative overriding, as well as an account of reasons against belief.

(4) Evidence and higher-order evidence: since evidence is widely taken to be defeasible, a plausible account of evidence should come with a corresponding plausible account of defeat. For instance, one important desideratum on any such account is that it explains the defeating power of higher-order evidence, namely of evidence that one's first-order beliefs are the output of a flawed process.[2]

(5) Closure and transmission: one popular solution to alleged failures of closure principles for knowledge and transmission principles for warrant is known as 'the defeat solution'. Roughly, the thought goes, closure and transmission hold prima facie, and the intuitions of failure are to be explained in terms of psychological defeat. This solution, of course, hangs on the assumption that there is such a

---

[2] Some philosophers believe that knowledge is not defeasible by higher-order evidence (e.g. Lasonen-Aarnio 2017, Williamson (forthcominga): the picture I put forth does not rest on the denial of this claim. Even sceptics of knowledge defeat by higher-order evidence are not full-on sceptics about the defeating power of higher-order evidence.

thing to begin with (i.e. that psychological defeat is a genuine epistemic category).

(6) Disagreement: one way to characterise the debate between conciliatory and steadfast views of disagreement is as centred around the question: can the testimony of one's peer carry defeating power? Steadfastism answers 'no', conciliationism answers 'yes'. The correct account of the nature of defeat can help settle the issue.

(7) Reductionism versus anti-reductionism about testimony: say that a suspect for murder S tells you that she did not do it. According to both of the main views in the epistemology of testimony, you are not justified to believe S. According to reductionism, that's because you always need positive, non-testimonial reasons to believe what you are being told. In contrast, according to anti-reductionism, you are prima facie justified to believe S, but your justification is defeated. The correct account of the nature of defeat will likely go a long way towards settling this issue.

Given these high theoretical stakes, investigations into the nature and normativity of defeat carry significant philosophical weight. Unfortunately, not many systematic, full accounts of defeat have been put forth on the market (although see Brown and Simion (2021) for the first full volume on defeat and Kelp (2023) for the first book-length treatment). In what follows, I will look at the classical accounts of defeat on the market – one internalist evidentialist, coming from John Pollock, and one externalist reliabilist, championed by Alvin Goldman – to help situate my account in the extant landscape.[3]

8.1.1 Traditional Evidentialism About Defeat

The first and what is now considered the classic view on the nature of defeat in epistemology is due to Pollock (1986). According to this view, d is a defeater of e's support for p for S if and only if (1) e is a reason to believe p for S and (2) $e \& d$ is not a reason to believe p for S (henceforth 'Pollock's view').

The account has a lot going for it: it nicely promises to cut across normative domains in virtue of being framed in terms of reasons; after all, epistemologists hardly enjoy an exclusivity on reasons. With Pollock's view

---

[3] For a comprehensive overview of extant accounts of defeat in the literature, see Simion (forthcoming).

in play, it is easy to see how we could generalise it to cover different targets (e.g. actions) and types (e.g. moral, prudential) of normativity. Second, Pollock's view makes good on the intuitive thought that defeaters are actualisers of the possibility of a positive normative status to be overridden or undercut; what the view says, in a nutshell, is that defeaters are the kind of things that render a permissible belief impermissible.

For our purposes here, there are two important limitations to Pollock's view: first, it does not account for partial defeat – nor is it trivial to see how it could be extended to do so. Since many cases of defeat resistance will be cases of partial defeat, the view will not deliver the needed theoretical resources for the data I am trying to explain. Second, the account remains silent on the nature of reasons and, most importantly, on what it is for something to be a reason *for S* to believe: however, in order to understand the impermissibility of defeat resistance, it is crucial to understand both of these things. We need to know what reasons are and which reasons are reasons *for S* to believe, since this is essential to understanding the impermissibility of S's resistance to defeat.

One way to spell out Pollock's view that suggests itself, given his evidentialist leanings, is a traditional, seemings-based recipe: on this account, reasons for S to believe are S's relevant seemings. Of course, as we have seen in Chapter 2, a view like this will get us into trouble with resistance cases rather rapidly: on the necessity direction, recall only the very sexist George, who zones out whenever a woman speaks to him. This guy doesn't host any relevant seemings – intuitively, however, his beliefs are defeated by women's testimony. Against the sufficiency direction, notably, cases of cognitive penetration will create trouble for a seemings-based defeat account (e.g. see Lyons 2011): the fact that it seems to me – due to sexist bias – that women don't know what they're talking about is not enough to defeat my justification to believe their testimony.

8.1.2 Defeaters as Reliable Processes

Reliabilist theories of justification have been extremely popular in the last three decades and come in a variety of forms, but the gist of the view is that a belief is justified if and only if it is formed via a (normally) reliable procedure or ability. Reliabilism is a theory of prima facie justification. As such, in line with normative theories in general, it needs a theory of defeat in order to hold water. The standard reliabilist account of defeat comes from Alvin Goldman:

> **The alternative reliable process account (ARP):** S's belief is defeated iff there are reliable (or conditionally reliable) belief-forming processes available to S such that, if S had used those processes in addition to the process actually used, S wouldn't have held the belief in question (Goldman 1979).

One can see how ARP is an elegant reliabilist translation of the Pollockian thought that defeat is the kind of normative entity that, when taken in conjunction with the extant epistemic support for the relevant belief, fails to render it justified.

Bob Beddor (2015) is the *locus classicus* for criticism of ARP; if Beddor is right, ARP is both too weak and too strong. Against ARP's sufficiency direction, Beddor offers the following case:

> **Thinking About Unger:** Harry sees a tree in front of him at t. Consequently, he comes to believe the proposition TREE: ⟨There is a tree in front of me⟩ at t. Now, Harry happens to be very good at forming beliefs about what Peter Unger's 1975 time-slice would advise one to believe in any situation. Call this cognitive process his Unger Predictor [...]. What's more, [...] whenever it occurs to Harry that Unger would advise him (Harry) to suspend judgement about p, this causes Harry to [...] suspend judgement about p. So if Harry had used his Unger Predictor, he would have come to [...] suspend judgement regarding TREE. (Beddor 2015, 152)

What this cases shows is that ARP is too weak normatively: contra ARP, for my belief that p to be defeated, it is not enough that I would change my mind about p in a counterfactual world due to employing some reliable process. Just because I would change my mind in world W, it does not follow that I *should* change my mind in world W: defeat is a normative notion.

More importantly for our purposes here, however, Beddor's case against ARP's necessity direction is, indeed, a paradigmatic case of evidence resistance. Here it is:

> **Job Opening:** Masha tells Clarence that her department will have a job opening in the fall. Clarence believes Masha; assuming that Masha is usually reliable, Clarence's belief counts as prima facie justified. Sometime later, Clarence speaks with the head of Masha's department, Victor, who informs him that the job search was cancelled due to budget constraints. Now suppose that Clarence harbours a deep-seated hatred of Victor that causes him to disbelieve everything that Victor says; what's more, no amount of rational reflection would rid Clarence of this inveterate distrust. Consequently, he continues to believe that there will be a job opening in the autumn.

This case shows that ARP is also too strong: just because, in all counterfactual words, I would irrationally and stubbornly hold on to my belief, it does not follow that I *should* do so. Once again, ARP is not normative enough to do the job it is supposed to do. Going back to our purposes here, Job Opening is a paradigmatic case of testimonial evidence resistance: it shows that APR's normative weakness results in difficulties for accounting for resistance to defeat.

Along similar lines, recall the case of Professor Racist:

> Case #6. **Misdirected Attention:** Professor Racist is teaching college-level maths. He believes people of colour are less intelligent than white people. As a result, whenever he asks a question, his attention automatically goes to the white students, such that he doesn't even notice the Black students who raise their hands. As a result, he believes Black students are not very active in class.

To see the problem that this cases poses for ARP, let us again ramp up the epistemically problematic aspects of the case and stipulate that Professor Racist is not only racist but also dogmatic (indeed, this assumption should not be very hard to make, since these two epistemic vices tend to be encountered together): even if he had seen the Black students raising their hands, he would have still strongly believed that they're not very active in class. If so, ARP predicts that there is no defeat at stake in this case: after all, there is now no alternative reliable process that is such that, had Professor Racist used it, he would have abandoned his belief that Black students are not very active in class. Not only is ARP then not predicting defeat in this case, but it predicts that Professor Racist is epistemically better off in this version of the case than in the original version. Since being racist and dogmatic is epistemically worse than being only racist, ARP remains unsatisfactory.[4]

Note, finally, that we can make the same stipulation of dogmatism in all of the other resistance cases as well, with the same unsatisfactory result.

---

[4] See Beddor (2015) for an excellent and comprehensive critique of ARP, Graham and Lyons (2021) for a rejoinder on ARP's behalf and Simion (forthcoming) for criticism of both. Beddor (2021) proposes a reasons-first reliabilism that unpacks reasons as inputs to reliable processes. Beddor's view will also struggle with resistance cases. After all, reliable processes are not infallible processes: they can fail on occasion, either by not taking up the right kind of stuff or by taking up the wrong kind of stuff. If so, the account does not have the resources to explain why testimony from a woman is a reason, while sexist beliefs are not.

As such, process reliabilists still owe us an explanation of what is going wrong in cases of defeat resistance.

The account I will develop next, somewhat unsurprisingly, complements the account of evidence as knowledge indicators developed in the previous chapter. On the view I will defend, conversely, defeaters are ignorance indicators. It is interesting, I think, to consider the view against its historical evidentialist and reliabilist predecessors: like the evidentialist, my account takes evidence and defeaters to have normative strength independently of whether they are being taken up via particular types of processes or abilities. Like the reliabilist, however, the account bottoms out in processes and abilities: a fact only constitutes a defeater if one is *in a position* to take it up via one's cognitive capacities.

8.2 Defeaters as Ignorance Indicators

In my view, defeaters are indicators of ignorance: they are facts that one is in a position to know and that lower one's evidential probability that p is the case:

> **Defeaters as ignorance indicators:** A fact d is a defeater for S's evidence e for p iff S is in an position to know d and S's evidential probability that p conditional on $e\&d$ is lower than S's evidential probability that p conditional on e.

Or, slightly more formally:

> **Defeaters as ignorance indicators:** A fact d is a defeater for S's evidence e for p iff S is in a position to know d, and $P(p/e\&d) < P(p/e)$.

Recall also that, on my view, S is in a position to know a fact e if S has a cognitive capacity with the function of generating knowledge that can (qualitatively, quantitatively, and environmentally) easily uptake e in cognisers of S's type. It is easy to see that the view of defeat defended here nicely predicts that the justification of some occurrent beliefs hosted by the characters in several of resistance cases is defeated by the presence of ignorance indicators. Take Bill, Dump's supporter: since the information coming from several sources around him is such that he is in a position to know it, and it lowers the evidential probability that Dump is a good president, Bill should lower his confidence that Dump is a good president. Similarly, Mary should lower her confidence that her husband is just making friends, and Professor Racist should not believe, as he does, that Black students are not very active in class.

In my view, rebutting and undercutting defeaters share one and the same central epistemic normative property: they are evidential probability decreasers. What differs is the mechanism by which they achieve this effect: rebutters lower one's evidential probability for p by raising one's evidential probability for not-p. In contrast, undercutters reduce the degree of confirmation that a particular piece of evidence e confers on p (see also Kotzen (2019) for a detailed formal treatment along these lines). This comes in stark contrast to literature that gives different treatment to first- and higher-order evidence or rebutting and undercutting defeat. I think mine is the right result, and we should, all else equal, prefer this unified treatment on grounds having to do with theoretical adequacy. Here are some quick reasons why scepticism about the defeating power of higher-order evidence does not work: one's evidence comes with a having relation and an evidential support relation (also known as degree of confirmation: how much a piece of evidence probabilifies p). Plausibly, one's confidence in p should match the degree of confirmation that one's evidence offers to p. Higher-order evidence/undercutting defeat works via raising/lowering the degree of confirmation that first-order evidence provides to p. Now, here is a case of higher-order evidence that increases the degree of confirmation of the first-order evidence: I believe p based on my neighbour George's testimony (alternatively, I have, e.g., 0.8 credence that p). Mary tells me that George is the top expert in the world on the matter. Her testimony is evidence that q: 'George's testimony gives very high support to p'. In probabilistic terms: if George's original testimony probabilifies p to x, Mary's testimony translates roughly as 'George's testimony probabilifies p to y & $y > x$' (how high y is will depend on Mary's epistemic credentials). So now that Mary has spoken, I am in a position to know something along the lines of r: 'I have a 0.8 credence that p based on George's testimony and the probability that p conditional on George's testimony is 0.9'. Intuitively, I should revise to 0.9.

Moving on to a corresponding case of undercutting defeat: I believe p (indeed, I know p) based on my neighbour George's testimony (alternatively, I host, e.g., 0.8 credence that p). Mary tells me that George is a well-known liar on p-issues. Her testimony is evidence that q: 'George's testimony gives lower support to p'. George's original testimony probabilifies p to x; Mary's testimony, just like before, amounts to: 'George's testimony probabilifies p to y & $y < x$' (it will depend on Mary's epistemic credentials how low y is). Just like before, I am in a position to know that r: 'I have a 0.8 credence that p based on George's testimony and the probability that p conditional on George's testimony is 0.4'. Intuitively,

I should revise to 0.4. Scepticism about the defeating power of higher-order evidence is wrong, and defeat affords unified treatment.

Going back to our central cases of evidence resistance – again, crucially, real-world, high-stakes cases of climate change denial and vaccine scepticism will sometimes be diagnosed by this account of evidence and defeat as evidence resistance: this will happen in cases of cognisers who have easily available evidence that climate change is happening and that vaccines are safe but fail to take it up and update their beliefs accordingly.

As previously shown, however, it is compatible with this account, however, that this is not always the case: not all evidence rejection is evidence resistance. Sometimes, cognisers inhabit an epistemic environment heavily polluted with misleading defeat: if reliable testifiers in one's community testify against p: 'climate change is happening', and one has every reason to trust them (say, because they have an exceptional track record of reliability as testifiers – although they get it wrong on this particular occasion), it can happen that one justifiably rejects evidence for p due to being in a position to know 'heavier' defeaters (i.e. evidential probability decreasers). Note, however, that these cases – cases of justified evidence rejection in virtue of misleading defeat – will be fairly specific cases epistemically: for example, cases in which the cogniser has more reliable (although misleading) testimony that not-p than evidence that p, or cases in which the cogniser has overwhelming undercutting defeaters (e.g. based on reliable although misleading testimony) for the source of p. While this may happen in fairly isolated communities, the more one has access to evidence for p, the less justified their evidence rejection will be.

Here is a question that arises for the account put forth: why think that there is such a thing as an ought governing our belief formation to take up defeat? After all, on the account proposed, defeaters are ignorance indicators (i.e. facts that lower evidential probability for one). Why should a system with the function of generating knowledge be under an obligation[5] to take up ignorance indicators, which, by stipulation, decrease closeness to knowledge?

Two things about this: first, note that defeaters are not merely ignorance indicators for p, but also either knowledge indicators for not-p (rebutting defeaters) or knowledge indicators for 'piece of evidence e does not confirm/offers weaker confirmation for p' (undercutters). This, in turn,

---

[5] Recall that I follow classic deontic logic in using 'ought' and 'obligation' interchangeably. Philosophers who think of obligations as being thicker than mere oughts, or as governing only human beings but not systems, artifacts, etc., should read 'obligation' as 'ought' throughout.

affords them the same normative explanation as that offered for garden variety evidence: defeaters exercise normative pressure on our cognitive systems in virtue of them being knowledge indicators.

Second, and furthermore, I think that there is more to the normative pressure of defeat than this merely general evidential normative pressure; in particular, I think that the normative pressure of defeaters for my belief that p can also be explained in a p-centric fashion. Here it goes: consider, for starters, a case in which I know that p at t_1, and (misleading) evidence that not-p becomes available to me at t_2. In a situation like this, crucially, whether I take up the defeating evidence or not, my knowledge that p is defeated (short of my knowledge constituting defeat defeat): I am now left, at best (depending on the relevant evidential weights), with a somewhat – but not fully – justified true belief that p. My full belief has thereby been rendered impermissible: I now hold a doxastic attitude that is stronger than what the evidence affords. Note, also, that this is so even if what I started with is not knowledge, but rather, for example, a justified credence of 0.6. Now that defeat is available in my environment, whether I take it up or not, my 0.6 credence is no longer permissible, since my level of justification has been lowered by defeat.[6] What is it that my cognitive system ought to do now that it's hosting an impermissible doxastic attitude? The answer that suggests itself is: abandon it, either altogether (if defeat is full defeat) or in favour of the weaker attitude that remains supported by the evidence.

Note, though, that abandoning the (now) impermissible doxastic attitude in conjunction with not taking up the relevant defeaters seems irrational. If I, at the same time, (mistakenly) continue to take my evidence to support a 0.6 credence and adjust to a 0.5 credence, something has gone amiss, rationality-wise. In sum, it would seem as though, if I don't take up the relevant defeat from the environment, I am faced with a normative dilemma: either I hold on to an impermissible doxastic attitude that is no longer supported by my evidence or I hold a novel doxastic attitude that enjoys propositional justification but not doxastic justification, for lack of proper basing. Grasping neither of these horns is knowledge conducive. If so, it would seem, the only path left for knowledge conduciveness is

---

[6] For readers who believe that knowledge is not defeasible by higher-order evidence, while other epistemic states may be – in line with, for example, Lasonen-Aarnio (2014) and Williamson (forthcomingb): the picture I put forth does not rest on the denial of this claim. That is because it is compatible with my picture that, for example, knowledge always constitutes defeat defeat.

taking up the relevant defeaters and adjusting my doxastic attitude in light of them.[7]

8.3 External Defeat and Norms of Evidence Gathering

Consider a doctor, X, who believes that p but missed a recent development in the field that (q =) the data that have been taken to support p don't really do so. X does not justifiably believe that p: q is a defeater for this belief, which undermines X's justification for believing p. Now contrast X with a layperson, Y, who had been told by their doctor that p and still believes that p. Despite the fact that there has been a recent development in the field of medicine, Y's belief that p continues to be justified. In particular, q does not undermine Y's justification for their belief that p. Since the central difference between X and Y is that X occupies a certain social role (i.e. they are a doctor), there is reason to think that social roles can be sources of defeat via giving subjects reasons to inquire (Goldberg 2018).

Note, first, that so far we have looked only at epistemic functions in individual agents. And while epistemic functions may arise in individual agents, they also arise in broader social systems. It is precisely this idea that will be of central importance in what follows.[8]

To begin with, I take social systems to be systems that feature multiple agents who are connected to one another in at least some ways. The social roles we are interested in are properties of agents in social systems. Being a doctor, teacher, parent, etc., is a property of an agent in a social system.[9]

One interesting feature of social roles is that many of them have constitutive functional properties in that what it is to be an X (doctor, teacher, baker, fireperson, etc.) is to have the particular function in question (to treat ill people, to teach people stuff, to make baked goods, to put out fires, etc.). To see this, note that we cannot even fully understand the roles in question without understanding their functions: to fully understand what a doctor is, you have to understand what the function of a doctor is (i.e. to

---

[7] For a discussion of the epistemic value of coherence, see Chapter 11.
[8] See Kelp and Simion (2021b) for a full treatment of normative defeat.
[9] Note that the existence of agents who occupy social roles need not imply the existence of other agents. We might want to allow that a doctor continues to be a doctor even if they are the only human being left alive. However, this does imply the existence of other agents at least at some point in the past. If there had only ever been one human being around, this person could not have been a doctor. At best, they may have engaged in healing practices, but they couldn't have been a doctor. We take this to be independently plausible. After all, social roles are just that: *social* roles.

treat ill people). It is easy enough to see that the same is true of a whole host of other social roles, including teachers, bakers, firepeople, among many others.

Given that many social roles have constitutive functional properties, the prospects for an analysis of the epistemic norms constituting these social roles already look bright. The question that we need to consider is: are the functions constitutive of these social roles generating any constitutive epistemic norms of proper functioning? If the answer to this question is yes, then the route to an account of epistemic norms constitutive of social roles is a going to be a short one. By the same token, an account of how social roles may lead to defeat may come into view.

To get an idea of how this might be, let's take another look at the case of the doctor. Note that having an up-to-date understanding of their field is part of the normal functioning of doctors in the social system that we occupy. More specifically, it is part of such normal functioning that doctors engage in inquiries into recent developments in the field, as a result of which they maintain an up-to-date understanding of the field and thereby know how to treat people. In fact, that doctors maintain an up-to-date understanding is a key element in the feedback loop that explains the continued existence of this important social role in the social system that we occupy[10]: doctors' understanding informs their treatment practices, and the fact that it is kept up to date enhances their success rate of these treatments, which in turn explains why the social role of doctor continues to exist in our social system. But since maintaining an up-to-date understanding of the field is part of the normal functioning of doctors in our social system, we get the by now familiar normative import. It is thereby part of such proper functioning. This, in turn, means that we get a norm that doctors violate if they fail to maintain an up-to-date understanding of their field and, by the same token, if they fail to engage in the inquiries needed to do so. And, of course, it is easy enough to see that the same holds, mutatis mutandis, for many other social roles, including teachers,

---

[10] These are, of course, not essential features of doctors, but merely constitutive features: doctors remain doctors even when they are in breach of some of the norms constitutive of their social role. This is a general feature of functionalist normativity: hearts remain hearts even when they malfunction. It is also a general feature of constitutive normativity more generally: one can break several constitutive norms of a game or language and still count as playing the game/speaking the language. Note, though, that too widespread a breach of constitutive norms with maximal systematicity will lead to discontinuing the constituted activity: if I only utter 'kakakakaka', I don't count as speaking English. Similarly, someone who doesn't have a medical degree, lacks any understanding of medicine, etc., will not count as being a doctor due to their being in too widespread a breach of the constitutive norms of the role.

lawyers, academics, and so on. In turn, since the norms in question are generated by the constitutive functions of these social roles, they will be constitutive norms.

It turns out, then, that we can explain normative defeat as a breach of a constitutive norm, sourced in the constitutive function of these social roles. Since our doctor X is a practicing doctor, they occupy the social role of doctor. As a result, they violate an epistemic norm associated with proper functioning for this role when they fail to maintain an up-to-date understanding of their field (e.g. by missing the research that indicates that q). In this way, it is epistemically proper for them to believe that q. And since q is a reason against believing that p, we get the desired result that X's justification for believing p is defeated.

How does this account of normative defeat map onto my general account of defeaters? Recall the proposed view: a fact d is a defeater for S's evidence e for p iff S is in an position to know d and S's evidential probability that p conditional on $e \& d$ is lower than S's evidential probability that p conditional on e. Recall also that, on my account, being in a position to know is spelled out in terms of availability, as restricted by the type of cogniser instantiated. What I want to suggest is that, in cases like that above, the social role individuates the type of cogniser at stake and the availability conditions follow the corresponding constitutive epistemic oughts: since cognisers like our doctor should be aware of recent developments in their field, the account will predict that these are available to them in the relevant sense – of course, with reasonable qualitative, quantitative, and environmental restrictions.

But won't this account suffer from a problem parallel to Goldberg's view? Recall that Goldberg wanted to explain the evidence one should have had in terms of social expectations. Recall, also, that we said that epistemically illegitimate (albeit reliable) social expectations make problems for Goldberg's account: if epistemic normativity is encroached by social normativity, reliable but epistemically problematic social expectations cannot be further explained in epistemic normative terms.

Won't my account have the same problem, in virtue of appealing to social roles? Can't there be social roles that are functionally constituted by norms that are bad, epistemically? Consider, for instance, the social role 'judge' in a judicial system where discrimination based on race is written into the laws of the land: isn't my account going to deliver the result that judges shouldn't update based on the testimony of, for example, Black testifiers?

It will not. To see this, note that one important advantage that my account has over Goldberg's is that epistemic normativity is not encroached upon by social normativity: the epistemic remains an independent normative domain with its own independent evaluative structure. On my view, some genuine epistemic norms – associated with promoting epistemic values, such as knowledge – constitute social roles. Compatibly, norms constituting social roles that are bad epistemically, in that they conflict with norms sourced in the proper functioning of our cognitive system – such as 'don't believe Black testifiers!' – are not epistemic norms: they are mere (bad) social norms with epistemic content.

8.4 Conclusion

This chapter developed an account of defeat that builds nicely on the account of evidence developed in the previous chapter. On this view, defeaters are ignorance indicators: they are facts that one is in a position to know and that decrease one's evidential probability. What differs is the mechanism by which they achieve this effect: rebutters lower one's evidential probability for p by raising one's evidential probability for not-p. In contrast, undercutters reduce the degree of confirmation that a particular piece of evidence e confers on p. Finally, the chapter developed a novel, functionalist account of normative defeat and the impermissibility of negligence in evidence gathering.

CHAPTER 9

Inquiry and Permissible Suspension

This chapter develops an account of permissible suspension that builds on the views of justification, evidence, and defeat defended in the previous chapters. The view is superior to extant competitors in that it successfully predicts epistemic normative failure in cases of suspension generated by evidence and defeat resistance. On this view, doxastically justified suspension is suspension generated by properly functioning knowledge-generating processes. In turn, properly functioning knowledge-generating processes uptake knowledge and ignorance indicators.

9.1 Suspension and the Knowledge Function

I have argued that generating knowledge is the function of our cognitive processes, and that the norms governing moves in inquiry – such as beliefs, suspensions, withholdings, credences, assertions, or pieces of reasoning – will drop out of this function.

Moves in the practice of inquiry – that is, all epistemically significant states and actions – aim either directly (plausibly: beliefs, assertions, reasonings) or indirectly (credences, suspensions, withholdings) at the aim of the practice of inquiry. The difference will lie with goal achievability: since beliefs, assertions, and conclusions of reasonings can be knowledgeable, in a way in which things like credences, suspensions, and withholdings cannot, belief formation aims directly at fulfilling the function of the practice (generating knowledge), while, at the same time, credence, withholding, and suspension aim at knowledge indirectly – they are transitional attitudes, in the sense in which these are attitudes held en route to knowledge but that are not in the running for knowledge.

On my view, such transitional attitudes[1] aim at getting us closer to knowledge: they aim directly at adjusting one's doxastic states to the available

---

[1] Staffel (2023) is an excellent discussion of transitional attitudes, but the terminology maps onto a different ontological category.

evidence, which, in turn, ultimately aims at the aim of inquiry – knowledge generation. In what follows, I put more flesh on the bones on this general thought.

Importantly, topics in the epistemology of credence, or degrees of belief, deserve a book-length treatment of their own, so I will not touch on this here.[2] This book restricts itself to full belief and suspension and how evidence and defeat resistance affect the permissibility thereof. In what follows, I offer a sketch of how the knowledge function of inquiry will generate norms for suspensions.

9.2 Justified Suspension

Suspension was, for the longest time, not very hot in epistemology: historically (from Descartes to Clifford, from internalist evidentialists to reliabilists and knowledge-first externalists), people worried mostly about the risks and sins involved in believing without justification, and they ignored the risks of failing to believe when one has plenty of evidence. Recent social and political difficulties sourced in science denialism brought the normativity of suspension to centre stage.

One might think that an account of suspension is straightforwardly predicted by the view of evidence defended here. In particular, one might expect that something like the following principle is correct:

Suspension–evidence link (SEL): A subject S is justifiedly suspended on p iff S has equally weighty evidence for and against p.

There are, however, many problems with SEL. First, there is a purely terminological problem: most often, the epistemic permissibility of suspending on p is taken to be synonymous with the epistemic permissibility of not forming a full belief that p. In this sense of suspension – which only affects full belief – SEL is false on the necessity direction: one need not have equally weighty support for p and not-p to permissibly withhold full belief in p. Any level of epistemic support short of full propositional justification for p will be sufficient for permissibly withholding full belief that p.

If so, we need to distinguish between (1) what makes full belief permissibly suspended – which is compatible with being permissibly more confident that p than that not-p – and (2) outright permissible neutrality[3]:

---

[2] See Kelp and Simion (2023b) for a full treatment.
[3] Thanks to Julia Staffel for many helpful discussions on this topic.

taking a fully neutral attitude with regard to p (e.g. suspending belief and forming a 0.5 credence, or withholding (not forming) full belief and holding a 0.5 credence, or withholding both belief and credence). To this effect, for ease of recognition, I will refer to the former variety as permissible belief suspension and to the latter as permissible neutrality. On this picture, we get two different permissibility principles. Here they are:

> **Full belief suspension–evidence link (SEL):** Suspending belief in p is epistemically permissible for S iff S does not have enough evidential support for a justified belief that p.
> **Neutrality–evidence link (NEL):** A subject S is justifiedly neutral on p iff S has equally weighty evidence for and against p.

SEL tells us when a subject S can permissibly suspend on p – although they may well be epistemically normatively constrained to form a fairly high credence that p. In contrast, NEL normates tout court neutrality: epistemically permissibly taking a neutral doxastic attitude with regard to p.

SEL and NEL seem fairly plausible at first glance, and they also give us a nice way to think about the nature of reasons to withhold/suspend and their relation to reasons to believe/against believing: on this account, a subject S has a reason to suspend just in case S does not have sufficient reason to fully believe, and, in turn, S has a reason to be neutral on p just in case S has equally weighty reasons for and against p.

Unfortunately, things aren't as easy as this: suspension and neutrality, just like any other doxastic attitude, afford two types of justification: propositional and doxastic (see also Lord and Sylvan 2021, 2022). In particular, the two will come apart in cases in which S will have sufficient evidence to suspend on p/be neutral on p but will nevertheless fail to do so epistemically permissibly.

The reason why this can happen is improper uptake and evidence handling: one can have evidence for/against p that one fails to uptake/update on or improperly uptakes/processes/updates on, which will result in a lack of doxastic justification for suspension/neutrality just as it results in a lack of doxastic justification for belief. To see how this can be the case, it is easy to imagine cases in which S's evidence is as per SEL/NEL, but S's suspension/neutrality either is not based on this evidence (but, say, on wishful thinking) or is based on this evidence in the wrong way (e.g. the evidence supports suspending/neutrality inductively, but S takes it to do so deductively).

If this is so, SEL and NEL are false. What we need are more fine-grained principles that distinguish between these varieties of justification for withholding/suspending. Here it goes, for propositional justification:

> **Propositionally justified full belief suspension:** Suspending belief on *p* is propositionally justified for S iff S does not have enough evidential support for a justified belief that *p*.
>
> **Propositionally justified neutrality:** A subject S's neutrality on *p* is propositionally justified iff S has equally weighty evidence for and against *p*.

De facto, then, propositionally justified neutrality will occur in cases in which the relevant evidential probability is at 0.5. In this, the view is evidence-based but not evidentialist (i.e. not evidence-first), since evidence is further unpacked in terms of facts that can be taken up by cognitive processes hosted by the relevant type of cogniser.

An account of doxastically justified neutrality falls outside of the scope of this book, since it will rest on the correct account of credence justification.[4] How about doxastically justified suspension? It should not come as a surprise to the reader, at this stage, that in my view this will be, once more, a matter of proper functioning. Here it goes:

> **Doxastically justified suspending:** S's suspension on *p* is doxastically justified iff formed via a properly functioning belief-forming capacity that has the function of generating knowledge.

What is the relationship between doxastically justified suspensions and the evidence for which they are held? Once more, pieces of evidence are pro tanto, prima facie justification-makers: they are inputs to the process of belief formation, and when the latter has the function of generating knowledge and is properly functioning, the resulting doxastic attitude is epistemically justified. When evidence is sufficient for full belief, a properly functioning belief-formation capacity with the function of generating knowledge will generate a full belief. When it is not enough, a properly functioning belief-formation capacity with the function of generating knowledge will generate a suspension.

This view of permissible suspension will deal well with the cases of impermissible suspension that made trouble for Sosa's virtue-theoretic view: George the sexist, for instance, will not be permissibly suspended on where Glasgow Central is, since he has undefeated evidence (Anna's testimony) that it is to the right. More precisely, since Anna's testimony raises his evidential probability that Glasgow Central is to the right and no

---

[4] See my work on justified credence (Kelp and Simion 2023b) for an account of doxastically justified neutrality.

other facts lower it, George should (at least) be more confident that Glasgow Central is to the right than that it is not.

Why should we believe that this account is the metaphysically correct account of suspension (i.e. why should we think that knowledge-generating belief-formation processes are the ones in charge of generating suspensions)? There are a few reasons for this. First, recall the normative picture defended here: I take it that generating knowledge is the function of our epistemic practice of inquiry, and that norms governing moves in inquiry – such as beliefs, suspensions, assertions, or pieces of reasoning – will drop out of this function. This normative picture fits snugly with a picture in which the cognitive capacities in charge of generating knowledge will be the same ones responsible for generating withholdings and suspensions when enough support for knowledge is not available: these processes will seek to form a belief if *and only if* the belief in question is knowledgeable (Sosa 2021). This function, in turn, will translate into them generating knowledgeable beliefs whenever knowledge is available, but also, as Ernie Sosa puts it, into forbearing when knowledge is not available. In this, as predicted, the normativity of suspension drops right out of the knowledge-generating function of our inquiring practice and of our cognitive systems.

9.3 Suspension and the Normativity of Inquiry

Before moving on, I would like to address a worry that the view of suspension – and, correspondingly, the account of the ought to believe – put forth here is too demanding, in that it would seem as though it asks of us to believe too many things: after all, it would seem as though, at all times, we are both in a position to know a very high number of facts from our immediate environment[5] and in a position to inquire into a variety of questions.

To the contrary, as I'm about to argue, an important theoretical advantage of the account of suspension proposed here is that, while being able to account for the epistemic impermissibility intuition in cases of resistance to evidence, it also nicely explains the permissibility of ignoring a multitude of facts in our environment to the aim of focusing on issues that we care (or that we should care) about inquiring into. If this is right, the account is just as strong and just as permissive as we want it to be.

To get this into clearer view, consider a puzzle about the normativity of inquiry notably put forth by Jane Friedman:

---

[5] Many thanks to Matt McGrath for pressing me on this. See e.g. Friedman 2020, Kelp 2021, Flores and Woodard 2023, Falbo 2023, Thornstad 2021, Whitcomb 2017, Willard-Kyle 2023 for recent work on the normativity of inquiry.

Inquiry and Permissible Suspension

The Chrysler Building
Say, for instance, that I want to know how many windows the Chrysler Building in Manhattan has. I decide that the best way to figure this out is to head down there myself and do a count. To do my counting, I set up outside of Grand Central Station. Say it takes me an hour of focused work to get the count done and figure out how many windows that building has. During that hour there are many other ways I could make epistemic gains. There is obviously a huge amount of facts around me that I can come to know. (Friedman 2020, 503)

Here is the puzzle: if some inquiry norms (i.e. norms of gathering evidence, or zetetic norms) are epistemic norms, as the account defended here predicts, then it might looks as though the following paradigmatic zetetic norm is an epistemic norm:

ZIP: If one wants to figure out [the answer to a question] Q, then one ought to take the necessary means to figuring out Q.

At the same time, the following is an epistemic norm par excellence:

Kp: If one is in a position to know a proposition, p, then one is permitted to come to know that p.

But, Friedman argues, it would seem as though in the Chrysler Building case, ZIP and Kp come into conflict; after all, as soon as I focus on Q (counting the windows), I am no longer able to pay attention to the myriad of other things happening around me. Because of this, there will be very many things happening around me that I am in a position to know but that I will, as a matter of fact, fail to know. I will, thereby, register a huge amount of epistemic loss. Since events like the one described in the Chrysler Building case are ubiquitous – whenever we inquire into a specific question, we seem to ignore many unrelated facts – it seems to follow that the epistemic domain is peppered with normative conflict and, indeed, failure. Since, according to Friedman, it is implausible that this might be so, one of ZIP or Kp has to go.

A few things about this: first and foremost, as currently stated, ZIP and Kp do not come into *normative* conflict – after all, in the current formulation, Kp is a permission, whereas ZIP is an obligation. Permissions and obligations cannot come into normative conflict, in that their normative strength cannot pull in two different directions: it is always permissible by the lights of both norms to do whatever the obligation requires.

That being said, on a view like mine, which incorporates justifiers as epistemic obligations, we can – and, indeed, Friedman herself does so later in her paper – reformulate Kp as an obligation and thereby get a revamped version of Friedman's puzzle:

> **ZIP:** If one wants to figure out Q, then one ought to take the necessary means to figuring out Q.
> **Kp*:** If one is in a position to know a proposition, *p*, then one ought to come to know that *p*.

While many epistemological accounts will not accept Kp* – indeed, as we have just seen, the vast majority of the literature we have looked at has difficulties accommodating epistemic oughts – and thus will not make the proper target of Friedman's puzzle, that is not the case with the account defended here: OTB, together with a plausible assumption that, at least most of the time, when there is sufficient evidence for one to come to believe that *p*, then one is in a position to know that *p*,[6] imply Kp*. As such, for now, it would seem as though my account owes Friedman an explanation of what is going on in Chrysler Building-type cases.

Before moving on, though, I want to take one last look at Friedman's puzzle, only this time focusing on ZIP. Note that, as stated, ZIP is a desire-conditional ought: given the scope of the deontic operator, the obligation only arises upon the desire to inquire being present. However, inquiry norms proper (i.e. norms constituting our practice of inquiry) are not plausibly desire conditional (Kelp 2021). Indeed, constitutive norms never are: think about games. Once you've engaged in playing chess, and short of ceasing to do so, it is not up to your desires anymore if you are allowed to move the bishop diagonally or not: it's a categorical rule of the game. Similarly, what is desire conditional is entering the zetetic domain to begin with, rather than being subject to its constitutive norms once already engaged in inquiry. In order to see this, it will be helpful to distinguish between zetetic norms (i.e. norms constituting inquiry) and norms about inquiry (i.e. norms regulating when one should take on inquiry in a particular domain).[7] An example of the latter is the norm 'if you want to be a biologist, go study biology'. Clearly, this is not a zetetic norm, although it is a norm about when one should inquire into a specific domain. In contrast, consider: 'biologists should know the latest findings in their field'. This, arguably, is a zetetic norm proper: now that one has

---

[6] Possible exceptions will be cases in which the agent can't come to know due to something intervening in the basing process.
[7] Thanks to Jane Friedman and Chris Kelp for many helpful discussions on this.

engaged in biological inquiry, one is under epistemic normative pressure to take up the latest evidence in the field. Let's restrict ZIP accordingly and outline the final revamped Friedman Puzzle:

ZIP*: If you engage in an inquiry aimed at figuring out Q, then you ought to take the necessary means to figuring out Q.

Kp*: If one is in a position to know a proposition, *p*, then one ought to come to know that *p*.

The final revamped Friedman Puzzle is, indeed, on the face of it, a puzzle for a view like mine, which takes epistemic justification to be epistemic obligation to believe. After all, it would seem as though, in the Chrysler Building case, there is a lot of evidence lying around about all of things happening around Central Station that I completely ignore. For instance, just as I count the windows on the Chrysler Building, there is a man with a green hat exiting the station. Clearly, the thought would go, given that the man is walking in plain view, I am in a position to know that he's exiting the station (*p*). If so, by Kp, I ought to come to know that he's exiting the station. However, at the same time, since I've engaged in counting the windows on the Chrysler Building, it seems as though now I am subject to an obligation to come to know the number of windows on the Chrysler Building. Since I can't do both at the same time, the thought would go, I'm faced by an inescapable normative conflict.

I believe that many views endorsing epistemic oughts to believe will face this problem (for more about normative conflicts and epistemic dilemmas, see Chapter 10); at the same time, as I'm about to argue, my account does not. Indeed, an important theoretical advantage of my account of evidence, defeat, and suspension is precisely that it not only accommodates intuitive epistemic obligations, but it also, conversely, nicely explains the permissibility of ignoring a multitude of facts in our environment to the aim of focusing on issues that we are inquiring into.

In a nutshell, the reason why my account escapes Friedman's puzzle is that, on my view, evidence, defeat, and permissible suspension are unpacked in terms of a notion of being in a position to know that predicts that I am not in a position to know that the man with the green hat left the station, nor any other such detail about what is going on at Central Station, at the time when I am counting the windows on the Chrysler Building. Recall the account:

Being in a position to know: S is in a position to know a fact *e* iff S has a cognitive capacity with the function of generating knowledge that can (qualitatively, quantitatively, and environmentally) easily uptake e in cognisers of S's type.

Recall, also, the rationale for the quantitative restriction on easy uptake: there are quantitative limitations on my information accessing and processing – the fact that there's a table somewhere towards the periphery of my visual field (in contrast of it being right in front of me, in plain view) is not something I can easily process. I lack the power to process everything in my visual field – it's just too much information.

Quantitative limitations on being in a position to know will make it so that I can only take up a limited number of the $e_1, e_2, e_3 \ldots e_n$ facts that lie within reach with my knowledge-generating capacities. On the account defended, I only shoulder an epistemic obligation to take up a subset of $e_1, e_2, e_3 \ldots e_n$ that is as large as my quantitative uptake limitations. *Availability rankings* will deliver the relevant set, on my view: the most easily available subset of facts that I can take up is the one that I ought to take up. Crucially, also, note that quantitative limitations on being in a position to know imply the denial of conjunction introduction for being in a position to know: being in a position to know p, q, r, and s individually does not imply being in a position to know $p\&q\&r\&s$.

If all of this is the case, and given that, by stipulation, I am not able to pay attention to everything that's going on at the train station while I'm engaged in counting the windows on the Chrysler Building, it follows that, as soon as I will have started counting, I am not in a position to know what is going on at the station anymore. I am not in a position to know that there are eighty-nine windows and a man with a green hat exited the station.

In turn, since, on my account, epistemic obligations are grounded in being in a position to know, I am also under no obligation to form any beliefs about what is going on at the station after I started my inquiry. As soon as I'm subject to ZIP* – because I will have engaged in my inquiry into the question of how many windows there are on the Chrysler Building – I am no longer subject to Kp, because I am not in a position to know what is happening at the station. Therefore, I am at no point subject to ZIP* and Kp* at the same time, and thereby neither to a ZIP*–Kp* normative conflict. My account escapes the Friedman Puzzle.

One might think this is a bit fast.[8] Of course, Sophie of *Sophie's Choice* is also not faced by a dilemma anymore once she has already chosen the

---

[8] Thanks a lot to Anna Mahtani for pressing me on this.

twin to save (at t_2). The interesting normative conflict, though, happens at t_1, when she needs to make the choice and she's faced with a normative dilemma. Similarly, one might think, the interesting normative version of the Friedman Puzzle concerns t_1, when one is supposed to choose between which epistemic obligation to fulfil: that of inquiring into the number of windows or that of forming beliefs about the man in the green hat. Or so the thought would go.

A few things about this. First, note that there is a difference between *Sophie's Choice* and the Friedman Puzzle (revamped): Sophie is subject to two unconditional obligations – to save her twins, respectively. In contrast, ZIP* is an obligation only conditional upon already engaging in the relevant inquiry. At t_1, therefore (i.e. before engaging in the relevant inquiry), I am under no epistemic obligation to count the windows: my only epistemic obligation concerns forming beliefs about what's going on around me (i.e. at the station). At t_2, a practical norm along the lines of ZIP simpliciter (i.e. sourced in my peculiar desire to find out how many windows there are on the Chrysler Building) overrides this epistemic obligation and makes it permissible for me to direct my attention towards the Chrysler Building and start my inquiry into the number of windows on the Chrysler Building. As soon as that occurs, I am no longer under an obligation to form beliefs about what's going on at the station because I am no longer in a position to know what is going on at the station. Since, on my account, at no time am I under the normative pressure of both ZIP* and Kp* in Friedman's case, my account does not face Friedman's puzzle.

9.4 Conclusion

One should suspend if and only if one does so via a properly functioning cognitive process that has the function of generating knowledge and that, in virtue of it being properly functioning, takes up one's available evidence and defeat. An important theoretical advantage of the account of suspension proposed here is that, while being able to account for the epistemic impermissibility intuition in cases of resistance to evidence, it also nicely explains the permissibility of ignoring a multitude of facts in our environment to the aim of focusing on issues that we care about inquiring into. If this is right, the account is just as demanding and just as permissive as we want it to be.

PART III
Theoretical Upshots

CHAPTER 10

Epistemic Oughts and Epistemic Dilemmas

The following chapters examine the theoretical upshots of the positive epistemological view proposed in this book. The account developed so far delivers the result that epistemic justifiers constitute epistemic oughts. In this chapter, I discuss the worry that such accounts threaten to give rise to widely spread epistemic dilemmas between paradigmatic epistemic norms. I argue for a modest scepticism about epistemic dilemmas. In order to do that, I first point out that not all normative conflicts constitute dilemmas: more needs to be the case. Second, I look into the moral dilemmas literature and identify a set of conditions that need to be at work for a mere normative conflict to be a genuine normative dilemma. Last, I argue that while our epistemic life is peppered with epistemic normative conflict, epistemic dilemmas are much harder to find than we thought.

10.1 Obligations to Believe and Epistemic Dilemmas

My account takes epistemic justification to be epistemic obligation. Nevertheless, it does not follow from my view that we are obliged to believe all of the things that, for example, happen in our visual fields at the same time. That is because what grounds obligations to believe is being in a position to know, and being in a position to know is limited quantitatively by our cognitive capacities.

We have also seen that, on my account, paradigmatic epistemic norms such as Kp will not come into conflict with zetetic norms, or norms of inquiry and gathering evidence. The question that arises at this point is: how about paradigmatic epistemic norms themselves? Will they not generate normative conflicts and, indeed, normative dilemmas?

First, recall that the account predicts that normative priority will be decided by availability rankings. As such, short of too many facts (i.e. more than I can uptake at once) enjoying the precise same availability ranking, the view will not result in normative dilemmas. Second, although epistemic dilemmas have been hotly discussed in recent epistemology, I remain unconvinced of their in-principle possibility. The following sections, indeed, will argue for a (modest) scepticism about epistemic dilemmas. If I am right, while our epistemic lives – in line with our normative lives more generally – encounter decidable epistemic conflict often, epistemic dilemmas are rather hard to come by.

10.2 What Dilemmas Are Not

What is a normative dilemma? On a first approximation, it seems plausible that one is facing a dilemma just in case two courses of action and two courses only are available to one, and whichever one chooses, one finds oneself in normative breach: there's no good way out, as it were. This seems promising. Let's spell it out:

Normative dilemma #1 (ND1): A state of affairs such that a subject S has only two available courses of action, both of which imply norm violation.

ND1 is false – and widely acknowledged[1] to be false – in that it is too inclusive: it defines conflicts rather than dilemmas. Not all normative conflicts are dilemmas: there are several well-theorised phenomena that prevent garden variety normative conflicts from becoming full-blown dilemmas.

First, in cases in which one norm overrides the other, conflict is present, whereas there's no dilemma as to the best action to pursue: it is the one recommended by the overriding norm. Indeed, it lies in the meaning of 'overriding' that such cases are cases of normative conflict without a dilemma. That's what it is for a norm to override another: to come into conflict with it and take precedence. If it takes precedence, there's no dilemma left to face the subject of the normative constraints in question: again, I face a moral conflict but not a moral dilemma when I decide to save the drowning child even at the cost of breaking my promise to meet you for lunch at noon. The norm of saving lives conflicts with the one of promise-keeping and renders one course of action, and only one, permissible – no dilemma here. Our definition needs tightening up if we are to distinguish dilemmas proper from mere normative conflicts. In addition to the conditions stipulated by ND1, at a minimum, it also needs to be the case that neither of the normative constraints are overridden.

---

[1] For an excellent overview of the relevant literature, see McConnell (2018).

Second, normative requirements can be overridden, but they can also be undercut. The difference between undercutting and overriding is that, roughly, while in cases of overriding we get reasons for and against a course of action phi, and the reasons against phi-ing are, for example, weightier than the reasons for phi-ing – such that the latter get overridden by the former – in cases of undercutting the counter-reasons speak, in the first instance, against the normative strength of the reasons in favour of phi-ing rather than directly against phi-ing. Your testimony that the train leaves at 8 a.m. is reason for me to go to the station before 8 a.m. My finding out that you are a compulsive liar undercuts this reason and renders it normatively inert. There is normative conflict between the two reasons, for sure. But the conflict fails to result in a dilemma: I know precisely what to do in this situation (i.e. not base my action on trust in your testimony).

Our definition needs to be tightened up if it is to distinguish between mere normative conflicts and normative dilemmas proper. At a minimum, on top of the conditions stipulated by ND1, we need to add an anti-overriding and an anti-undercutting condition. Here is a second pass:

Normative dilemma #2 (ND2): A state of affairs such that a subject S has only two available courses of action, both of which imply *active* norm violation.

In ND2, what is meant by 'active norm' is a norm that remains efficacious within the context after all things normative are considered. What ND2 implies is that, for a dilemma to be instantiated, (1) the two normative constraints need to be equally weighty (on pain of overriding taking place) and (2) it should not be the case that the one sheds doubt on the normative credentials of the other.

On closer inspection, though, ND2 is still too broad: sometimes, two active (equally weighty, non-undercut) norms can come into conflict, while a dilemma is not instantiated in virtue of the fact that one takes qualitative precedence over the other. Of course, overriding and undercutting are also ways in which norms can take precedence; they are not the only ways, however. Overriding is a quantitative matter: weightier normative constraints prevail. Precedence relations, however, can also be qualitative: they can be exhibited between active, non-overridden norms as well. A paradigmatic such case is one in which one of the norms is derivative of the other. Here is such a case:

Promise-breaker George: George is a promise-breaker: whenever possible, he will reliably break his promises to others. One day,

> George promises his colleague, Anna, to call her on Thursday at precisely 12 o'clock, and, as per usual, he doesn't care much about keeping his promise. On Thursday, he looks at his watch, comes to believe it's 11.45 a.m., and decides to take a nap before making the call, thinking that he will be at most thirty to forty minutes late. Luckily, though, George's watch is broken: it's actually only 10.45 a.m. After taking his nap, George ends up calling Anna at precisely 12 o'clock.

Promise-breaker George is in breach of a bunch of conceivable norms in this scenario (Williamson forthcominga): he has a bad disposition – he is a promise-breaker; he acts in ways that would, had his watch not been broken, have resulted in breaking his promise; in general, he seems to be rather inconsiderate and untrustworthy.[2] But here is one thing that cannot be said about George: that he broke his promise to Anna. Morally lucky George did no such thing. Indeed, he called Anna at precisely 12 o'clock as promised.

What is happening in this case is an instance of breach of a number of norms that derive from what we may call, following Williamson (forthcominga), the 'primary' norm of promise-keeping ('keep your promises!'; e.g. 'don't be a promise-breaker!', 'don't act like a promise-breaker would!') without breach of the primary norm.

What is crucial to note about this case is that George cannot comply with both the primary norm of promise-keeping – 'keep your promises!' – and, for example, the derived norm 'do what a promise-keeper would do!'. Meeting one will ensure he is in breach of the other. In that, one would think, the case looks initially promising for a dilemmatic case. Had George not been in breach of some of the derived norms, he would have been the victim of moral bad luck and would have ended up in breach of the primary norm at stake: had he, for example, called Anna at what he thought – according to his broken watch – was 12 o'clock, he would have failed to keep his promise (since he would have, in fact, called her at 11 o'clock). Last but not least, note also that this is not a case of either overriding or undercutting: the norms at stake here – both primary and derived – are standing, active norms. It's easy to see this from the fact that, whichever of them George would be in breach of, he would intuitively be the proper subject of blame. It's worthy of blame to break your promises, but so is to be the kind of person who would do so and to act accordingly.

---

[2] See Kelp and Simion (2023a) for an account of trustworthiness in terms of a disposition to comply with one's obligations.

Still, George is not faced with a moral dilemma here: the primary norm of promise-keeping, as its description suggests, has priority. To see this, note that we describe the case as one of moral *good* luck. Had the norm of promise-keeping not taken precedence, it's a mystery why we wouldn't describe the case in neutral terms (should the norm of promise-keeping be as stringent as the norm requiring one to be the kind of person who keeps promises, etc.) or negative terms (should what we have dubbed 'derived' norms take precedence).

What George's case suggests is that we need a further (and final) restriction on our account of dilemmas: a state of affairs will qualify as a dilemma if and only if a subject S has only two available courses of action, both of which imply *active* norm violation, where neither of the norms at stake is derivative of the other. Here is a simpler way to put this:

> **Genuine normative dilemma (GND):** A state of affairs such that a subject S has only two available courses of action, both of which imply norm violation, where neither of the norms at stake takes precedence over the other.

In turn, as we have seen, taking precedence can come in many shapes, including overriding, undercutting, or normative primacy. William Styron's (1979) *Sophie's Choice* presents a useful example of such a genuine moral dilemma. Sophie Zawistowska has been asked to choose which of her two children, Eva or Jan, will be sent to the gas chamber in Auschwitz. An SS doctor, Fritz Jemand von Niemand, will grant a dispensation to only one of Sophie's children. If she does not choose which one should live, Dr von Niemand will send both to their deaths.

In Sophie's case, the moral norm asks of her to make a choice rather than not; otherwise, the worst scenario obtains: both children will die. So withholding from acting is not an option. The two options are: sacrifice Eva, or sacrifice Jan. Both options represent breaches of standing, non-overridden (the two options are equally bad, no norm is weightier than the other), non-undercut moral (and prudential) norms, neither of which takes priority over the other. Indeed, plausibly, the moral norm at stake on both horns of the dilemma is one and the same: 'don't put the life of your child in danger!'. In this, *Sophie's Choice* is a GND.

10.3 Epistemic Non-dilemmas

This section puts the results above to use: it looks at several cases featured in the epistemological literature as alleged examples of epistemic dilemmas and argues that they are garden variety normative conflicts rather than genuine dilemmas.

Let's start with a very straightforward case:

Rebutting defeat: My four-year-old hears me coughing and tells me I have a cold. My doctor disagrees: it's bronchitis.

Here's a garden variety epistemic normative conflict that is not a normative dilemma. Rather, it's a straightforward case of normative overriding: I have stronger reason to trust my doctor's testimony than my four-year-old son's. Indeed, note that epistemological terminology implies that this is a non-dilemmatic normative conflict: after all, this is a classic case of full rebutting defeat acting against the epistemic reason provided by my son's testimony. The presence of full rebutting defeat, however, implies that the reasons against my belief that it's a cold are weightier than those in favour: otherwise, full defeat would not be instantiated. The presence of defeat, then, precludes this variety of normative epistemic conflict from being a genuine dilemma. Indeed, this is, of course, a mere epistemic incarnation of the case in which I am late for lunch because I stop to save the child: a classic case of normative overriding.

What about a case where two equally reliable, equally trustworthy, etc., sources (plug in your favourite view of the epistemology of testimony) offer conflicting testimonies? No problem at all: uncontroversially, the epistemically correct thing to do is to suspend/withhold belief[3]; again, there is no epistemic dilemma here. Indeed, strictly speaking, we should expect epistemology to be, if anything, most often the proper home of normative trilemmas rather than dilemmas: after all, in epistemology, there's always the possibility to suspend belief.

So far so good: one wouldn't expect much in the way of controversy to be triggered by this fairly straightforward diagnosis of rebutting defeat.

But here is a type of case hotly discussed under the heading of an epistemic dilemma, starting back in the early 1990s:

Evidence-undermining belief: As S considers some proposition, p, it is clear to S that an effect of S's believing p would be to undermine the evidence S has, which otherwise is sufficient epistemic reason for S to believe p.

---

[3] The difference between withholding and suspending belief will be of no consequence throughout this chapter. I will therefore use them interchangeably.

Evidence-undermining belief is a type of case extensively discussed in several epistemological works (e.g. Conee 1987, 1992, Sorensen 1987, Richter 1990, Foley 1991, Kroon 1993, Odegard 1993). Here, for example, is Odegard's take on the normative landscape present in this type of case:

> Clearly we should not deny the belief, since this would be to deny a belief for which we have adequate evidence, both prior to adopting a position on it and when we adopt a position on it. But we should not affirm the belief either, for this would be to affirm a belief for which we would not have adequate evidence when we held it [. . .]. Yet it can seem that we should not withhold on the belief either, since in withholding on it we fail to adopt a belief for which we have adequate evidence when we consider it for adoption. So it can seem that whatever happens, we do something that we should not do. (Odegard 1993, 161)

The discussion in the Section 10.2, however, should by now have made it clear that Odegard's trilemmic diagnosis here is mistaken. What we have here is a straightforward case of normative undercutting: the normative force of the evidence that the subject has for thinking that p is undercut by the evidence that the subject has for thinking that as soon as they adopt a belief in p, this would undermine the normative strength of the evidence for p. This is a straightforward case of undercutting defeat. Indeed, here is Conee's diagnosis along the same lines:

> When believing would result in a loss of crucial evidence for the believed proposition, adopting the belief would not bring about knowledge of the proposition. Foreseeing this sort of loss excludes having an epistemic reason to believe when contemplating the proposition. (Conee 1993, 478)

If this is a case of undercutting defeat, however, it cannot, in principle, constitute a normative dilemma, for roughly the same reason why cases of rebutting defeat cannot constitute dilemmas: that is what it means for evidence to be defeated – it is for it to lose its initial normative strength. Fully undercut evidence no longer supports one's belief in the target proposition. The case cannot be at the same time one of full undercutting defeat and a dilemma.

How about partial undercutting defeat? Can't it be that the dilemma arises when the undercutter only partially affects the first-order evidence? Consider:

> **Logic problem:** Anna is a logic student who is evaluating a tautology (T). Anna is certain that (T) is true. However, her logic professor, Chad, then tells her that before she began the exam, she was slipped a reason-distorting

drug that impairs one's ability to solve logic problems; those who are affected by the drug only reach the right conclusions 50 per cent of the time. As it turns out, though, unbeknownst to both Anna and Chad, the drug was just a placebo and Anna's logic reasoning abilities were not affected in the least. (Adapted from Leonard 2020)

Chad's testimony provides Anna with higher-order evidence to the effect that there is a 50 per cent chance that she botched her assessment of what this first-order evidence actually supports. Her first-order evidence is thus partially undercut. What is Anna supposed to believe? According to some,[4] Anna is faced by a dilemma that requires a lot of epistemic fine-tuning to explain away.

However, note that, again, insofar as we accept the case as one of undercutting defeat, it can't be that this is a dilemma rather than a mere normative conflict (and if we don't thus accept it, no dilemma arises): its being a case of partial defeat implies that the higher-order evidence partially neutralises the normative force of the first-order evidence. The fact that the defeat is merely partial does nothing to change this: by the way the case is built, at least on a first approximation, Anna is left with 50 per cent first-order normative support for her belief that (T). If so, there is no dilemma here: Anna should suspend belief, since she has equal support for (T) and non-(T).

To see this further, let's see what would have to be the case for this to be a genuine dilemmatic case. For a genuine dilemmatic normative conflict to be instantiated, we would have to think that something like the following principle (Worsnip 2018) holds:

> Possibility of Iterative Failure (PIF). It is possible that:
>
> i. S's evidence supports D(p); and
> ii. S's evidence supports believing that her evidence does not support D(p),

where D(p) is a possible doxastic attitude for a subject S towards a proposition p. I find PIF implausible, for the following reason (which I expanded on in Chapter 8): evidence about what evidence supports will normatively affect what evidence supports, in one way or another: sometimes, when weightier than the first-order evidence, it will defeat its normative strength. Andy's testimony that p: 'the train leaves at 8 a.m.' is a reason for me to believe that the train leaves at 8 a.m. Testimony from the much more reliable (trustworthy, etc.) Mary that Andy is a compulsive

---

[4] See Leonard (2018) for an overview and discussion.

liar is a reason for me to believe that Andy's testimony is less weighty than I thought and thus lower my confidence in p. This need not always be the case, of course. It may be that defeat goes the other way – in cases in which the first-order evidence is weightier. My a priori justification that there are no round cubes will likely defeat my four-year-old's testimony that I'm confused, since he just saw a round cube at his friend's house. At other times, the two sources can also be equally weighty, in which case, again, the proper thing to do is to suspend. The important point, though, is that higher-order evidence interacts normatively with first-order evidence, which renders PIF implausible.[5]

Do we have any reason to believe PIF to be true, in spite of this prima facie plausible evidentiary situation? Alex Worsnip argues that we do; according to Worsnip, rejecting PIF commits one to an implausibly strong claim about justification: denying (PIF), according to him, requires denying that one can have, all things considered, misleading evidence about what one's evidence supports; in other words, justified false beliefs about what one's evidence supports are impossible. That is a strong claim, as any claim that a particular kind of justified false belief is impossible would be (Worsnip 2018).

Let's state this clearly. According to Worsnip, the following claim holds:

Non-PIF implies no justified false beliefs about evidential support (NJFBES): If non-PIF, then one cannot have justified false beliefs about what one's evidence supports.

I agree with Worsnip that NJFBES is implausibly strong.[6] I disagree, though, with the claim that the denial of PIF implies it. In particular, denying PIF is perfectly compatible with having a justified false belief that your evidence *does* support p. Rather, what the denial of PIF implies is the weaker:

No justified false beliefs about lack of evidential support (NJFBLES): One cannot have a justified false belief that one's evidence does not support p.

NJFBLES might be hard to recognise at first, but, as opposed to its more ambitious cousin NJFBES, it is not a particularly controversial claim: it's

---

[5] See Chapter 8 for an extensive critical discussion of scepticism targeting this claim.
[6] Note, though, that traditionalist evidentialists might have to accept it. If one's justification is strictly a function of one's evidence, then it seems to follow that one cannot have justified false beliefs about what one's evidence supports.

merely stating that undercutting defeat via higher-order evidence is a genuine phenomenon. As soon as you have justification for thinking your evidence does not support *p*, either the higher-order justification negatively affects the normative strength of your first-order evidence, making it true that you don't have evidential support for *p*, or, if weightier, your first-order evidence affects the normative strength of the higher-order justification, making it false that you are justified. If you think there is such a thing as undercutting defeat, you hold NJBLES to be true (and for people who don't, see the discussion in Chapter 8 on scepticism about the defeating power of higher-order evidence, as well as the discussion below on knowledge-first, level-splitting views). If so, the fact that denying PIF does imply NJFBLES (but not NJFBES) is not a problem for denying PIF but at worst a natural feature, and it is more likely a theoretical virtue of prior plausibility (given the widely spread popularity of undercutting defeat).

To sum up: for all of the above cases, I have argued that if we accept that they are cases of defeat, their being epistemic dilemmas becomes an in-principle impossibility, since their being cases of defeat implies that they are cases of either normative overriding or normative undercutting. How about if one wants to deny the very idea of defeat? Here is another type of case featuring what seems to be undercutting defeat that has been discussed in more recent literature:

> **Maths:** A competent mathematician has just proved a surprising new theorem. She shows her proof to several distinguished senior colleagues, who all tell her that it involves a subtle fallacy. She cannot quite follow their explanations of her mistake. In fact, the only mistake is in their objections, obscured by sophisticated bluster; her proof is perfectly valid. (Williamson forthcomingb, 1)

In this case, too, if we accept that what is going on is undercutting defeat, we are left with mere normative conflict without normative dilemma: depending on the weight of the colleagues' testimony, the mathematician's first-order support for the theorem will be more or less diminished. The amount of warrant left will support either belief (if only marginally affected) or disbelief (if seriously affected), or else suspension.

Several authors in the knowledge-first camp, though, argue against undercutting defeat for knowledge. According to people like Maria Lasonen-Aarnio (2014) and Tim Williamson (forthcomingb), insofar as our mathematician knows that the theorem in question holds, misleading higher-order evidence will have no impact on the normative credentials of their belief: they should hold steadfast. In turn, these philosophers explain the intuition of the impermissibility of such dogmatic doxastic behaviour via appeal to epistemic blameworthiness. According to Lasonen-Aarnio, the intuition that dogmatism is suspicious doxastic behaviour even in the presence of knowledge is to be explained by the fact that ignoring evidence is, generally speaking, a bad epistemic disposition that is worthy of blame. As such, while our mathematician is not in breach of the norm of belief in this case – since they are a knower – they are blameworthy for displaying a bad epistemic disposition in ignoring available evidence.

Does this take on these cases create problems for our diagnosis of them as non-dilemmatic normative conflicts? The answer is 'no'. Insofar as one holds that there is some sort of priority ordering between the two norms coming into conflict – the knowledge norm of belief on the one hand and the norm prescribing against a disposition to ignore evidence on the other – the case is not an epistemic dilemma. Recall the case of George the promise-breaker: just like in that case, insofar as one takes one of these norms to have primacy over the other, GND is not instantiated.

Now, it is plain to see that according to the no-defeat champions, the knowledge norm takes primacy in Maths: first, because they hold that the mathematician should hold steadfast in this case – which suggests that the knowledge norm takes primacy over the dispositionalist norm – and second because they hold that the mathematician is in mere blameworthy norm compliance rather than in genuine norm violation. If so, by the lights of this variety of undercutting defeat deniers, there will be no dilemma instantiated in this case.

We have seen that both champions and foes of undercutting defeat will have to deny that cases like Maths instantiate epistemic dilemmas. Note, though, that there is still a bit of theoretical distance between this result and an in-principle impossibility of cases like these being dilemmatic: after all, there is one possibility left in the logical space. One could deny undercutting defeat and at the same time hold that the first- and second-order norms in this case have equal normative strength: none takes primacy. If so, one would think, we would have an instance of GND in this case: an epistemic *Sophie's Choice*.

Fortunately, though, that's not quite right. Our epistemic lives are easier than our moral lives: what is often an epistemically available option, but is not always a morally or prudentially available option, is suspending. By stipulation, Sophie does not have the option not to make any choice between her children: if she refuses to choose, they will both be killed. In cases of epistemic conflict, however, suspending belief is often an available option. As such, mere normative strength parity will not be enough to generate a dilemma.

This will be the case in both cases of (alleged) undercutting and rebutting defeat: for the theorist who rejects defeat and upholds normative parity, what is going on in these cases is a conflict between two equally weighty norms – one requiring belief and one disbelief in the relevant target proposition. If so, epistemology has an easy answer to these cases: the subject must, *ceteris absentibus*, suspend.

What the discussion so far suggests is that epistemic dilemmas are hard to come by. What we would need to generate an epistemic *Sophie's Choice* is, for example, an equally weighty reason against believing that p and believing that non-p and an even stronger reason against suspending belief. Here it is:

Genuine epistemic dilemma (GED): A state of affairs such that believing that p, believing that non-p, and suspending on p all imply epistemic norm violation, where the norm forbidding one of the three options is weightier than the remaining two and neither of the remaining two norms takes precedence over the other.

Alternatively, we can also have a genuine epistemic trilemma, should the norms in question be equally weighty:

Genuine epistemic trilemma (GET): A state of affairs such that believing that p, believing that non-p, and suspending on p all imply epistemic norm violation, where none of the norms at stake take precedence over the others.

Note how far we've come from our first pass at isolating dilemmas proper from mere normative conflicts: normative conflicts are ubiquitous in epistemology; di/trilemmatic conflicts, however, are less so, if they exist at all.

Could we get something like GED/GET in our epistemic life? One thing to notice, from the start, is that what we would need is a proper *epistemic* reason against suspending. Stipulating that you're bound to either believe or disbelieve because a villain is holding a gun to your head and threatens to kill you if you suspend, even though your evidence equally supports p and non-p, will not generate an epistemic dilemma, but rather an inter-normative conflict with an easy way out: all things considered, you should randomly believe whatever just to save your life. Epistemically, though, you should suspend.

I would like to end this chapter on a more optimistic note than I have proceeded with so far: I would like, that is, to propose two cases that, at least at first glance, look to me like better candidates for an epistemic di/trilemma than what we have been looking at so far. I am not myself convinced that they will hold water ultimately (which is why I dub them, modestly, 'attempted epistemic di/trilemmas'). But it does seem to me, in the light of the results in this chapter, that they stand a better chance at instantiating di/trilemmatic normative conflict proper than the cases that we have been looking at. Because of this, I think they are worth putting on the table for further discussion. Here they are:

> **Attempted epistemic trilemma (AET):** Mary, John, and Anna are equally reliable, equally trustworthy testifiers, and you know them to be such (again, plug in whatever else you need to instantiate epistemic justification on your favourite view of testimony). Mary tells you that p: the train leaves at 8 a.m. John tells you that non-p: the train does not leave at 8 a.m. Anna tells you that you don't have equally weighty evidence for p and non-p (alternatively, Anna tells you that it's epistemically impermissible for you to suspend belief on whether the train leaves at 8 a.m.).

And, correspondingly:

> **Attempted epistemic dilemma (AED):** Mary and John are equally reliable, equally trustworthy testifiers, and you know them to be such. Mary tells you that p: the train leaves at 8 a.m. John tells you that non-p: the train does not leave at 8 a.m. Anna is the most reliable (trustworthy, etc.) testifier you know. Anna tells you that you don't have equally weighty evidence for p and non-p (alternatively, Anna tells you that it's epistemically impermissible for you to suspend belief on whether the train leaves at 8 a.m.).

There are a few things to notice about these cases. First, note that the cases need not be spelled out as featuring testimony; the choice here is driven by convenience. Parallel cases can be described with any other sources of knowledge. Nor does it have to be the case that one and only one type of source is at stake: a combination would do, too. Second, about AED: it is meant to be the epistemic equivalent of *Sophie's Choice* structurally. Third, note that AED and AET are only di/trilemmas if we assume that an undercutting defeat-denying view is false, and thus that the higher-order evidence provided by Anna affects the justification you get from the first-order evidence generated by Mary and John. Otherwise, the case will be one of permissible suspension, and thus no dilemma will be instantiated.

Are AED and AET genuine epistemic di/trilemmas? Again, I'm not fully convinced: it may depend on what the correct view of evidential weight will be (e.g. the correct view of evidential weight might make it such that what one should do in these cases is suspend on everything: *p*, non-*p*, and the issue of what your evidence supports). I do believe, though, that these cases are worthy of serious attention, in that, as opposed to other cases that are historically popular in the literature, they do instantiate a di/trilemmatic structure proper: it looks as though, that is, whatever one decides to do – doxastically speaking – in these cases, one is in breach of equally strong, standing norms, neither of which takes priority over the other. (Compatibly, of course, structure might not be all that there is to epistemic dilemmatic conflict.)

10.4 Conclusion

I have defended modest scepticism about epistemic dilemmas: they're hard to find. My scepticism, to be clear, only falls short of being radical insofar as the attempts I made at mimicking a *Sophie's Choice* structure for the epistemic – or similar attempts – can be made to work. I am not myself convinced that they will, however. If they turn out to fail, I want to claim that we have reason to be very pessimistic about the in-principle possibility of an epistemic dilemma. I have also argued that an account like mine, taking justifiers to be obligations, will not deliver the theoretically suspicious result that the epistemic domain is peppered with dilemmas, but rather the more modest result that, just as in other normative domains, the epistemic sometimes faces us with normative conflict: sometimes, I can't make it to lunch in time and save the child from drowning – something has to give. Epistemically, things look pretty similar.

CHAPTER 11

Scepticism as Resistance to Evidence

The view of evidence, defeat, and suspension put forth here delivers the result that paradigmatic scepticism about knowledge and justification is an instance of resistance to evidence. This chapter argues that this result is correct. In order to do that, I look at extant neo-Moorean responses to purported instances of failure of knowledge closure (Pryor 2004, Williamson 2007) and warrant transmission and argue that they are either too weak – in that they concede too much to the sceptic – or too strong – in that they cannot accommodate the intuition of reasonableness surrounding sceptical arguments. I propose a novel neo-Moorean explanation of the data, relying on my preferred account of defeat and permissible suspension, on which the sceptic is in impermissible suspension but in fulfilment of their contrary-to-duty epistemic obligations.

11.1 Two Neo-Mooreanisms

Moore sees his hands in front of him and comes to believe that HANDS: 'hands exist' based on his extraordinarily reliable perceptual belief-formation processes. Moore's belief is warranted, if any beliefs are: Moore is an excellent believer. Indeed, Moore knows that hands exist. In spite of his laudable epistemic ways, Dretske (1971) thinks Moore shouldn't feel free to do whatever it pleases him to do with this belief, epistemically speaking; in particular, Dretske thinks that, in spite of his warranted belief that HANDS, Moore should refrain from reasoning to some propositions he knows to be entailed by HANDS, such as WORLD: 'there is an external world'. He thinks that this is an instance of closure failure for knowledge: we don't always know the stuff that we know our knowledge to entail. In better news, conversely, that's why the sceptic is wrong to think that my not knowing that I'm not a brain in a vat implies that I don't know any of the ordinary things I take myself to know.

Wright (2002, 2003, 2004) agrees: Moore shouldn't reason to WORLD from HANDS. However, that's not because closure fails, but because the stronger principle of warrant transmission fails: the problem here, according to Wright, is not that we sometimes fail to know the stuff that we know is entailed by what we know. Rather, the issue is that the warrant Moore has for HANDS fails to transmit to WORLD. Compatibly, though, Moore may still be entitled to believe WORLD on independent grounds. If Moore is entitled to believe HANDS, then perhaps he must also be entitled to believe WORLD. But it doesn't follow that his warrant to believe WORLD is his warrant to believe HANDS. Rather, it may be that Moore needs to be independently entitled to believe WORLD to begin with if he is to be entitled to believe HANDS.

Many philosophers are on board with rejecting at least one of these principles – be it merely warrant transmission or closure as well. At the same time, since closure and warrant transmission constitute a bedrock of our epistemic ways – indeed, they are crucial vehicles for expanding our body of knowledge – one cannot give them up without a working restriction recipe: if closure and/or warrant transmission don't hold unrestrictedly, when do they hold? It is fair to say that the jury is still out on this front, and a satisfactory restriction recipe does not seem to be within easy reach.[1]

That being said, several philosophers take the alternative route of resisting the failure claims altogether and thus fully dismiss the data: according to them, closure and warrant transmission are too important theoretical tools to be abandoned on grounds of misguided intuitions. They reject the intuition that something fishy is going on in Moore's argument and argue that scepticism is just an instance of cognitive malfunction: the sceptic's cognitive system malfunctions in that it fails to get rid of their unjustified sceptical beliefs in favour of the justified Moorean conclusion. I call these people 'radical neo-Mooreans'. Here is Williamson:

> Our cognitive immunity system should be able to destroy bad old beliefs, not just prevent the influx of bad new ones. But that ability sometimes becomes indiscriminate, and destroys good beliefs too. (Williamson 2007, 681)

I like radical neo-Mooreanism a lot. The majority reaction to this move, however, is that it is less than fair to the sceptic; indeed, this view

---

[1] But see Kelp (2019) for my favourite proposal.

(intuitively unfairly) categorises scepticism, without qualification, in the same normative boat with other epistemic malfunctions, such as wishful thinking. It is undeniable, though, that in the case of the sceptic, but not in the case of the wishful thinker, we think that there is something reasonable – even if not quite right – about their resistance to Moore's argument. This intuitive difference cries out for an explanation.

At the other side of the neo-Moorean spectrum, we find concessive neo-Mooreans (e.g. Pryor 2004, 2012); these philosophers accept both closure and transmission in Moorean inferences and try to come up with alternative explanations of the data (i.e. with an alternative account of what is intuitively amiss with Moore's argument). In the next section, I look closer at the concessive neo-Moorean explanation of this datum.

11.2 Against Concessive Neo-Mooreanism

According to Jim Pryor (2004), while Moore is right to reason from HANDS to WORLD, he wouldn't be very convincing were he to do so in conversation with a sceptic. The problem behind the intuitive fishiness of Moore's reasoning pattern is pragmatic, not epistemic: it is lack of dialectical force, not lack of warrant transmission, that's triggering the uneasiness intuition. In the cases of alleged failure of closure and/or transmission, warrant transmits, but the argument fails dialectically due to psychological higher-order defeat.[2] The sceptic about WORLD will not be convinced by Moore's argument in its favour from HANDS. Here is Pryor:

> For a philosopher with such beliefs [i.e. sceptical beliefs], it'd be epistemically defective to believe things just on the basis of her experiences – even if those experiences are in fact giving her categorical warrant to so believe. (Pryor 2012, 286)

Why would it be thus epistemically defective? According to Pryor, the sceptic's unjustified sceptical beliefs rationally obstruct them from believing based on Moore's argument via psychological defeat. In particular, Pryor thinks that Moore's argument gives the sceptic propositional justification for the conclusion, but it fails to generate doxastic justification due to the psychological defeat generated by the sceptic's previously acquired sceptical beliefs. Since the sceptical beliefs are not justified, according to

---

[2] To my knowledge, the first to have introduced the category of psychological (or doxastic) defeat is Jennifer Lackey (e.g. 2006, 438). For excellent recent work on defeat, see Brown and Simion (2021).

Pryor, they don't defeat the propositional justification generated by Moore's argument. They do, however, rationally obstruct the sceptic from justifiably believing the conclusion of Moore's argument, and in this they defeat the sceptic's doxastic justification.

The point, then, in a nutshell, is that even though it transmits warrant, the Moorean argument fails to convince the rational sceptic in virtue of the conflict between the Moorean claims and the sceptic's previously held beliefs. The sceptic has propositional justification but does not have doxastic justification for HANDS and WORLD.

In what follows, I will take issue with this claim at several junctures. First and foremost, though, it is worth clarifying what exactly the content of the sceptical beliefs that allegedly do the defeating work here is. I want to start off by noting that it is implausible to think that the sceptical belief at stake in the literature is (or should be) something like non-WORLD: 'the external world does not exist'. After all, what we are talking about – and the philosopher that is worth engaging with – is a reasonable sceptic who, for example, believes in underdetermination (i.e. who thinks that, for all they know, they may well be a brain in a vat), not someone who is anxiously fully confident that they're a brain in a vat. The reasonable sceptic that is worth engaging with thinks that, for all the evidence that they have, there may well be no external world. If so, the reasonable sceptic will, at best, have a 0.5 credence that non-WORLD, or else they will suspend belief on the issue. Not much will hang on this below, but since I am interested in being maximally charitable to concessive neo-Mooreanism, I will, for the most part, discuss the reasonable sceptic rather than the maximally anxious sceptic in what follows. Everything I will say, though, will apply mutatis mutandis to the anxious sceptic as well.

Now here is a widely endorsed thesis in philosophy: justification is normative. The following is an attractive way of capturing this thought: one's phi-ing is prima facie practically, morally, epistemically, etc., justified if and only if one prima facie practically, morally, epistemically, etc., permissibly phis. Plausibly enough, then, one's belief that p is epistemically justified if and only if one epistemically permissibly believes that p. Justifiers are considerations that support belief, in that, if all else goes well (i.e. proper basing, no defeat, good processing, etc.), enough justifiers render a belief epistemically permissible.

Where does defeat fit within this picture? Just like justification, defeat is a normative category, in that it affects the permissibility of belief. Unlike justification, however, its function is to counter rather than support believing. If justifiers support belief – they contribute to rendering it permissible – defeaters contribute to rendering it impermissible. It is plausible, then, to think that defeat is the arch-enemy of justification: if justification is normative with a positive valence – in that it renders belief permissible – (full) defeat is normative with a negative valence, in rendering belief impermissible. In reason terms, if you wish, justifiers are normative reasons for belief, whereas defeaters are normative reasons against believing.

Now let's go back to Pryor's account of what goes on in the exchange between Moore and the sceptic. Recall that, according to Pryor, even though Moore's argument does provide the sceptic with propositional justification, it fails to provide them with doxastic justification, in virtue of their unjustified sceptical beliefs defeating the latter but not the former. As such, according to Pryor, the sceptic's belief that HANDS (and WORLD) based on Moore's argument would be rendered unjustified via defeat.

The problem with this picture is that it's not clear how an unjustified belief can have defeating force to begin with. To be clear, I am not claiming that we do not often resist information that we are presented with because of our previously held unjustified beliefs. Indeed, we often resist information presented to us for bad reasons (e.g. due to wishfully believing that it is not true; think, for instance, of cases of resistance to evidence due to partisanship in virtue of friendship, cases of people in abusive relationships who refuse to acknowledge the abuse, etc.). The question at stake when it comes to defeat, though, is not one concerning the *possibility* of resistance to evidence but of permissibility: since justification and defeat are normative, they can only be instantiated in cases in which permissibility is at stake. Cases of wishful thinking are paradigmatic cases in which the hearer is, to use Pryor's term, 'obscured' from believing information that is presented to them due to their wishes. Clearly, though, wishful thinking cases are impermissibility cases: the hearer should not, as a matter of fact, resist the testimony in question, even though they do. Again, to follow Pryor's terminology, these are cases in which the believer is not 'rationally obscured' from forming said beliefs but merely 'obscured'. Or, to put it in reason terms, their unjustified, wishful thinking-based beliefs are mere *motivating* reasons for resisting testimony but not *normative* reasons.

If all of this is so, the question that arises is: is the sceptic being 'rationally obscured', as Pryor would have it, from adopting a belief based on Moore's testimony by their previously held unjustified sceptical beliefs or rather, just like the wishful thinker, merely 'obscured' from so doing?

Since defeat is a normative category, and since, by Pryor's own stipulation, the sceptic's sceptical beliefs are unjustified, it would seem as though they do not qualify as justification defeaters proper, but rather as mere motivating reasons for resisting Moore's argument. The non-normative cannot defeat the normative: motivating reasons cannot outweigh normative reasons normatively. Just because I wish really hard to steal your purse, it does not follow that it is permissible to steal your purse: my motivating reasons, no matter how strong, in favour of stealing cannot outweigh the normative reasons against stealing, since they don't factor into the overall permissibility calculus to begin with.

Why, then, is it intuitive and, according to Pryor, right to think that, once one has adopted a belief that non-p (or a doubt about whether p, or a 0.5 credence that non-p), it would be importantly epistemically defective to adopt a subsequent belief that p? Take the following standard case of higher-order defeat: I come to believe that the walls in your studio are white but illuminated by a red light to look red. Subsequently, upon arriving at your studio, it seems problematic for me to adopt the belief 'the wall in front of me is red' based on my corresponding perceptual experience as of a red wall. Why is this so? In particular, why is it that, even if we stipulate that my initial belief that the wall is white and illuminated to look red is unjustified, it would seem that, now that I hold it, I shouldn't just trust my perceptual experience?

Maybe the answer to this question has something to do with the order in which the beliefs have been acquired; that is, maybe a difference in extant doxastic states is an epistemologically significant difference. Indeed, Pryor himself alludes to an answer along these lines. According to him, were the sceptic to believe based on Moore's testimony that HANDS, and thereby WORLD, their belief would be irrational because it would not cohere with their previously held sceptical beliefs. According to Pryor, since irrationality precludes justification, were the sceptic to believe what Moore says, their belief would also be unjustified:

> I will count a belief as rational when it's a belief that none of your other beliefs or doubts rationally oppose or rationally obstruct you from believing. [...] A rational commitment is a hypothetical relation between your beliefs; it doesn't 'detach'. That is, you can have a belief in P, that belief can rationally commit you to believe Q, and yet you be under no categorical requirement to believe Q. Suppose you believe Johnny can fly. This belief rationally commits you to the belief that someone can fly. If you're not justified in believing that Johnny can fly, though, you need not have any justification for the further belief. You may even have plenty of evidence and be fully justified in

believing that no one can fly. But your belief that Johnny can fly still rationally commits you to the belief that someone can fly. Given your belief about Johnny, if you refrain from believing that someone can fly, you'll thereby exhibit a rational failing. (Pryor 2004, 363–364)

Since rational failings are incompatible with justification, Pryor takes it that this hypothetical type of normativity that he associates with rationality – of the form 'if you believe that p, then you are rationally committed to believing that q' – will affect the permissibility of belief tout court: were the sceptic to believe what Moore tells them, their belief would be irrational – since they are antecedently committed to believing the opposite – and thereby unjustified.

There are two problems with this normative assessment, though. First and foremost, note that there are two ways of resolving cognitive dissonance due to holding two conflicting beliefs B_1 and B_2: one can either abandon B_1 or abandon B_2. Coherence doesn't tell us which one we should choose: it merely tells us that one needs to go.[3] There are two ways of proceeding in cases in which one is presented with information B_2 that runs counter to one's extant belief B_1: one can resist adopting B_2 or, alternatively, one can abandon B_1. Again, coherence doesn't recommend any particular course of action: it just tells us that we need to choose between them.

One thing that Pryor could reply at this juncture is: time makes a difference, epistemically. The previously held belief takes precedence over the incoming information; this is what explains why the sceptic is rational to resist Moore's argument.

The question that arises, though, is: why should we think that time is of such devastating epistemological significance? Just because the sceptical belief precedes Moore's testimony temporally, why is it that we should think that it also gets normative priority? After all, consider the following pair of cases (adapted from Jessica Brown 2018)[4]:

Case 1: A reliable testifier A, who knows that p, asserts that p. At the very same time as receiving A's testimony, the hearer also receives contrary testimony from another reliable testifier, B, that not-p.

Case 2: We slightly change Case 1 so that the testimony from B arrives just a bit later than the testimony from A, but for whatever reason the hearer does not form any belief about p before the testimony from B arrives.

---

[3] See also Graham and Lyons (2021) for similar points.   [4] See also Goldberg (2021).

In these cases, the evidentiary and doxastic situation is constant: one testimony item for p and one against p, and there is no difference in mental states. Clearly, the time difference will not make any epistemic difference: in both Case 1 and Case 2, the hearer has equally strong evidence for and against p. They should suspend belief. But now consider:

Case 3: This differs from Case 2 only in the following respect: as a result of receiving A's testimony, the hearer forms the belief that p before receiving B's testimony.

Note that there is no temporal difference between Case 2 and Case 3. As such, even by the lights of the philosopher who believes that time can make an epistemic difference, there should be no difference in epistemic assessment either. But if there is no epistemic difference between Cases 1 and 2, nor any epistemic difference between Cases 2 and 3, it follows that there is no epistemic difference between Cases 1 and 3 either. If so, what the hearer should do in both cases is suspend rather than give priority to the first belief they formed and dismiss the second.

Let's take stock. We have seen that considerations pertaining to coherence cannot explain why we should think that the sceptic is rational to resist Moore's argument: coherence is indifferent between resisting Moore's argument and abandoning the previously held sceptical belief. We have also seen that time does not make an epistemic difference either. If so, just because a belief is antecedently held, it does not follow that it takes epistemic priority. All of this suggests that the sceptic has no epistemic normative reason to give priority to their sceptical belief and thereby resist Moore's argument.

Furthermore, recall that, on Pryor's view, Moore's argument is justification conferring, whereas the sceptical belief is unjustified. If so, there *is* epistemic normative reason for the sceptic to adopt the conclusion of Moore's argument, and there is *no* epistemic normative reason to hold onto the sceptical belief – albeit, of course, the sceptic may well have a merely motivating reason to do so. All in all, it would seem, the sceptic ought (epistemically) to abandon their sceptical belief and adopt the conclusion of Moore's argument. The concessive neo-Moorean solution to the sceptical puzzle is wrong: while Moore's argument may well often fail to convince the sceptic, this is not because it lacks dialectical power, but rather because the sceptic is epistemically impermissibly resisting its conclusion in virtue of their previously held unjustified sceptical beliefs.

11.3 A New Radical Neo-Mooreanism

Let's take stock again: we've seen that radical neo-Mooreanism – claiming that the sceptic's resistance to Moore's argument is an instance of epistemic malfunction – is thought by many to fail to offer a fully satisfactory explanation of the datum, in that it places the sceptic in the same boat with wishful thinkers, epistemically speaking. However, intuitively, we find the sceptic to be reasonable, even if wrong, when they resist Moore's inference.

Concessive neo-Mooreanism does better on this front. According to this philosopher, the intuition of epistemic permissibility concerning the sceptic's resistance to Moore's argument is to be explained in terms of psychological defeat: Moore's argument is warrant conferring but dialectically defective. Alas, on closer investigation, this account was shown to run into normative trouble: given that the sceptical belief is unjustified, it remains unclear why the sceptic should favour it over the warranted conclusion of the Moorean argument.

In what follows, I will develop a new neo-Mooreanism. My view falls squarely within the radical neo-Moorean camp, in that it takes transmission to hold in Moorean inferences and finds no flaw – epistemic or dialectical – with Moore's argument. However, as opposed to extant radical neo-Mooreanism, it does predict that there is something epistemically good about the sceptic's doxastic response that sets them apart from believers merely displaying full-on cognitive malfunctions, such as wishful thinking.

Recall that, on the account developed here, evidence consists of facts that are knowledge indicators, in that they enhance closeness to knowledge: it consists of facts that one is in a position to know and that increase one's evidential probability (i.e. the probability on one's total body of evidence) of p being the case. The fact that there is a table in front of me is a piece of evidence for me that there is a table in front of me. It is a knowledge indicator: it raises the probability on my evidence that there is a table in front of me, and I'm in a position to know it.

As such, not just any psychological facts will constitute evidence that there is a table in front of me: my having a perception as of a table will fit the bill in virtue of having the relevant indicator property. The fact that I wish that there was a table in front of me will not fit the bill, even if, unbeknownst to me, my table wishes are strongly correlated with the presence of tables: wishes are not knowledge indicators, for they don't raise my evidential probability of p being the case. For the same reason, mere beliefs, as opposed to justified and knowledgeable beliefs, will not be evidence material; they lack the relevant indicator property.

Conversely, defeaters are indicators of ignorance: they are facts that one is in a position to know and that lower one's evidential probability that p is the case.

Going back to our sceptic: just like the wishful thinker, on this view of evidence and defeat, the sceptic has no epistemic reason to believe their preferred sceptical hypothesis. There are no knowledge indicators available to them to this effect. There are no facts that raise the evidential probability of the sceptical hypotheses within their reach. Furthermore, Moore's assertion that HANDS provides the sceptic with evidence that there are hands, as Moore's testimony to this effect is a knowledge indicator. Also, as the sceptic's sceptical belief is not an ignorance indicator (i.e. it does not lower the relevant evidential probability), it does not qualify as a defeater for HANDS. In this, the sceptic is in double breach of justification-conferring epistemic norms: they have unjustified sceptical beliefs, and they resist knowledge indicators on offer because of them. The sceptic does not have defeaters for HANDS; rather, they have mere motivating reasons to this effect: evidentially irrelevant facts (i.e. the fact that they believe non-WORLD/doubt WORLD) that lead her to unjustifiably reject HANDS.

What is it, then, that explains our intuition of reasonableness in the sceptic case and the lack thereof in the case of the wishful thinker? Recall that, according to the view developed here, the sceptic ought not to hold sceptical beliefs to begin with, ought to come to believe that WORLD based on Moore's argument, and thereby ought to draw the inference to WORLD with Moore and abandon their antecedently held sceptical beliefs. If they fail to do all that, they are in breach of the justification-conferring epistemic norm: their resistance to Moore's argument is epistemically impermissible.

Now, here is, however, a well-known fact about norms, generally speaking: sometimes, when we engage in impermissible actions, this gives rise to contrary-to-duty obligations. Consider the following normative claims:

(1) It ought to be that John does not break the neighbour's window.
(2) If John breaks the neighbour's window, it ought to be that he apologises.

(1) is a *primary obligation*, saying what John ought to do unconditionally. In contrast, (2) is a *contrary-to-duty obligation* about (in the context of (1)) what John ought to do conditional on his violating his primary obligation.

(1) is a norm of many sorts: social, prudential, moral, and one of politeness. Should John break the neighbour's window, there would be nothing good about it. That being said, John would be even worse off if, should he break the neighbour's window, he would also fail to go and apologise to the neighbour.

Our functionalist normative schema has the resources needed to explain this datum: input-independent proper functioning – of the type that governs hearts – remains a dimension of functional evaluation in its own right, independently of whether the general proper functioning of the trait in question is input dependent or not. Just like we can ask whether a heart is doing what it's supposed to do with the stuff that it takes up – be it blood or orange juice – we can also ask whether the lungs are doing the stuff that they're supposed to do with the stuff that they have taken up – be it oxygen or carbon dioxide. There's going to be an evaluative difference, then, between two pairs of lungs that are both improperly functioning simpliciter (i.e. in the input-dependent sense, in that they take up the wrong kind of stuff from the environment) in terms of how they process their input gas: are they carrying the input gas through the respiratory system, and subsequently through the lining of the air sacs, to the blood cells? The pair of lungs that do are better than the pair of lungs that don't in that, even though strictly speaking both are malfunctioning overall, the former are at least displaying input-independent proper functioning.

What explains our intuition of reasonableness in the sceptic's case, I claim, is not an epistemic norm simpliciter but rather an epistemic contrary-to-duty imperative: now that the sceptic is in breach of the justification-conferring epistemic norm, short of abandoning their unjustified beliefs, the next best thing for them to do is to embrace the commitments following from their unjustified beliefs and reject the commitments that follow from their negation. The next best thing for the sceptic, now that they believe/have a 0.5 credence that non-WORLD and reject HANDS, both impermissibly, short of abandoning their impermissible beliefs, is to reject whatever follows from HANDS. The sceptic's cognitive system, just like the wishful thinker's and just like lungs taking up carbon dioxide from the environment, is overall malfunctioning on several counts: it takes up improper inputs (the sceptic's sceptical beliefs) and rejects excellent inputs (Moore's testimony that HANDS). That being so, though, the sceptic's cognitive system does something right in terms of input-independent functioning: it processes the (bad) stuff that it has taken up in the right way. The sceptic's cognitive system would be even worse were they, now that they believe/have a 0.5 credence that non-HANDS, to go ahead and infer that WORLD.

Before I close, I would like to consider a possible objection to my view. So far, I have been assuming, with Pryor and Williamson, that the sceptic's sceptical beliefs/doubts are unjustified. One could worry, though, that my view of evidence might allow for the (reasonable) sceptic to have induction-based evidence for their 0.5 credence that non-WORLD. After all, the sceptic could reason as follows: (1) when I can't tell the difference between pears and apples, I can't come to know that there's an apple in front of me. (2) When I can't tell the difference between John and his twin brother, Tim, I can't come to know that John is in front of me. (3) Therefore, when I can't tell the difference between x and y, I can't come to know that x is the case. (4) I can't tell the difference between WORLD and non-WORLD. (5) Therefore, I don't know that WORLD. In turn, if the sceptic believes that (5), on pain of Moorean paradoxicality, they can't believe that WORLD.

There are two points to consider about this. First, crucially, the envisaged sceptic is wrong, as (1) is notably too strong: I can come to know that there's a pear in front of me in a world where there are no apples, or where apples are extremely rare, even if I can't tell the difference between pears and apples. That being said, of course, (1) may well be justified inductively, which would lead to (5) being justified inductively. Second, though, note that Moorean paradoxicality, just like incoherence, tells us nothing about which of the two beliefs should be abandoned: it merely predicts that one needs to go. Why think WORLD needs to go rather than (5)? Furthermore, notice that in everyday testimonial cases it's the previously held ignorance belief that should be abandoned: I believe I don't know whether you are thirty-two years old, you tell me that you are thirty-two years old, and I thereby come to know that you are thirty-two years old and abandon my belief that I don't know that you are thirty-two years old. That's how it normally goes.

Here is a last attempt: maybe the sceptic's inductively justified belief that they can't tell the difference between WORLD and non-WORLD acts as an undercutting defeater for Moore's testimony that HANDS? This could work. The problem, though, is that undercutting defeaters need to exhibit particular strength properties in order to successfully undercut. For instance, my three-year-old's testimony that Dretske is wrong about closure failure because he took a hallucinogenic drug before writing his paper 'Epistemic Operators' will not successfully undercut my evidence that closure fails sourced in Dretske's paper. Why not? My three-year-old is just not a very reliable testifier on the issue – not reliable enough to undercut Dretske's written testimony at any rate. The testimony from my three-year-old does not lower my evidential probability conditional on Dretske's testimony that closure fails. If so, what would need to happen in the case of the sceptic for their induction-based sceptical belief to undercut Moore's testimony would be that the former is weighty enough, epistemically. Why, though, should we think that the sceptic's induction has such devastating epistemic effects against Moore's testimony? Also, recall that the inductive argument only warrants the reasonable sceptical belief 'I don't know that WORLD', not the anxious sceptical belief that 'non-WORLD'. Of course, though, the former is much weaker than the latter and thus has much less defeat power.[5]

11.4 Conclusion

This chapter has developed a novel, functionalist variety of radical neo-Mooreanism. I have argued with Williamson that, just like the wishful thinker, the sceptic is displaying epistemic malfunction in rejecting Moore's testimony. On my account, that is because their cognitive processes fail to pick up knowledge indicators. I have also shown, however, that the intuition that there's something reasonable about the sceptic who resists going through Moore's inference is right: the sceptic is in compliance with a contrary-to-duty obligation akin to input-independent well-functioning.

To be clear: this account does not make any concessions to the sceptic in terms of justification-conferring epistemic norms (i.e. primary epistemic obligations): no justification for sceptical beliefs, nor any defeat against Moore's testimony, is instantiated in the context. The account merely explains why we find the sceptic reasonable (albeit wrong) to resist Moore's inference from HANDS to WORLD: they are in compliance with their contrary-to-duty epistemic obligations. Now that they have broken the window, as it were, the sceptic might as well go ahead and apologise.

---

[5] Thanks to Chris Kelp for pressing me on this.

CHAPTER 12

Knowledge and Disinformation

Ideally, we want to resist mis/disinformation but not evidence. If this is so, we need accounts of misinformation and disinformation to match the epistemic normative picture developed so far. This chapter develops a full account of the nature of disinformation. The view, if correct, carries high-stakes upshots, both theoretically and practically. First, it challenges several widely spread theoretical assumptions about disinformation – such as that it is a species of information, a species of misinformation, essentially false or misleading, or essentially intended/aimed/having the function of generating false beliefs in/misleading hearers. Second, it shows that the challenges faced by disinformation tracking in practice go well beyond mere fact checking. I begin with an interdisciplinary scoping of the literature in information science, communication studies, computer science, and philosophy of information to identify several claims constituting disinformation orthodoxy. I then present counterexamples to these claims and motivate my alternative account. Finally, I put forth and develop my account: disinformation as ignorance-generating content.

12.1 Information and Disinformation

Philosophers of information, as well as information and communication scientists, have traditionally focused their efforts in three main directions: offering an analysis of information, a way to measure it, and investigating prospects for analysing epistemic states – such as knowledge and justified belief – in terms of information. Misinformation and disinformation have traditionally occupied the backseat of these research efforts.[1] The

---

[1] While fully-fledged accounts of the nature of disinformation are still thin on the ground, a number of information scientists and philosophers of information have begun to address the problem of disinformation (Hernon 1995, Skinner and Martin 2000, Calvert 2001, Lynch 2001, Piper 2002, Fallis 2009, Walsh 2010, Rubin and Conroy 2012, Whitty et al., 2012, Karlova and Fisher 2013).

assumption has mostly been that a unified account of the three is going to become readily available as soon as we figure out what information is. As a result, for the most part, misinformation and disinformation have received dictionary treatment: for whatever the correct analysis of information was taken to be, misinformation and disinformation have either been taken to constitute the false variety thereof (misinformation) or the intentionally false/misleading variety thereof (disinformation) – by theorists endorsing non-factive accounts of disinformation – or, alternatively, something like information minus truth (misinformation) or information minus truth spread with an intention to mislead (disinformation) in the case of theorists endorsing factive accounts of information.

This is surprising in more than one way: first, it is surprising that philosophers of any brand would readily and unreflectively endorse dictionary definitions of pretty much anything – not to mention entities with such high practical stakes associated with them – such as mis/disinformation. Second, it is surprising that not more effort on the side of information, communication, and computer scientists has been spent on identifying a correct account of the nature of disinformation given the increasingly high stakes of issues having to do with the spread of disinformation that threaten our democracies, our trust in expertise, our uptake of health provision, and our social cohesion. We are highly social creatures, dependent on each other for flourishing in all walks of life. Our epistemic endeavours make no exception: due to our physical, geographical, and psychological limitations, most of the information we have is sourced in social interactions. We must inescapably rely on the intellectual labour of others, from those we know and trust well, to those whose epistemic credentials we take for granted online. Given the staggering extent of our epistemic dependence – one that recent technologies have only served to amplify – having a correct account of the nature of mis/disinformation, in order to be able to reliably identify it and escape it, is crucial.

Disinformation is widespread and harmful, epistemically and practically. We are currently facing a global information crisis that the Secretary-General of the World Health Organization (WHO) has declared an 'infodemic'. Furthermore, crucially, there are two key faces to this crisis: two ways in which disinformation spreads societal ignorance: One concerns the widespread *sharing of disinformation* (e.g. fake cures, health superstitions, conspiracy theories, political propaganda, etc.), especially online and via social media, which contribute to dangerous and risky political and social behaviour. Separately, though at least as critical to the wider infodemic we face, is the prevalence of disinformation-generated resistance to evidence: even when the relevant information available is reliably sourced and accurate, many information consumers fail to take it on board or otherwise resist or discredit it (Klintman 2019) due to the rising lack of trust and scepticism generated by the ubiquity of disinformation. An important pay-off, then, of a correct analysis of the nature of disinformation is an understanding of how to help build and sustain more resilient trust networks. It is urgent that we gain such answers and insights: according to the 2018 Edelman Trust Barometer, UK public trust in social media and online news has plummeted to below 25 per cent, and trust in government is at a low of 36 per cent. This present crisis in trust of corresponds with a related crisis of distrust, in that the dissemination and uptake of disinformation, particularly on social media, have risen dramatically over the past few years (Lynch 2001, Levinson 2017, Barclay 2022).

12.2 Against Disinformation Orthodoxy

In what follows, I will scope the scientific and philosophical literature, identify three very widely spread – and rarely defended – assumptions about the nature of disinformation, and argue against their credentials.

(1) **Assumption §1:** Disinformation is a species of information (e.g. Shannon 1948, Carnap and Bar-Hillel 1952, Frické 1997, Fallis 2009, 2015, Cevolani 2011, D'Alfonso 2011, Dinneen and Brauner 2015).

These theorists take information to be non-factive and disinformation to be the false and intentionally misleading variety thereof. On accounts like these, information is something like meaning: 'the cat is on the mat', on this view, caries the information that *the cat is on the mat* in virtue of the fact that it means that the cat is on the mat. Disinformation, on this view, consists in spreading 'the cat is on the mat' in spite of knowing it to be false and with the intention to mislead.

Why think in this way? Two rationales can be identified in the literature, one practical and one theoretical.

12.2.1 The Practical Rationale

Factivity doesn't matter for the information scientist. In the early days of information science, the thought behind this went roughly as follows: for the information scientist, the stakes associated with the factivity/non-factivity of information are null – after all, what the computer scientist/

communication theorist cares about is the quantity of information that can be packed into a particular signal/channel. Whether the relevant content will be true or not makes little difference to the prospects of answering this question.

It is true that, when it comes to how much data one can pack into a particular channel, factivity doesn't make much difference. However, times have changed, and so have the questions the information scientist needs to answer: the 'infodemic' has brought with it concerted efforts to fight the spread of disinformation online and through traditional media. We have lately witnessed an increased interest in researching and developing automatic algorithmic detection of misinformation and disinformation, such as PHEME (2014), Kumar and Geethakumari's (2014) 'Twitter algorithm', Karlova and Fisher's (2013) diffusion model, and the Hoaxy platform (Shao et al. 2016), to name a few. Interest from developers has also been matched by interest from policymakers: the European Commission has brought together major online platforms, emerging and specialised platforms, players in the advertising industry, fact-checkers, and research and civil society organisations to deliver a strengthened Code of Practice on Disinformation (European Commission 2022). The American Library Association (2005) has issued a 'Resolution on Disinformation, Media Manipulation, and the Destruction of Public Information'. The UK Government has recently published a call for evidence into how to address the spread of disinformation via employing trusted voices. These are, of course, only a few examples of disinformation-targeting initiatives. If all of these and others are to stand any chance at succeeding, we need a correct analysis of disinformation. The practical rationale is false.

12.2.2 The Theoretical Rationale

Natural language gives us clear hints as to the non-factivity of information: we often hear people utter things like 'the media is spreading a lot of fake information'. We also utter things like 'the library contains a lot of information' – however, clearly, there will be a fair share of false content featured in any library (Fallis 2015). If this is correct, the argument goes, natural language suggests that information is not factive – there can be true and false varieties thereof. Therefore, disinformation is a species of information.

The first problem with the natural language rationale is that the cases in point are underdeveloped. Take the library case: I agree that we will often say that libraries contain information in spite of the likelihood of false content. This, however, is compatible with information being factive: after all, the claim about false content, as far as I can see, is merely an existential claim. There being some false content in a library is perfectly compatible with it containing a good amount of information alongside it. Would we still say the same were we to find out that this particular library contains only falsehoods? I doubt it. If anything, at best, we might utter something like: 'this library contains a lot of fake information.'

Which brings me to my more substantial point: natural language at best cannot decide the factivity issue either way and at worst suggests that information is factive. Here is why: first, it is common knowledge in formal semantics that, when a complex expression consists of a intensional modifier and a modified expression, we cannot infer a type–species relation – or, indeed, to the contrary, in some cases, we might be able to infer that a type–species relation is absent. This latter class includes the so-called privative modifiers such as 'fake', 'former', and 'spurious', which get their name from the fact that they license the inference to 'not x' (McNally 2016). If so, the fact that 'information' takes 'fake' as modifier suggests, if anything, that information is factive, in that fake acts as privative: it suggests that it is not information to begin with. As Dretske (1981) well puts it, mis/disinformation is as much a type of information as a decoy duck is a type of duck (see also Mingers (1995) and Floridi (2004, 2005a, 2005b) for defences of factivity). If information is factive and disinformation is not, however, the one is not the species of the other. The theoretical rationale is false: meaning and disinformation come apart on factivity grounds. As Dretske well puts it:

> signals may *have* a meaning, but they *carry* information. What information a signal carries is what it is capable of telling us, telling us truly, about another state of affairs. [...] When I say I have a toothache, what I say means that I have a toothache whether it's true or false. But when false, it fails to carry the information that I have a toothache. (Dretske 1981, 44, emphases in original)

Natural language semantics also gives us further, direct reason to be sceptical about disinformation being a species of information: several instances of dis-prefixed properties that fail to signal type–species relations – disbarring is not a way of becoming a member of the bar, displeasing is not a form of pleasing, and displacing is not a form of placing. More on this below.

(2) **Assumption §2:** Disinformation is a species of misinformation (e.g. Floridi 2007, 2008, 2011, Fallis 2009, 2015).

Misinformation is essentially false content, and the mis- prefix modifies as 'badly', 'wrongly', 'unfavourably', 'in a suspicious manner', 'opposite or lack of', or 'not'. In this, misinformation is essentially non-information, in the same way in which fake gold is essentially non-gold.

As opposed to this, for the most part, dis- modifies as 'deprive of' (a specified quality, rank, or object), 'exclude', or 'expel from'. In this, paradigmatically,[2] dis- does not negate the prefixed content, but rather it signals un-doing: if misplacing is placing in the wrong place, displacing is taking out of the right place. Disinformation is not a species of misinformation any more than displacing is a species of misplacing. To think otherwise is to engage in a category mistake.

Note also that disinformation, as opposed to misinformation, is not essentially false: I can, for instance, disinform you via asserting true content and generating false implicatures. I can also disinform you via stripping you of justification via misleading defeaters.

Finally, note also that information/misinformation exists out there, whereas disinformation is us-dependent: there is information/misinformation in the world without anyone being informed/misinformed (Dretske 1981), whereas there is no disinformation without audience. Disinformation is essentially audience-involving.[3]

(3) **Assumption §3:** Disinformation is essentially intentional/functional (e.g. Fetzer 2004b, Floridi 2007, 2008, 2011, Mahon 2008, Fallis 2009, 2015).

The most widely spread assumption across disciplines is that disinformation is intentionally spread misleading content, where the relevant way to think about the intention at stake can be quite minimal, as having to do with content that has the function to mislead (Fallis 2009, 2015). I think this is a mistake generated by paradigmatic instances of disinformation. I also think it is a dangerous mistake, in a world of the automated spread of disinformation that has little to do with any intention on the part of the programmer, to operate with such a restricted concept of disinformation. To see this, consider a black-box artificial intelligence (AI) that, in the absence of any intention to this effect on the part of the designer, learns how to and proceeds to widely spreading false claims about COVID-19

---

[2] Not essentially, however. Disagreeable and dishonest are cases in point, where the dis- prefix modifies as 'not-'. The underlying rationale for the paradigmatic usage, however, is solidly grounded in the Latin and later French source of the English version of the prefix (the Latin prefix meaning 'apart', 'asunder', 'away', 'utterly', or having a privative, negative, or reversing force).
[3] See Grundmann (2020) for an audience-orientated account of fake news.

vaccines in the population in a systematic manner. Intention is missing in this case, as is function: the AI has not been designed to proceed in this way (no design function), and it does not do so in virtue of some benefit or another generated for either itself or any human user (no etiological function). Furthermore, and most importantly, AI is not the only place where the paradigmatic and the analytic part ways: I can disinform you unintentionally (where, furthermore, the case is one of genuine disinformation rather than mere misinformation). Consider the following case: I am a trusted journalist in village V, and, unfortunately, I am the kind of person who is unjustifiably very impressed by there being any scientific disagreement whatsoever on a given topic. Should even the most isolated voices express doubt about a scientific claim, I withhold belief. Against this background, I report on V TV (the local TV station in V) that there is disagreement in science about climate change and the safety of vaccines. As a result, whenever V inhabitants encounter expert claims that climate change is happening and vaccines are safe, they hesitate to update accordingly.

A couple of things about this case: first, this is not a case of false content/misinformation spreading – after all, it is true that there is disagreement on these issues (albeit very isolated). Second, there is no intention to mislead present in the context, nor any corresponding function. Third, and crucially, however, it is a classic case of disinformation spreading.

Finally, consider the paradigmatic spread of conspiracy theories. Their advocates are, paradigmatically, believers, and their intention is to inform rather than mislead. Since spreading conspiracy theories is a central case of disinformation spread – indeed, I submit, if our account of disinformation cannot accommodate this case, we should go back to the drawing board – we need a new account of the nature of disinformation that does not require any intention or function to mislead.

12.3 A Knowledge-First Account of Disinformation

In what follows, I will offer a knowledge-first account of disinformation that aims to vindicate the findings of the previous section.

Traditionally, in epistemology (e.g. Dretske 1981) and philosophy of information alike, the relation between knowledge and information has been conceived on a right-to-left direction of explanation (i.e. several theorists have attempted to analyse knowledge in terms of information). Notably, Fred Dretske thought knowledge was information-caused true belief. More recently, Luciano Floridi's (2004) network theory involves an argument for the claim that, should information be embedded within a network of questions and answers, then it is necessary and sufficient for it to count as knowledge. Accounts like these, unsurprisingly, encounter the usual difficulties in analysing knowledge.

The fact that information-based analyses of knowledge remain unsuccessful, however, is not good reason to abandon the theoretical richness of the intuitive tight relation between the two. In extant work (Simion and Kelp forthcoming), I have developed a knowledge-based account of information that explores the prospects of the opposite, left-to-right direction of explanation: according to this view, very roughly, a signal s carries the information that p iff it has the capacity to generate knowledge that p.[4] On this account, then, information carries its functional nature up its sleeve, as it were: just like a digestive system is a system with the function to digest and the capacity to do so under normal conditions, information has the function to generate knowledge and the capacity to do so under normal conditions (i.e. given a suitably situated agent).

Against this background, I find it very attractive to think of disinformation as the counterpart of information: roughly, as stuff that has the capacity to generate or increase ignorance (i.e. to fully/partially strip someone of their status as knower, or to block their access to knowledge, or to decrease their closeness to knowledge). Here is the account I want to propose:

> Disinformation as ignorance-generating content (DIGC): X is disinformation in a context C iff X is a content unit communicated at C that has a disposition to generate or increase ignorance at C in normal conditions.

Normal conditions are understood in broadly etiological functionalist terms (e.g. Graham 2012, Simion 2019b, 2021a) as the conditions under which our knowledge-generating cognitive processes have acquired their

---

[4] My co-author and I owe inspiration for this account to Fred Dretske's excellent book *Knowledge and the Flow of Information* (1981). While Dretske himself favours the opposite direction of analysis (knowledge in terms of information), at several points he says things that sound very congenial to our preferred account and that likely played an important role in shaping our thinking on this topic. On page 44 of this book, for instance, Dretske claims that '[r]oughly speaking, information is that commodity capable of yielding knowledge, and what information a signal carries is what we can learn from it'. Sandy Goldberg pointed out to me that Gareth Evans as well may well have had something in the vicinity in mind in his *Varieties of Reference* (1982), in the chapter on communication, when he said that we can exploit epistemic principles about knowledge transmission in testimony cases to derive the semantics of the words used in those knowledge-transmitting cases (roughly, the words mean what they must if such knowledge is to be transmitted).

function of generating knowledge. The view is contextualist in that the same communicated content will act differently depending on contextual factors such as the evidential backgrounds of the audience members, the shared presuppositions, extant social relations, and social norms. Importantly, as with dispositions more generally, said content need not actually generate ignorance in the context – after all, dispositions are sometimes masked.

Now, generating ignorance can be done in a variety of ways – which means that disinformation will come in diverse incarnations. In what follows, I will make an attempt at offering a comprehensive taxonomy of disinformation. (The ambition to exhaustiveness is probably beyond the scope of this chapter, or even of an isolated philosophical project such as mine; however, it will be useful to have a solid taxonomy as a basis for a fully-fledged account of disinformation: at a minimum, any account should be able to incorporate all varieties of disinformation we will have identified.[5]) Here it goes:

(1) Disinforming via spreading content that has the capacity of *generating false belief*. The paradigmatic case of this is the traditionally recognised species of disinformation: intentionally spread false assertions with the capacity to generate false beliefs in hearers.

(2) Disinforming via misleading defeat. This category of disinformation has the capacity of stripping the audience of held knowledge/being in a position to know via defeating justification.

(3) Disinforming via content that has the capacity of inducing epistemic anxiety (Nagel 2010). This category of disinformation has the capacity of stripping the audience of knowledge via belief defeat. The paradigmatic way to do this is via artificially raising the stakes of the context/introducing irrelevant alternatives as being relevant: 'Are you really sure that you're sitting at your desk? After all, you might well be a brain in a vat'; or 'Are you really sure he loves you? After all, he might just be an excellent actor, in which case you will have wasted years of your life.' The way in which this variety of disinforming works is via falsely implicating that these error possibilities are relevant in the context when in fact they are not. In this, the audience's body of evidence is changed to include misleading justification defeaters.

---

[5] See Simion (2019a, 2021a, 2021b), Simion and Kelp (2022), and Kelp and Simion (2023a) for knowledge-centric accounts of trustworthiness and testimonial entitlement. See Kelp and Simion (2017, 2021) for functionalist accounts of the distinctive value of knowledge.

(4) Confidence-defeating disinformation. This has the capacity to reduce justified confidence via justification/doxastic defeat: you are sure that your name is Anna, but I introduce misleading (justification/doxastic) defeaters, which gets you to lower your confidence. You may remain knowledgeable about p: 'my name is Anna' in cases in which the confidence lowering does not bring you below the knowledge threshold. Compatibly, however, your knowledge – or evidential support – concerning the correct likelihood of p is lost: you now take/are justified to take the probability of your name being Anna to be much lower than it actually is.

(5) Disinforming via exploiting pragmatic phenomena. Pragmatic phenomena can be easily exploited to the end of disinforming in all of the ways above: true assertions carrying false implicatures will display this capacity to generate false beliefs in the audience. I ask: 'Is there a gas station anywhere near here? I'm almost out of gas.' And you reply: 'Yeah, sure, just one mile in that direction!', knowing perfectly well that it's been shut down for years. Another way in which disinformation can be spread via making use of pragmatic phenomena is by introducing false presuppositions. Finally, both justification and doxastic defeat will be achievable via speech acts with true content but problematic pragmatics, even in the absence of generating false implicatures.

What all of these ways of disinforming have in common is that they generate ignorance – by generating either false beliefs, knowledge loss, or a decrease in warranted confidence. One important thing to notice, which was also briefly discussed in the previous section, is that this account, and the associated taxonomy, is strongly audience-involving, in that disinformation has to do with the capacity to have a particular effect – generating ignorance – in the audience. Importantly, though, this capacity will heavily depend on the audience's background evidence/knowledge: after all, in order to figure out whether a particular piece of communicated content has the disposition to undermine an audience in their capacity as knowers, it is important to know their initial status as knowers. Here is, then, on my view, in more precise terms, what it takes for a signal to carry a particular piece of disinformation for an audience A:

> **Agent disinformation:** A signal r carries disinformation for an audience A wrt p iff A's evidential probability that p conditional on r is less than A's unconditional evidential probability that p and p is true.

What is relevant for agent disinformation with regard to p is the probability that p on the agent's evidence. And A's evidence – and, correspondingly, what underlies A's evidential probability – lies outwith A's skull: it consists in probability raisers that A is in a position to know. Recall the account defended in Chapter 7:

> **Evidence as knowledge indicators:** A fact e is evidence for p for S iff S is in a position to know e and $P(p/e) > P(p)$.

In turn, we have seen that, on this account, a fact e being such that I am in a position to know it has to do with the capacity of my properly functioning knowledge-generating capacity to take up e:

> **Being in a position to know:** S is in a position to know a fact e if S has a cognitive capacity with the function of generating knowledge that can (qualitatively, quantitatively, and environmentally) easily uptake e in cognisers of S's type.

This completes my account of disinformation. On this account, disinformation is the stuff that undermines one's status as a knower. It does so via lowering their evidential probability for p – the probability on the p-relevant facts that they are in a position to know – for a true proposition. It can, again, do so by merely communicating to A (semantically, pragmatically, etc.) that not-p when in fact p is the case. Alternatively, it can do so by (partially or fully) defeating A's justification for p, A's belief that p is the case, or A's confidence in p.

One worry that the reader may have at this point goes along the following lines: isn't the account in danger of over-generating disinformation? After all, I might be wrong about something I tell you through no fault of my own; isn't it harsh to describe me as thereby spreading disinformation? Furthermore, every true assertion that I make in your presence about p being the case may, for all I know, serve as (to some extent) defeating evidence for a different proposition q, which may well be true. I truthfully tell you it's raining outside, which, unrelatedly and unbeknownst to me, together with your knowledge about Mary not liking the rain, may function as partial rebutting defeat for 'Mary is taking a walk' – which may well, nevertheless, be true. Is it now appropriate to accuse me of having thereby disinformed you? Intuitively, that seems wrong.[6]

Here are also a couple of parallel cases from Sandy Goldberg (in conversation): say that S is widely (but falsely) thought to be an inveterate

---

[6] Many thanks to Sandy Goldberg, Julia Staffel, and Martin Smith for pressing me on this.

liar, so that whenever S says that p, everyone immediately concludes that $\sim p$. Prior to encountering S, A has a credence of 0.2 in p (this is what A's evidence supports prior to encountering S's testimony). S testifies (truly) that p, and A, who, like everyone else in the entire community, takes S to be a liar, drops her credence in p to 0.1. If S's reputation as a liar is assumed to be common knowledge, such that everyone knows of it and would update accordingly, it seems that S's true testimony would meet my analysis of agent disinformation. Conversely, one can imagine cases in which S says something false, explicitly aiming to disinform, but others (who know of S's lying ways) come to true conclusions on the basis of the fact that S said so. On my account, this will not count as a case of disinformation.

Three things about these cases: first, note, once more, that intentions don't matter for disinforming. As such, restricting disinforming via defeat to intentional/functional cases will not work for the same reasons that created problems for the intention/function condition on disinformation more broadly – we want an account of disinformation to be able to predict that asserters generating doubt about, for example, climate change via spreading defeaters to scientific evidence, even if they do it without any malicious intention, are disinforming the audience.

Second, note that it is independently plausible that, just as any bad deed can be performed blamelessly, one can also disinform blamelessly; if so, given garden variety epistemic and control conditions on blame, any plausible account of disinformation will have to accommodate non-knowledgeable and non-intentional instances of disinformation. Conversely, like with all intentions, intentions to disinform can also fail: one may aim to disinform and fail to do so. Indeed, it would be theoretically strange if an intention to disinform will be analytically successful.

Finally, note that we don't need to restrict the account in order to accommodate the datum that disinformation attribution, and the accompanying criticism, would sound inappropriate in the cases above. We can use simple Gricean pragmatics to predict as much via the maxim of relevance: since the issue of whether Mary was going for a walk was not under discussion, and nor was it remotely relevant in our conversational context, flat out accusing you of disinforming me when you assert truthfully that it's raining is pragmatically impermissible (although strictly speaking true with regard to Mary's actions).

Going back to the account, note that, interestingly, on this view, one and the same piece of communication can, at the same time, be a piece of information and a piece of disinformation: information, as opposed to disinformation, is not context-relative. Content with knowledge-generating potential (i.e. that can generate knowledge in a possible agent) is information. Compatibly, the same piece of content, in a particular context, can be a piece of disinformation insofar as it has a disposition to generate ignorance under normal conditions. I think this is the right result: me telling you that *p*: 99 per cent of Black people at Club X are staff members is me informing you that *p*. Me telling you that *p* in the context of you inquiring as to whether you can give your coat to a particular Black man is a piece of disinformation since it carries a strong disposition (due to the corresponding relevance implicature) to generate the unjustified (and maybe false) belief in you that this particular Black man is a member of staff (Gendler 2011).

Finally, and crucially, my account allows that disinformation for an audience A can exist in the absence of A's hosting any relevant belief/credence: (partial) defeat of epistemic support that one is in a position to know is enough for disinformation. Even if I (irrationally) don't believe that vaccines are safe or that climate change is happening to begin with, I am still vulnerable to disinformation in this regard in that I am vulnerable to content that has, under normal conditions, a disposition to defeat epistemic support available to me that vaccines are safe and climate change is happening. In this, disinformation, on my view, can generate ignorance even in the absence of any doxastic attitude – by decreasing closeness to knowledge via defeating available evidence. This, I submit, is a very nice result: in this, the account explains the most dangerous variety of disinformation available out there – disinformation targeting the already epistemically vulnerable.

12.4 Conclusion

Disinformation is not a type of information and disinforming is not a way of informing: while information is content with knowledge-generating potential, disinformation is content with a disposition to generate ignorance under normal conditions in the context at stake. This way of thinking about disinformation, crucially, tells us that it is much more ubiquitous and hard to track than it is currently taken to be in policy and practice: mere fact-checkers just won't do. Some of the best disinformation detection tools at our disposal will fail to capture most types of disinformation. To give but a few examples (but more research on this is clearly needed): the PHEME project aims to algorithmically detect and categorise rumours in social network structures (such as X (formerly Twitter) and Facebook) and to do so, impressively, in near real time. The rumours are mapped according to four categories, including 'disinformation, where something untrue is spread with malicious intent' (Søe 2016). Similarly, Kumar and Geethakumari's project (2014) had developed an algorithm that ventures to detect and flag whether a tweet is misinformation or disinformation. In their framework, 'Misinformation is false or inaccurate information, especially that which is deliberately intended to deceive [and d]-isinformation is false information that is intended to mislead, especially propaganda issued by a government organization to a rival power or the media' (Kumar and Geethakumari 2014, 3). In Karlova and Fisher's (2013) diffusion model, disinformation is taken to be deceptive information. Hoaxy is 'a platform for the collection, detection, and analysis of online misinformation, defined as "false or inaccurate information"' (Shao et al. 2016, 745). Examples targeted, however, include clear cases of disinformation such as rumours, false news, hoaxes, and elaborate conspiracy theories (Shao et al. 2016).

It becomes clear that these excellent tools are just the beginning of a much wider effort that is needed in order to capture disinformation in all of its facets rather than mere paradigmatic instances thereof. At a minimum, pragmatic deception mechanisms, as well as evidential probability-lowering potentials, will need to be tracked against an assumed (common) evidential background of the audience.

Concluding Remarks
The Way Forward in Policy and Practice[*]

Disinformation is widespread and harmful, epistemically and practically. We are currently facing a global information crisis that the Secretary-General of the World Health Organization (WHO) has declared an 'infodemic'.[1] Furthermore, crucially, there are two key facets to this crisis (i.e. two ways in which disinformation spreads societal ignorance): one concerns the widespread sharing of disinformation (e.g. fake cures, health superstitions, conspiracy theories, political propaganda, etc.), especially online and via social media, which contributes to dangerous and risky political and social behaviour. Separately, though at least as critical in the wider infodemic we face, is the prevalence of resistance to evidence: even when the relevant information available is reliably sourced and accurate, many information consumers fail to take it on board or otherwise resist or discredit it due to the rising lack of trust and scepticism generated by the polluted epistemic environment (i.e. by the ubiquity of disinformation). What we need, then, is an understanding of how to help build and sustain more resilient trust networks in the face of disinformation. To this effect, we need a better understanding of the nature and mechanisms of disinformation and of the triggers of evidence resistance.

Evidence Resistance

We have increasingly sophisticated ways of acquiring and communicating knowledge, but efforts to spread this knowledge often encounter resistance to evidence. Resistance to evidence consists in a disposition to reject evidence coming from highly reliable sources. This disposition deprives

---

[*] From White Paper: 'Trust, Disinformation, and Evidence Resistance' (2022, with Chris Kelp). Submitted in response to the UK Parliament Call for Evidence: 'Fighting Disinformation with Trustworthy Voices'. Published on the UK Parliament website here: https://committees.parliament.uk/writtenevidence/111503/pdf/.

[1] www.who.int/health-topics/infodemic#tab=tab_1.

us of knowledge and understanding and comes with dire practical consequences; recent high-stakes examples include climate change denial and vaccine scepticism.

Until very recently, the predominant hypothesis in social epistemology and social psychology principally explained evidence resistance with reference to politically motivated reasoning: on this view, a thinker's prior political convictions (including politically directed desires and attitudes about political group membership) best explain why they are inclined to reject expert consensus when they do. Typically, epistemologists who have explored the consequences of this empirical hypothesis take its merits at face value.

However, on closer and more recent inspection, the hypothesis is both empirically and epistemically problematic. Empirically, there are worries that in extant studies political group identity is often confounded with prior (often rationally justified) beliefs about the issue in question; and, crucially, reasoning can be affected by such beliefs in the absence of any political group motivation. This renders much existing evidence for the hypothesis ambiguous. Epistemologically, the worry is that the hypothesis is ineffective at making crucial distinctions among a number of phenomena, such as (1) concerning epistemic status: between irrational resistance to evidence and rationally justified evidence rejection; (2) concerning triggers: between instances of motivated reasoning on the one hand and epistemically deficient reasoning featuring cognitive biases and unjustified premise beliefs on the other; and (3) concerning strategies for addressing the phenomenon of evidence resistance: between targeting widely spread individual irrationality on the one hand and targeting an unhealthy epistemic environment on the other.

Furthermore, difficulties in answering the question as to what triggers resistance to evidence have a very significant negative impact on our prospects of identifying the best ways to address resistance to evidence. If resistance to evidence has one main source (e.g. a particular type of mistake in reasoning, such as motivated reasoning), the strategy to address this problem will be unidirectional and targeted mostly at the individual level. In contrast, should we discover that a pluralistic picture is more plausible when it comes to what triggers resistance to evidence – whereby this phenomenon is, for example, the result of a complex interaction of social, emotive, and cognitive phenomena – we would have to develop much more complex interventions at both individual and societal levels.

My results suggest that the widespread irrationality hypothesis assumed by the politically motivated reasoning account of evidence resistance is incorrect: humans are very reliable cognitive machines in spite of relatively isolated instances of biased cognitive processing or heuristics-based reasoning. Irrational resistance to evidence is rare and is an instance of input-level epistemic malfunctioning that is often encountered in biological traits the proper function of which is input-dependent: just like our respiratory systems are biologically malfunctioning when they fail to take up easily available oxygen from the environment, our cognitive systems are epistemically malfunctioning when they fail to take up easily available evidence from the environment.

What is often encountered in the population, however, is rationally justified evidence rejection due to overwhelming (misleading) evidence present in the (epistemically polluted) environment of the agent. When agents rationally reject reliable scientific testimony, they often do so in virtue of two types of epistemic phenomena: rebutting epistemic defeat and undercutting epistemic defeat. Rebutting epistemic defeat consists, often, in testimony from sources one is rational to trust that contradicts scientific testimony on the issue. These sources will be rationally trusted by the agent because of an excellent track record of testimony: they are overall reliable testifiers in the cognitive agent's community (which is why it is rational for the agent to trust them), but they are mistaken about the matter at hand. Reliability is not infallibility – it admits of failure.

One often-encountered trigger for rational evidence rejection is undercutting epistemic defeat. Undercutting epistemic defeat is evidence that suggests that a particular testimonial source is not trustworthy: relevant examples include misleading evidence against the reliability of a particular source of scientific testimony or a particular media outlet or against the trustworthiness of a particular public body. In vaccine-sceptic communities, for instance, we often encounter worries that the scientific community or the NHS does not have the relevant communities' interests in mind when they recommend vaccine uptake. These worries, in turn, are, once more, often rationally sourced in otherwise-reliable testimony (testifiers within the agent's community that the agent trusts due to their excellent track record but that are wrong on this particular occasion).[2]

These results, in turn, illuminate the best strategies to address the phenomenon of evidence resistance. Two major types of interventions are required:

---

[2] See, for example, *Scotland, African Voices: The Covid19 Vaccine Debate* (2022; documentary film, co-developed with Josephine Adekola, PI). Full documentary available here: https://youtu.be/h1yNAZffpOg.

(1) For combatting rational evidence rejection: engineering enhanced social epistemic environments. This requires combatting rebutting defeaters via evidence flooding. Evidence-resistant communities, inhabiting polluted epistemic environments, cannot be reached via the average communication strategies designed to reach the mainstream population inhabiting a friendly epistemic environment (with little to no misleading evidence). What is required is: (1.1) quantitatively enhanced reliable evidence flow. This is a purely quantitative measure aimed at outweighing rebutting defeaters in the agent's environment. More evidence in favour of the scientifically well-supported facts will, in rational agents, work to outweigh the misleading evidence they have against the facts. (1.2) Qualitatively enhanced reliable evidence flow. This is a qualitative measure that aims to outweigh misleading evidence via evidence from sources that the agent trusts – that are trustworthy vis-à-vis the agent's environment (see below on context-variant trustworthiness). (1.3) Quantitatively and qualitatively enhanced evidence aimed at combatting undercutting defeat (misleading evidence against the trustworthiness of reliable sources). This involves flooding evidence-resistant communities with evidence from sources that they trust in favour of the reliability of sources they fail to trust due to misleading undercutting defeaters.

(2) For combatting (relatively isolated) cases of irrational evidence resistance due uptake cognitive malfunction: increasing availability of cognitive flexibility training (e.g. in workplaces and schools, alongside anti-bias training; Chaby et al. 2019, Sassenberg et al. 2022). Cognitive flexibility training helps with enhancing open-mindedness to evidence that runs against one's held beliefs and with opening up alternative decision pathways.

Disinformation

My results show that disinformation need not come in the form of false content but rather consists of content with a disposition to generate ignorance under normal conditions in the context at stake. This predicts that disinformation is much more ubiquitous and harder to track than it is currently taken to be in policy and practice: mere fact-checkers just won't be able to adequately protect us against disinformation because disinforming does not require making false claims. Disinformation is ignorance-generating content: content X is disinformation in a context C iff X is a content unit communicated at C that has a disposition to generate ignorance at C under normal conditions. The same communicated content will act differently depending on contextual factors such as the evidential backgrounds of the audience members, the shared presuppositions, extant social relations, and social norms. Generating ignorance can be done in a variety of ways – which means that disinformation will come in diverse incarnations, including false content, true content with false implicatures, false presuppositions, epistemic anxiety-inducing content, misleading evidence, and defeat.

What all of these ways of disinforming have in common is that they generate ignorance – either by generating false beliefs or by generating knowledge loss. Importantly, this capacity to generate ignorance will heavily depend on the audience's background evidence/knowledge. A signal r carries disinformation for an audience A wrt p iff A's evidential probability that p conditional on r is less than A's unconditional evidential probability that p and p is true.

Some of the best disinformation-detection tools at our disposal, targeting mainly false content, will fail to capture most types of disinformation. They are just the beginning of a much wider effort that is needed in order to capture disinformation in all of its facets rather than mere paradigmatic instances thereof, which involve false assertions. At a minimum, we need to build fact-checkers that track pragmatic deception mechanisms as well as evidential probability-lowering potentials against an assumed (common) evidential background of the audience.

Bibliography

Adams, F. and de Moraes, J. A. (2016). 'Is there a philosophy of information?', *Topoi*, Vol. 35, No. 1, pp. 161–171.
Adekola, J., Fischbacher-Smith, D., Okey-Adibe, T., and Audu, J. (2022). 'Strategies to build trust and COVID-19 vaccine confidence and engagement in Scotland', *International Journal of Disaster Risk Science*, Vol. 13, pp. 890–902.
Adriaans, P. (2012). 'Information', in E. N. Zalta (ed.), *Stanford Encyclopedia of Philosophy*, fall 2013 edition. Palo Alto, CA: Stanford University. Available at: http://plato.stanford.edu/archives/fall2013/entries/information.
Adriaans, P. and van Benthem, J. (eds.) (2008). *Philosophy of Information*. Amsterdam and Oxford: Elsevier B.V.
Alston, W. (2002). 'Plantinga, naturalism, and defeat', in J. Beilby (ed.), *Naturalism Defeated? Essays on Plantinga's Evolutionary Argument against Naturalism*. Ithaca, NY: Cornell University Press, pp. 176–203.
  (2005). *Beyond Justification: Dimensions of Epistemic Evaluation*. Ithaca, NY: Cornell University Press.
American Library Association. (2005). 'Resolution on disinformation, media manipulation and the destruction of public information'. Available at: www.ala.org/aboutala/sites/ala.org.aboutala/files/content/governance/policymanual/updatedpolicymanual/ocrpdfofprm/52-8disinformation.pdf.
Ancell, A. (2019). 'The fact of unreasonable pluralism', *Journal of the American Philosophical Association*, Vol. 5, No. 4, pp. 410–428.
Baehr, J. (2009). 'Evidentialism, vice, and virtue', *Philosophy and Phenomenological Research*, Vol. 78, pp. 545–567.
  (2011). *The Inquiring Mind: On Intellectual Virtues and Virtue Epistemology*. Oxford: Oxford University Press.
  (2017). 'Four dimensions of an intellectual virtue', in C. Mi, M. Slote, and E. Sosa (eds.), *Moral and Intellectual Virtues in Western and Chinese Philosophy*. London: Routledge, pp. 86–98.
Baker-Hytch, M. and Benton, M. (2015). 'Defeatism defeated', *Philosophical Perspectives*, Vol. 29, No. 1, pp. 40–66.
Ballantyne, N. and Coffman, E. J. (2011). 'Uniqueness, evidence, and rationality', *Philosophers Imprint*, Vol. 11, No. 18, pp. 1–13.

Barclay, D. A. (2022). *Disinformation: The Nature of Facts and Lies in the Post-truth Era*. Lanham, MD: Rowman & Littlefield.
Bates, M. J. (2006). 'Fundamental forms of information', *Journal of the American Society for Information Science and Technology*, Vol. 57, No. 8, pp. 1033–1045.
Battaly, H. (2010). 'Epistemic self-indulgence', *Metaphilosophy*, Vol. 41, No. 1–2, pp. 214–234.
  (2014). 'Varieties of epistemic vice', in J. Matheson and R. Vitz (eds.), *The Ethics of Belief*. Oxford: Oxford University Press, pp. 51–76.
Beddor, B. (2015). 'Process reliabilism's troubles with defeat', *Philosophical Quarterly*, Vol. 65, No. 259, pp. 145–159.
  (2021). 'Reasons for reliabilism', in J. Brown and M. Simion (eds.), *Reasons, Justification, and Defeat*. Oxford: Oxford University Press, pp. 146–176.
Benton, M. (2014). 'Knowledge norms', in J. Fieser and B. Dowden (eds.), *Internet Encyclopedia of Philosophy*. Available at: www.iep.utm.edu/kn-norms.
Bergmann, M. (2006). *Justification without Awareness*. New York: Oxford University Press.
Bird, A. (2007). 'Justified judging', *Philosophy and Phenomenological Research*, Vol. 74, pp. 81–110.
Blair, D. C. (1992). 'Information retrieval and the philosophy of language', *Computer Journal*, Vol. 35, No. 3, pp. 200–207.
  (2003). 'Information retrieval and the philosophy of language', *Annual Review of Information Science and Technology*, Vol. 37, No. 1, pp. 3–50.
Blair, J. P., Levine, T., and Shaw, A. (2010). 'Content in context improves deception detection accuracy', *Human Communication Research*, Vol. 36, pp. 423–442.
Bond, C. F. and DePaulo, B. M. (2006). 'Accuracy of deception judgments', *Personality and Social Psychology Review*, Vol. 10, pp. 214–234.
BonJour, L. (1985). *The Structure of Empirical Knowledge*. Cambridge, MA: Harvard University Press.
Brookes, B. C. (1980). 'The foundations for information science: part I. Philosophical aspects', *Journal of Information Science*, Vol. 2, pp. 125–133.
Brown, J. (2012). 'Assertion and practical reasoning: common or divergent epistemic standards?', *Philosophy and Phenomenological Research*, Vol. 84, No. 1, pp. 123–157.
  (2018). *Fallibilism: Evidence and Knowledge*. Oxford: Oxford University Press.
Brown, J. and Simion, M. (2021). *Reasons, Justification, and Defeat*. Oxford: Oxford University Press.
Bucher, T. (2017). 'The algorithmic imaginary: exploring the ordinary affects of Facebook algorithms', *Information, Communication & Society*, Vol. 20, No. 1, pp. 30–44.
Buckland, M. K. (1991). 'Information as thing', *Journal of the American Society for Information Science*, Vol. 42, No. 5, pp. 351–360.

Budd, J. M. (2011). 'Meaning, truth, and information: prolegomena to a theory', *Journal of Documentation*, Vol. 67, No. 1, pp. 56–74.
Buller, D. J. (1998). 'Etiological theories of function: a geographical survey', *Biology and Philosophy*, Vol. 13, No. 4, pp. 505–527.
Burge, T. (2010). *Origins of Objectivity*. Oxford: Oxford University Press.
Burrell, J. (2016). 'How the machine "thinks": understanding opacity in machine learning algorithms', *Big Data & Society*, Vol. 3, No. 1, pp. 1–12.
Calvert, P. J. (2001). 'Scholarly misconduct and misinformation on the World Wide Web', *Electronic Library*, Vol. 19, No. 4, pp. 232–240.
Capurro, R. and Hjørland, B. (2003). 'The concept of information', *Annual Review of Information Science and Technology*, Vol. 37, No. 1, pp. 343–411.
Carnap, R. and Bar-Hillel, Y. (1952). *An Outline of a Theory of Semantic Information, Technical Report No. 247*. Cambridge, MA: Research Laboratory of Electronics, MIT.
Carson, T. L. (2010). *Lying and Deception*. New York: Oxford University Press.
Carter, J. A. and McKenna, R. (2020). 'Skepticism motivated: on the skeptical import of motivated reasoning', *Canadian Journal of Philosophy*, Vol. 50, No. 6, pp. 702–718.
Carter, J. A. and Navarro, J. (2017). 'The defeasibility of knowledge-how', *Philosophy and Phenomenological Research*, Vol. 95, No. 3, pp. 662–685.
Cevolani, G. (2011). 'Strongly semantic information and verisimilitude', *Etica and Politica/Ethics and Politics*, Vol. 13, No. 2, pp. 159–179.
Chaby, L. E., Karavidha, K., Lisieski, M. J., Perrine, S. A., and Liberzon, I. (2019). 'Cognitive flexibility training improves extinction retention memory and enhances cortical dopamine with and without traumatic stress exposure', *Frontiers in Behavioral Neuroscience*, Vol. 13, p. 24.
Chandler, J. (2013). 'Defeat reconsidered', *Analysis*, Vol. 73, No. 1, pp. 49–51.
Choi, S. and Fara, M. (2018). 'Dispositions', in E. N. Zalta (ed.), *Stanford Encyclopedia of Philosophy*, fall 2018 edition. Palo Alto, CA: Stanford University. Available at: https://plato.stanford.edu/archives/fall2018/entries/dispositions.
Chrisman, M. (2008). 'Ought to believe', *Journal of Philosophy*, Vol. 105, No. 7, pp. 346–370.
Christensen, D. (2010). 'Higher-order evidence', *Philosophy and Phenomenological Research*, Vol. 81, No. 1, pp. 185–215.
Coates, A. (2012). 'Rational epistemic akrasia', *American Philosophical Quarterly*, Vol. 1, No. 2, pp. 113–124.
Comesaña, J. (2010). 'Evidentialist reliabilism', *Nous*, Vol. 94, pp. 571–601.
  (2020). *Being Rational and Being Right*. Oxford: Oxford University Press.
Conee, E. (1987). 'Evident, but rationally unacceptable', *Australasian Journal of Philosophy*, Vol. 65, pp. 316–326.
  (1992). 'The truth connection', *Philosophy and Phenomenological Research*, Vol. 52, pp. 657–669.
  (2009). 'Peerage', *Episteme*, Vol. 6, No. 3, pp. 313–323.

Conee, E. and Feldman, R. (2004). *Evidentialism: Essays in Epistemology*. Oxford: Oxford University Press.

Cornelius, I. (2002). 'Theorizing information for information science', *Annual Review of Information Science and Technology*, Vol. 36, No. 1, pp. 393–425.

Crawford, K. (2016). 'Can an algorithm be agonistic? Ten scenes from life in calculated publics', *Science, Technology, & Human Values*, Vol. 71, No. 1, pp. 77–92.

Crupi, V. (2021). 'Confirmation', in E. N. Zalta (ed.), *Stanford Encyclopedia of Philosophy*, spring 2021 edition. Palo Alto, CA: Stanford University. Available at: https://plato.stanford.edu/archives/spr2021/entries/confirmation.

Cummins, R. (1975). 'Functional analysis', *Journal of Philosophy*, Vol. 72, No. 20, pp. 741–765.

D'Alfonso, S. (2011). 'On quantifying semantic information', *Information*, Vol. 2, No. 1, pp. 61–101.

Davies, M. (2003). 'The problem of armchair knowledge', in S. Nuccetelli (ed.), *New Essays on Semantic Externalism and Self-Knowledge*. Cambridge, MA: MIT Press, pp. 23–55.

(2004). 'Epistemic entitlement, warrant transmission, and easy knowledge', *Aristotelian Society Supplement*, Vol. 78, pp. 213–245.

Day, R. E. (2001/2008). *The Modern Invention of Information. Discourse, History, and Power*, Paperback Gricean edition. Carbondale: Southern Illinois University Press.

Dinneen, J. D. and Brauner, C. (2015). 'Practical and philosophical considerations for defining information as well-formed, meaningful data in the information sciences', *Library Trends*, Vol. 63, No. 3, pp. 378–400.

Dogramaci, S. and Horowitz, S. (2016). 'An argument for uniqueness about evidential support', *Philosophical Issues*, Vol. 26, No. 1, pp. 130–147.

Dretske, F. (1970). 'Epistemic operators', *Journal of Philosophy*, Vol. 67, pp. 1007–1023.

(1971). 'Conclusive reasons', *Australasian Journal of Philosophy*, Vol. 49, pp. 1–22.

(1981). *Knowledge and the Flow of Information*. Cambridge, MA: MIT Press.

(1983). 'Précis of knowledge and the flow of information', *The Behavioral and Brain Sciences*, Vol. 6, pp. 55–63.

(1988). *Explaining Behavior*. Cambridge, MA: MIT Press.

Dutant, J. and Littlejohn, C. (2021). 'Defeaters as indicators of ignorance', in J. Brown and M. Simion (eds.), *Reasons, Justification, and Defeat*. Oxford: Oxford University Press, pp. 223–246.

European Commission (2022). Code of Practice on Disinformation. Available at: https://digital-strategy.ec.europa.eu/en/policies/code-practice-disinformation#:~:text=The%20Code%20will%20strengthen%20the,challenges%20related%20to%20such%20techniques.

Evans, G. (1982). *Varieties of Reference*. Oxford: Clarendon Press.

Ewing, A. C. (1947). *The Definition of Good*. London: Macmillan.

Falbo, A. (2023). 'Should epistemology take the zetetic turn?', *Philosophical Studies*, Vol. 180, pp. 2977–3002.
Fallis, D. (2009). A Conceptual Analysis of Disinformation, Preprint from iConference, Tucson, AZ. Available at: www.ideals.illinois.edu/bitstream/handle/2142/15205/fallis_disinfo1.pdf?sequence=2.
  (2010). 'Lying and deception', *Philosophers' Imprint*, Vol. 10, No. 11, pp. 1–42.
  (2011). 'Floridi on disinformation', *Etica & Politica*, Vol. 13, No. 2, pp. 201–214.
  (2014). 'The varieties of disinformation', in L. Floridi and P. Illari (eds.), *The Philosophy of Information Quality*. Cham, Heidelberg, New York, Dordrecht, and London: Springer, pp. 135–161.
  (2015). 'What is disinformation?', *Library Trends*, Vol. 63, No. 3, pp. 401–426.
Fantl, J. (2018). *The Limitations of the Open Mind*. Oxford: Oxford University Press.
Fantl, J. and McGrath, M. (2002). 'Evidence, pragmatics, and justification', *Philosophical Review*, Vol. 111, pp. 67–94.
Feldman, R. (2000). 'The ethics of belief', *Philosophy and Phenomenological Research*, Vol. 60, No. 3, pp. 667–695.
  (2004). 'The ethics of belief', in E. Conee and R. Feldman (eds.), *Evidentialism*. Oxford: Oxford University Press, pp. 166–196.
  (2008). 'Modest deontologism in epistemology', *Synthese*, Vol. 161, pp. 339–355.
Fetzer, J. H. (2004a). 'Information: does it have to be true?', *Minds and Machines*, Vol. 14, pp. 223–229.
  (2004b). 'Disinformation: the use of false information', *Minds and Machines*, Vol. 14, pp. 231–240.
Flores, C. and Woodard, E. (2023). 'Epistemic norms on evidence gathering', *Philosophical Studies*, 180 (9), 2547–2571.
Floridi, L. (2004). 'Outline of a theory of strongly semantic information', *Minds and Machines*, Vol. 14, No. 2, pp. 197–221.
  (2005a). 'Is semantic information meaningful data?', *Philosophy and Phenomological Research*, Vol. LXX, No. 2, pp. 351–370.
  (2005b). 'Semantic conceptions of information', in E. N. Zalta (ed.), *Stanford Encyclopedia of Philosophy*, Spring 2013 edition. Palo Alto, CA: Stanford University. Available at: http://plato.stanford.edu/archives/spr2013/entries/information-semantic/.
  (2007). 'In defence of the veridical nature of semantic information', *European Journal of Analytic Philosophy (EUJAP)*, Vol. 3, No. 1, pp. 31–41.
  (2008). 'Trends in the philosophy of information', in P. Adriaans and J. van Benthem (eds.), *Philosophy of Information*. Amsterdam and Oxford: Elsevier B.V., pp. 113–131.
Floridi, L. (2011). *The Philosophy of Information*. Oxford: Oxford Scholarship Online. Available at: www.oxfordscholarship.com.
Foley, R. (1991). 'Evidence and reasons for belief', *Analysis*, Vol. 51, pp. 98–102.

Fox, C. J. (1983). *Information and Misinformation: An Investigation of the Notions of Information, Misinformation, Informing, and Misinforming.* Westport, CT, and London: Greenwood Press.

Frances, B. and Matheson, J. (2019). 'Disagreement', in E. N. Zalta (ed.), *The Stanford Encyclopedia of Philosophy*, winter 2019 edition. Palo Alto, CA: Stanford University. Available at: https://plato.stanford.edu/archives/win2019/entries/disagreement/.

Frické, M. (1997). 'Information using likeness measures', *Journal of the American Society for Information Science*, Vol. 48, No. 10, pp. 882–892.

Fricker, M. (2007). *Epistemic Injustice: Power & the Ethics of Knowing.* Oxford: Oxford University Press.

Friedman, J. (2017). 'Why suspend judging?', *Nous*, Vol. 51, pp. 302–326.

  (2020). 'The epistemic and the zetetic', *Philosophical Review*, Vol. 129, No. 4, pp. 501–536.

Furner, J. (2004). 'Information studies without information', *Library Trends*, Vol. 52, No. 3, pp. 427–446.

  (2010). 'Philosophy and information studies', *Annual Review of Information Science and Technology*, Vol. 44, No. 1, pp. 154–200.

  (2014). 'Information without information studies', in F. Ibekwe-SanJuan and T. M. Dousa (eds.), *Theories of Information, Communication and Knowledge.* Dordrecht, Heidelberg, New York, and London: Springer Science+Business Media B.V., pp. 143–179.

Garner, J. K. (2009). 'Conceptualizing the relations between executive functions and self-regulated learning', *Journal of Psychology*, Vol. 143, No. 4, pp. 405–426.

Geach, P. T. (1956). 'Good and evil', *Analysis*, Vol. 17, pp. 32–42.

Gendler, T. (2011). 'On the epistemic costs of implicit bias', *Philosophical Studies*, Vol. 156, No. 1, pp. 33–63.

Gerken, M. (2011). 'Warrant and action', *Synthese*, Vol. 178, pp. 529–547.

Gettier, E. L. (1963). 'Is justified true belief knowledge?', *Analysis*, Vol. 23, pp. 121–123.

Gillespie, T. (2014). 'The relevance of algorithms', in T. Gillespie, P. J. Boczkowski, and K. A. Foot (eds.), *Media Technologies: Essays on Communication, Materiality, and Society.* Cambridge, MA: MIT Press, pp. 167–193.

Gilovich, T., Griffin, D. W., and Kahneman, D. (eds.) (2002). *Heuristics and Biases: The Psychology of Intuitive Judgment.* Cambridge: Cambridge University Press.

Godfrey-Smith, P. (1989). 'Misinformation', *Canadian Journal of Philosophy*, Vol. 19, No. 4, pp. 533–550.

Goffey, A. (2008). 'Algorithm', in M. Fuller (ed.), *Software Studies: A Lexicon.* Cambridge, MA: MIT Press, pp. 15–20.

Goldberg, S. (2022). 'What is a speaker owed?', *Philosophy and Public Affairs*, Vol. 50, No. 3, pp. 375–407.

  (2016). 'On the epistemic significance of evidence you should have had', *Episteme*, Vol. 13, No. 4, pp. 449–470.

(2017). 'Should have known', *Synthese*, Vol. 194, pp. 2863–2894.
(2018). *To the Best of Our Knowledge: Social Expectations and Epistemic Normativity*. Oxford: Oxford University Press.
(2021). 'The normativity of knowledge and the scope and sources of defeat', in J. Brown and M. Simion (eds.), *Reasons, Justification, and Defeat*. Oxford: Oxford University Press, pp. 18–38.
Goldman, A. I. (1979). 'What is justified belief?', in G. Pappas (ed.), *Justification and Knowledge*. Boston, MA: D. Reidel, pp. 1–25.
(1988). 'Strong and weak justification', in J. Tomberlin (ed.), *Philosophical Perspectives*, Vol. 13. Atascadero, CA: Ridgeview, pp. 51–69.
Graham, P. (2010). 'Testimonial entitlement and the function of comprehension', in A. Haddock, A. Miller, and D. Pritchard (eds.), *Social Epistemology*. New York: Oxford University Press, pp. 148–174.
(2012). 'Epistemic entitlement', *Nous*, Vol. 46, No. 3, pp. 449–482.
(2014). 'Functions, warrant, history', in A. Fairweather and O. Flanagan (eds.), *Naturalizing Epistemic Virtue*. Cambridge: Cambridge University Press, pp. 15–35.
(2015). 'Epistemic normativity and social norms', in D. Henderson and J. Greco (eds.), *Epistemic Evaluation. Purposeful Epistemology*. Oxford: Oxford University Press, pp. 247–273.
Graham, P. and Lyons, J. (2021). 'The structure of defeat: Pollock's evidentialism, Lackey's framework, and prospects for reliabilism', in J. Brown and M. Simion (eds.), *Reasons, Justification, and Defeat*. Oxford: Oxford University Press, pp. 39–68.
Greco, D. and Hedden, B. (2016). 'Uniqueness and metaepistemology', *Journal of Philosophy*, Vol. 113, No. 8, pp. 365–395.
Grice, H. P. (1967/1989/1991a). 'Logic and conversation', *Studies in the Way of Words*, Paperback edition. Cambridge, MA, and London: First Harvard University Press, pp. 22–40.
(1967/1989/1991b). 'Meaning', in *Studies in the Way of Words*, Paperback edition. Cambridge, MA, and London: First Harvard University Press, pp. 213–223.
(1967/1989/1991c). *Studies in the Way of Words*, paperback edition. Cambridge, MA, and London: First Harvard University Press.
Griffin, B., McGaw, E., and Care, E. (eds.) (2012). *Assessment and Teaching of 21st Century Skills*. Dordrecht: Springer.
Grundmann, T. (2020). 'Fake news: the case for a purely consumer-oriented explication', *Inquiry*. DOI: 10.1080/0020174X.2020.1813195.
Halavais, A. (2004). The Isuzu experiment. Available from: http://alex.halavais.net/the-isuzu-experiment.
Hancock, J. T. (2007). 'Digital deception: when, where and how people lie online', in A. Joinson, K. McKenna, T. Postmes, and U.-D. Reips (eds.), *Oxford Handbook of Internet Psychology*. Oxford: Oxford University Press, pp. 289–301.
Harman, E. (2011). 'Does moral ignorance exculpate?', *Ratio*, Vol. 24, No. 4, pp. 443–468.

Haselton, M. G. (2007). 'Error management theory', in R. F. Baumeister and K. D. Vohs (eds.), *Encyclopedia of Social Psychology*, Vol. 1. Thousand Oaks, CA: SAGE Publications, pp. 311–312.

Haselton, M. G. and Buss, D. M. (2000). 'Error management theory: a new perspective on biases in cross-sex mindreading', *Journal of Personality and Social Psychology*, Vol. 78, No. 1, pp. 81–91.

(2009). 'Error management theory and the evolution of misbeliefs', *Behavioral and Brain Sciences*, Vol. 32, pp. 522–523.

Haselton, M. G. and Nettle, D. (2006). 'The paranoid optimist: an integrative evolutionary model of cognitive biases', *Personality and Social Psychology Review*, Vol. 10, pp. 47–66.

Hawthorne, J. (2004). *Knowledge and Lotteries*. Oxford: Oxford University Press.

Hawthorne, J. and Srinivasan, A. (2013). 'Disagreement without transparency: some bleak thoughts', in D. Christensen and J. Lackey (eds.), *The Epistemology of Disagreement: New Essays*. Oxford: Oxford University Press, pp. 9–30.

Hazlet, A. (2017). 'On the special insult of refusing testimony', *Philosophical Explorations*, Vol. 20, Suppl. 1, pp. 37–51.

Hernon, P. (1995). 'Disinformation and misinformation through the internet: findings of an exploratory study', *Government Information Quarterly*, Vol. 12, No. 2, pp. 133–139.

Hjørland, B. (2007). 'Information: objective or subjective/situational?', *Journal of the American Society for Information Science and Technology*, Vol. 58, No. 10, pp. 1448–1456.

Horowitz, S. (2014). 'Epistemic akrasia', *Nous*, Vol. 48, No. 4, pp. 718–744.

Huemer, M. (2007). 'Compassionate phenomenal conservatism', *Philosophy and Phenomenological Research*, Vol. 74, No. 1, pp. 30–55.

Hughes, N. (2019). 'Dilemmic epistemology', *Synthese*, Vol. 196, pp. 4059–4090.

Ichikawa, J. (2014). 'Justification is potential knowledge', *Canadian Journal of Philosophy*, Vol. 44, pp. 184–206.

(forthcoming). *Epistemic Courage*. Oxford: Oxford University Press.

Jackson, F. (1998). *From Metaphysics to Ethics*. New York: Oxford University Press.

Jenkins-Ichikawa, J. (2020). 'Contextual injustice', *Kennedy Institute for Ethics Journal*, Vol. 30, No. 1, pp. 1–30.

Jope, M. (2019). 'Closure, credence and rationality: a problem for non-belief hinge epistemology', *Synthese*, Vol. 198, pp. 3565–3575.

Kahan, D. (2013). 'Ideology, motivated reasoning, and cognitive reflection', *Judgement and Decision Making*, Vol. 8, pp. 407–424.

(2014). 'Making climate-science communication evidence-based – all the way down', in M. Boykoff and D. Crow (eds.), *Culture, Politics and Climate Change*. New York: Routledge, pp. 203–220.

Kahan, D., Hoffman, D., Evans, D., Devins, N., Lucci, E., and Cheng, K. (2016). '"Ideology" or "situation sense"? An experimental investigation of motivated reasoning and professional judgment', *University of Pennsylvania Law Review*, Vol. 164, No. 349, pp. 349–438.

Kahan, D., Jenkins-Smith, H., and Braman, D. (2011). 'Cultural cognition of scientific consensus', *Journal of Risk Research*, Vol. 14, No. 2, pp. 147–174.

Kahneman, D., Slovic, P., and Tversky, A. (eds.) (1982), *Judgment Under Uncertainty: Heuristics and Biases*. Cambridge: Cambridge University Press.

Karlova, N. A. and Fisher, K. E. (2013). 'A social diffusion model of misinformation and disinformation for understanding human information behavior', *Information Research*, Vol. 18, No. 1, p. 573.

Kearney, M. D., Chiang, S. C., and Massey, P. M. (2020). 'The Twitter origins and evolution of the COVID-19 "plandemic" conspiracy theory', *Harvard Kennedy School Misinformation Review*, Vol. 1, No. 3. DOI: 10.37016/mr-2020-42.

Kelly, T. (2010). 'Peer disagreement and higher-order evidence', in R. Feldman and T. A. Warfield (eds.), *Disagreement*. Oxford: Oxford University Press, pp. 111–174.

  (2016). 'Evidence', in E. N. Zalta (ed.), *Stanford Encyclopedia of Philosophy*, winter 2016 edition. Palo Alto, CA: Stanford University. Available at: https://plato.stanford.edu/archives/win2016/entries/evidence/.

Kelp, C. (2018). *Good Thinking: A Knowledge-First Virtue Epistemology*. New York: Routledge.

  (2019). 'Inquiry and the transmission of knowledge', *Philosophy and Phenomenological Research*, Vol. 99, pp. 298–310.

  (2020). 'Internalism, phenomenal conservatism, and defeat', *Philosophical Issues*, Vol. 30, pp. 192–204.

  (2021). *Inquiry, Knowledge, Understanding*. Oxford: Oxford University Press.

  (2022). 'Defeat and proficiencies'. *Philosophical Issues*, Vol. 32, pp. 82–103.

  (2023). *The Nature and Normativity of Defeat*. Cambridge: Cambridge University Press.

Kelp, C. and Simion, M. (2017). 'Criticism and blame in action and assertion', *Journal of Philosophy*, Vol. 114, No. 2, pp. 76–93.

  (2021a). *Sharing Knowledge: A Functionalist Account of Assertion*. Cambridge: Cambridge University Press.

  (2021b). *What Is Normative Defeat?* Manuscript.

  (2023a). 'What is trustworthiness?', *Nous*, Vol. 57, No. 3, pp. 667–683.

  (2023b). *Justification as the Proper Route to Knowledge*. Manuscript.

Klintman, M. (2019). *Knowledge Resistance: How We Avoid Insight from Others*. Manchester: Manchester University Press.

Kornblith, H. (2001). 'Epistemic obligation and the possibility of internalism', in A. Fairweather and L. Zagzebski (eds.), *Virtue Epistemology: Essays on Epistemic Virtue and Responsibility*. New York: Oxford University Press, pp. 231–248.

  (2015). 'The role of reasons in epistemology', *Episteme*, Vol. 12, No. 2, pp. 225–239.

Kotzen, M. (2019). 'A formal account of epistemic defeat', in B. Fitelson, R. Borges, and C. Branden (eds.), *Themes from Klein: Knowledge, Scepticism, and Justification*. Synthese Library 404. New York: Springer, pp. 213–234.

Kraut, R. (1980). 'Humans as lie detectors: some second thoughts', *Journal of Communication*, Vol. 30, pp. 209–216.

Krohs, U. and Kroes, P. (eds.) (2009). *Functions in Biological and Artificial Worlds.* Cambridge, MA: MIT Press.

Kroon, F (1993). 'Rationality and epistemic paradox', *Synthese*, Vol. 84, pp. 377–408.

Kumar, K. P. K. and Geethakumari, G. (2014). 'Detecting misinformation in online social networks using cognitive psychology', *Human-Centric Computing and Information Sciences*, Vol. 4, No. 1, pp. 1–22.

Kunda, Z. (1987). 'Motivated inference: self-serving generation and evaluation of causal theories', *Journal of Personality and Social Psychology*, Vol. 53, No. 4, pp. 636–647.

Kunst, H., Groot, D., Latthe, P. M., Latthe, M., and Khan, K. S. (2002). 'Accuracy of information on apparently credible websites: survey of five common health topics', *British Medical Journal*, Vol. 324, No. 7337, pp. 581–582.

Lackey, J. (2006). 'Knowing from testimony', *Philosophy Compass*, Vol. 1, No. 5, pp. 432–448.

(2008). *Learning from Words*. Oxford: Oxford University Press.

(2011). 'Assertion and isolated second hand knowledge', in J. Brown and H. Cappelen (eds.), *Assertion: New Philosophical Essays*. Oxford: Oxford University Press, pp. 251–276.

(2014). 'Deficient testimonial knowledge', in T. Henning and D. Schweikard (eds.), *Knowledge, Virtue and Action*. London: Routledge, pp. 30–52.

(2018). 'Credibility and the distribution of epistemic goods', in K. McCain (ed.), *Believing in Accordance with the Evidence: New Essays on Evidentialism*. New York: Springer, pp. 145–168.

(2020). 'The duty to object', *Philosophy and Phenomenological Research*, Vol. 101, No. 1, pp. 35–60.

Lasonen-Aarnio, M. (2010). 'Unreasonable knowledge', *Philosophical Perspectives*, Vol. 24, pp. 1–21.

(2014). 'Higher-order evidence and the limits of defeat', *Philosophy and Phenomenological Research*, Vol. 88, pp. 314–345.

Leonard, N. (2020). 'Epistemic dilemmas and rational indeterminacy', *Philosophical Studies*, Vol. 177, No. 3, pp. 573–596.

(2023). 'Epistemological problems of testimony', in E. N. Zalta and U. Nodelman (eds.), *Stanford Encyclopedia of Philosophy*, spring 2023 edition. Palo Alto, CA: Stanford University. Available at: https://plato.stanford.edu/archives/spr2023/entries/testimony-episprob/.

Levine, T. R., Park, H. S., and McCornack, S. A. (1999). 'Accuracy in detecting truths and lies: documenting the "veracity effect"', *Communication Monographs*, Vol. 66, No. 2, pp. 125–144.

Levinson, P. (2017). 'Fake news in real context', *Explorations in Media Ecology*, Vol. 18, No. 1, pp. 173–177.

Levy, N. (2021). *Bad Beliefs: Why They Happen to Good People*. Oxford: Oxford University Press.

Littlejohn, C. (2020). 'A plea for epistemic excuses', in F. Dorsch and J. Dutant (eds.), *The New Evil Demon Problem*. Oxford: Oxford University Press.

Littlejohn, C. and Turri, J. (2015). *Epistemic Norms*. Oxford: Oxford University Press.
Lord, C. G., Ross, L., and Lepper, M. R. (1979). 'Biased assimiliation and attitude polarization: the effects of prior theories on subsequently considered evidence', *Journal of Personality and Social Psychology*, Vol. 37, No. 11, pp. 2098–2109.
Lord, E. and Sylvan, K. (2021). 'Suspension, higher-order evidence, and defeat', in J. Brown and M. Simion (eds.), *Reasons, Justification, and Defeat*, Oxford: Oxford University Press, pp. 116–145.
  (2022). 'On suspending properly', in L. R. G. Oliveira and P. Silva (eds.), *Propositional and Doxastic Justification*. London: Routledge, ch. 9, pp. 141–161.
Lovden, M., Backman, L., Lindenberger, U., Schaefer, S., and Schmiedek, F. (2010). 'A theoretical framework for the study of adult cognitive plasticity', *Psychological Bulletin*, Vol. 136, No. 4, pp. 659–676.
Lynch, C. A. (2001). 'When documents deceive: trust and provenance as new factors for information retrieval in a tangled web', *Journal of the American Society for Information Science and Technology*, Vol. 52, No. 1, pp. 12–17.
Lyons, J. (2011). 'Circularity, reliability, and the cognitive penetrability of perception', *Philosophical Issues*, Vol. 21, No. 1, pp. 289–311.
Mahon, J. (2008). 'The definition of lying and deception', in E. N. Zalta (ed.), *Stanford Encyclopedia of Philosophy*, fall 2019 edition. Palo Alto, CA: Stanford University. Available at: http://plato.stanford.edu/archives/fall2009/entries/lying-definition/.
Mai, J.-E. (2013). 'The quality and qualities of information', *Journal of the American Society for Information Science and Technology*, Vol. 64, No. 4, pp. 675–688.
Maitra, I. (2011). 'Assertion, norms, and games', in J. Brown and H. Cappelen (eds.), *Assertion: New Philosophical Essays*. Oxford: Oxford University Press, pp. 277–296.
Matheson, J. (2011). 'The case for rational uniqueness', *Logos & Episteme*, Vol. 2, No. 3, pp. 359–373.
McConnell, T. (2018). 'Moral dilemmas', in E. N. Zalta (ed.), *Stanford Encyclopedia of Philosophy*, fall 2018 edition. Palo Alto, CA: Stanford University. Available at: https://plato.stanford.edu/archives/fall2018/entries/moral-dilemmas/.
McGrath, M. (2013). 'Phenomenal conservatism and cognitive penetration: the "bad basis" counterexamples', in C. Tucker (ed.), *Seemings and Justification*. New York: Oxford University Press, pp. 225–247.
McNally, L. (2016). 'Modification', M. Aloni and P. Dekker (eds.), *Cambridge Handbook of Formal Semantics*. Cambridge: Cambridge University Press, pp. 442–466.
McNamara, P. and Van De Putte, F. (2022). 'Deontic logic', in E. N. Zalta and U. Nodelman (eds.), *Stanford Encyclopedia of Philosophy*, fall 2022 edition. Palo Alto, CA: Stanford University. Available at: https://plato.stanford.edu/archives/fall2022/entries/logic-deontic/.

Mearsheimer, J. J. (2011). *Why Leaders Lie*. New York: Oxford University Press.
Melnyk, A. (2008). 'Conceptual and linguistic analysis: a two-step program', *Noûs*, Vol. 42, No. 2, pp. 267–291.
Mercier, H. (2020). *Not Born Yesterday. The Science of Who We Trust and What We Believe*. Princeton, NJ: Princeton University Press.
Millikan, R. G. (1984). *Language, Thought, and Other Biological Categories*. Cambridge, MA: MIT Press.
Mingers, J. C. (1995). 'Information and meaning: foundations for an intersubjective account', *Information Systems Journal*, Vol. 5, No. 4, pp. 285–306.
Miracchi, L. (2015). 'Competence to know', *Philosophical Studies*, Vol. 172, No. 1, pp. 29–56.
  (2017). 'When evidence isn't enough: suspension, evidentialism, and knowledge-first virtue epistemology', *Episteme*, Vol. 16, No. 4, pp. 413–437.
Miscevic, N. (2016). 'Epistemic value. Curiosity, knowledge and response-dependence', *Croatian Journal of Philosophy*, Vol. 16, pp. 393–417.
  (2017). 'Curiosity – the basic epistemic virtue', in C. Mi, M. Slote, and E. Sosa (eds.), *Moral and Intellectual Virtues in Western and Chinese Philosophy*. London: Routledge, pp. 144–163.
Molden, D. C. and Higgins, E. T. (2012). 'Motivated thinking', in K. J. Holyoak and R. G. Morrison (eds.), *The Oxford Handbook of Thinking and Reasoning*. Oxford: Oxford University Press, pp. 390–409.
Monmonier, M. (1991). *How to Lie with Maps*. Chicago, IL: University of Chicago Press.
Montmarquet, J. (1993). *Epistemic Virtue and Doxastic Responsibility*. Lanham, MD: Rowman and Littlefield.
Moore, G. E. (1939). 'Proof of an external world', *Proceedings of the British Academy*, Vol. 25, pp. 273–300.
  (1993). *Principia Ethica*, revised edition. Cambridge: Cambridge University Press.
Moran, R. (2006). 'Getting told and being believed', *The Philosopher's Imprint*, Vol. 5, No. 5, pp. 1–29.
Nagel, J. (2010). 'Epistemic anxiety and adaptive invariantism', *Philosophical Perspectives*, Vol. 24, No. 1, pp. 407–435.
Neander, K. (1991). 'The teleological notion of function', *Australasian Journal of Philosophy*, Vol. 69, pp. 454–468.
Nesta, F. and Blanke, H. (1991). 'Warning: propaganda!', *Library Journal*, Vol. 116, No. 9, pp. 41–43.
Newman, M. L., Pennebaker, J. W., Berry, D. S., and Richards, J. M. (2003). 'Lying words: predicting deception from linguistic styles', *Personality and Social Psychology Bulletin*, Vol. 29, No. 5, pp. 665–675.
Nisbett, R. and Ross, L. (1980). *Human Inference: Strategies and Shortcomings of Social Judgment*. Hoboken, NJ: Prentice-Hall.
Odegard, D. (1993). 'Resolving epistemic dillemas', *Australasian Journal of Philosophy*, Vol. 71, No. 2, pp. 161–168.
PHEME (2014). About PHEME. Available at: www.pheme.eu.

Piper, P. S. (2002). 'Web hoaxes, counterfeit sites, and other spurious information on the Internet', in A. P. Mintz (ed.), *Web of Deception*. Medford, NJ: Information Today, pp. 1–22.

Plantinga, A. (2000). *Warranted Christian Belief*. New York: Oxford University Press.

Pollock, J. (1986). *Contemporary Theories of Knowledge*. Savage, MD: Rowman and Littlefield.

Pratchett, T., Stewart, I., and Cohen, J. (1999). *The Science of Discworld*. London: Ebury Press.

Primiero, G. (2016). 'Information in the philosophy of computer science', in L. Floridi (ed.), *The Routledge Handbook of Philosophy of Information*, London: Routledge, pp. 151–175.

Pritchard, D. (2015). *Epistemic Angst: Radical Skepticism and the Groundlessness of Our Believing*. Princeton, NJ: Princeton University Press.

Pryor, J. (2000). 'The skeptic and the dogmatist', *Nous*, Vol. 34, pp. 517–549.
  (2004). 'What's wrong with Moore's argument?', *Philosophical Issues*, Vol. 14, pp. 349–378.
  (2012). 'When warrant transmits', in A. Coliva (ed.), *Mind, Meaning, and Knowledge: Themes from the Philosophy of Crispin Wright*. Oxford: Oxford University Press, pp. 269–303.

Rabinowicz, W. and Rönnow-Rasmussen, T. (2004). 'The strike of the demon: on fitting pro-attitudes and value', *Ethics*, Vol. 114, pp. 391–423.

Raleigh, T. (2017). 'Another argument against uniqueness', *Philosophical Quarterly*, Vol. 67, No. 267, pp. 327–346.

Reddy, S. (2013). '"I don't smoke, doc," and other patient lies', *Wall Street Journal*. Available at: http://online.wsj.com/article/SB10001424127887323478004578306510461212692.html.

Richter, R. (1990). 'Ideal rationality and handwaving', *Australasian Journal of Philosophy*, Vol. 68, pp. 147–156.

Roberts, R. and Wood, W. (2007). *Intellectual Virtues: An Essay in Regulative Epistemology*. Oxford: Clarendon Press.

Robinson, L. and Bawden, D. (2014). 'Mind the gab: transitions between concepts of information in varied domains', in F. Ibekwe-SanJuan and T. M. Dousa (eds.), *Theories of Information, Communication and Knowledge*. Dordrecht, Heidelberg, New York, and London: Springer Science + Business Media B.V., pp. 121–141.

Rowe, M. W. (2012). 'The problem of perfect fakes', *Royal Institute of Philosophy Supplements*, Vol. 71, pp. 151–175.

Rubin, V. L. and Conroy, N. (2012). 'Discerning truth from deception: human judgments and automation efforts', *First Monday*, Vol. 17, No. 3. Available at: http://firstmonday.org/ojs/index.php/fm/article/view/3933/3170.

Rudy-Hiller, F. (2018). 'The epistemic condition for moral responsibility', in E. N. Zalta (ed.), *Stanford Encyclopedia of Philosophy*, fall 2018 edition. Palo Alto, CA: Stanford University. Available at: https://plato.stanford.edu/archives/fall2018/entries/moral-responsibility-epistemic/.

Ryan, S. (2003). 'Doxastic compatibilism and the ethics of belief', *Philosophical Studies*, Vol. 114, No. 1/2, pp. 47–79.
Sandvig, C. (2015). 'Seeing the sort: the aesthetic and industrial defense of "the algorithm"', *Journal of the New Media Caucus*. Available at: http://median.newmediacaucus.org/art-infrastructures-information/seeing-the-sort-the-aesthetic-and-industrial-defense-of-the-algorithm/.
Sassenberg, K., Winter, K., Becker, D., Ditrich, L., Scholl, A., and Moskowitz, G. (2022). 'Flexibility mindsets: reducing biases that result from spontaneous processing', *European Review of Social Psychology*, Vol. 33, No. 1, pp. 171–213.
Scanlon, T. (1998). *What We Owe to Each Other*. Cambridge, MA: Harvard University Press.
Scarantino, A. and Piccinini, G. (2010). 'Information without truth', *Metaphilosophy*, Vol. 41, No. 3, pp. 313–330.
Schauer, F. and Zeckhauser, R. (2009). 'Paltering', in B. Harrington (ed.), *Deception: From Ancient Empires to Internet Dating*. Palo Alto, CA: Stanford University Press, pp. 38–54.
Schellenberg, S. (2018). *The Unity of Perception: Content, Consciousness, Evidence*. Oxford: Oxford University Press.
Schroeder, M. (2012). 'Value theory', in E. N. Zalta (ed.), *Stanford Encyclopedia of Philosophy*, summer 2012 edition. Palo Alto, CA: Stanford University. Available at: http://plato.stanford.edu/archives/sum2012/entries/value-theory/.
Shannon, C. E. (1948). 'A mathematical theory of communication', *The Bell System Technical Journal*, Vol. 27, pp. 379–423.
Shao, C., Ciampaglia, G. L., Flammini, A., and Menczer, F. (2016). 'Hoaxy: a platform for tracking online misinformation', WWW'16 Companion, Montréal and Québec, 11–15 April, pp. 745–750. Available at: http://dx.doi.org/10.1145/2872518.2890098.
Sidgwick, H. (1907). *The Methods of Ethics*, 7th edition. Indianapolis, IN: Hackett.
Siegel, S. (2012). 'Cognitive penetrability and perceptual justification', *Nous*, Vol. 46, No. 2, pp. 201–222.
  (2017). *The Rationality of Perception*. Oxford: Oxford University Press.
Silins, N. (2005). 'Deception and evidence', in J. Hawthorne (ed.), *Philosophical Perspectives, Vol. 19, Epistemology*. Oxford: Blackwell, pp. 375–404.
Simion, M. (2016). 'Perception, history and benefit', *Episteme*, Vol. 13, No. 1, pp. 61–76.
  (2018a). 'The explanation proffering norm of moral assertion', *Ethical Theory and Moral Practice*, Vol. 21, No. 3, pp. 477–488.
  (2018b). 'No epistemic norm for action', *American Philosophical Quarterly*, Vol. 55, No. 3, pp. 231–238.
  (2019a). 'Knowledge-first functionalism', *Philosophical Issues*, Vol. 29, No. 1, pp. 254–267.
  (2019b). 'Saying and believing: the norm commonality assumption', *Philosophical Studies*, Vol. 176, No. 8, pp. 1951–1966.

(2019c). 'Assertion: the context shiftiness dilemma', *Mind & Language*, Vol. 34, pp. 503–517.
(2020). 'A priori perceptual entitlement, knowledge-first', *Philosophical Issues*, Vol. 30, No. 1, pp. 311–323.
(2021a). *Shifty Speech and Independent Thought: Epistemic Normativity in Context*. Oxford: Oxford University Press.
(2021b). 'Testimonial contractarianism: a knowledge-first social epistemology', *Nous*, Vol. 55, No. 4, pp. 891–916.
(2021c). 'Knowledge and reasoning', *Synthese*, Vol. 199, pp. 10371–10388.
(2022a). 'Review of Juan Comesana, *Being Rational and Being Right*, Oxford University Press 2020', *Mind*, Vol. 131, No. 523, pp. 1007–1017.
(2022b). 'Sosa on permissible suspension. Book Symposium on Ernest Sosa's "Epistemic Explanations: A Theory of Telic Normativity"', *Res Philosophica*, Vol. 99, No. 4, pp. 453–466.
(2023a). 'Resistance to evidence and the duty to believe', *Philosophy and Phenomenological Research*. DOI: 10.1111/phpr.12964.
(2023b). 'Knowledge and disinformation', *Episteme*. DOI: 10.1017/epi.2023.25.
(forthcoming). 'Defeat', in K. Sylvan (ed.), *The Blackwell Companion to Epistemology*. Hoboken, NJ: Wiley-Blackwell.
Simion, M. and Kelp, C. (2017). 'Commodious knowledge', *Synthese*, Vol. 194, No. 5, pp. 1487–1502.
(forthcoming). 'Information, misinformation, and disinformation: a knowledge-first account', in M. Popa-Wyatt (ed.), *Vices of the Mind: Mis/Disinformation and Other Epistemic Pathologies*. Cambridge: Cambridge University Press.
Simion, M., Kelp, C., and Ghijsen, H. (2016). 'Norms of belief', *Philosophical Issues*, Vol. 26, No. 1, pp. 375–392.
Simion, M., Schnurr, J., and Gordon, E. (2021). 'Epistemic norms, closure, and no-belief hinge epistemology'. *Synthese*, Vol. 198, pp. 3353–3564.
Skinner, S. and Martin, B. (2000). 'Racist disinformation on the World Wide Web: initial implications for the LIS community', *The Australian Library Journal*, Vol. 49, No. 3, pp. 259–269.
Skyrms, B. (2010). *Signals: Evolution, Learning, and Information*. Oxford: Oxford University Press.
Slote, M. (1989). *Beyond Optimizing*. Cambridge, MA: Harvard University Press.
Sober, E. (1994). *From a Biological Point of View: Essays in Evolutionary Philosophy*. New York: Cambridge University Press.
Søe, S. O. (2016). 'The urge to detect, the need to clarify. Gricean perspectives on information, misinformation, and disinformation', PhD thesis, Faculty of Humanities, University of Copenhagen.
Sorensen, R. (1987). 'Anti-expertise, instability, and rational choice', Australasian Journal of Philosophy, Vol. 65, pp. 301–315.
Sosa, E. (2016). *Judgment and Agency*. Oxford: Oxford University Press.
(2021). *Epistemic Explanations*. Oxford: Oxford University Press.

(2022). 'On epistemic explanations: responses to two critics', *Res Philosophica*, Vol. 99, No. 4, pp. 475–483.
Sowards, S. W. (1988). 'Historical fabrications in library collections', *Collection Management*, Vol. 10, No. 3–4, pp. 81–88.
Sperber, D., Clement, F., Heintz, C., Mascaro, O., Mercier, H., Origgi, G., and Wilson, D. (2010). 'Epistemic vigilance', *Mind & Language*, Vol. 25, No. 4, pp. 359–393.
Staffel, J. (2023). 'Transitional attitudes and the unmooring view of higher order evidence', *Nous*, Vol. 57, No. 1, pp. 238–260.
Steup, M. (2000). 'Doxastic voluntarism and epistemic deontology', *Acta Analytica*, Vol. 15, pp. 25–56.
  (2008). 'Doxastic freedom', *Synthese*, Vol. 161, No. 3, pp. 375–392.
Stokke, A. (2013). 'Lying, deceiving, and misleading', *Philosophy Compass*, Vol. 8, No. 4, pp. 348–359.
Striphas, T. (2015). 'Algorithmic culture', *European Journal of Cultural Studies*, Vol. 18, No. 4–5, pp. 395–412.
Sturgeon, S. (2014). 'Pollock on defeasible reasons', *Philosophical Studies*, Vol. 169, No. 1, pp. 105–118.
Styron, W. (1979) *Sophie's Choice*. New York: Random House
Sudduth, M. (2018). Defeaters in epistemology. Internet Encyclopaedia of Philosophy. Available at: www.iep.utm.edu/ep-defea/#SH1b.
Sullivan-Bisset, E. (2017). 'Malfunction defended', *Synthese*, Vol. 194, No. 7, pp. 2501–2522.
Sutton, J. (2005). 'Stick to what you know', *Nous*, Vol. 39, No. 3, pp. 359–396.
  (2007). *Beyond Justification*. Cambridge, MA: MIT Press.
Sylvan, K. (2022). 'Suspending properly' (with E. Lord), in L. R. G. Oliveira and P. Silva (eds.), *Propositional and Doxastic Justification*. London: Routledge, pp. 137–158.
Sylvan, K. and Lord, E. (2021). 'Suspension, higher-order evidence, and defeat', (with E. Lord), in J. Brown and M. Simion (eds.), *Reasons, Justification, and Defeat*. Oxford: Oxford University Press, pp. 116–145.
Sylvan, K. and Sosa, E. (2018). 'The place of reasons in epistemology', in D. Star (ed.), *The Oxford Handbook of Reasons and Normativity*, Oxford: Oxford University Press, pp. 555–574.
Taber, C. S. and Lodge, M. (2006). 'Motivated skepticism in the evaluation of political beliefs,' *American Journal of Political Science*, Vol. 50, No. 3, pp. 755–769.
Tanesini, A. (2021). *The Mismeasure of the Self: A Study in Vice Epistemology*. Oxford: Oxford University Press.
Tappin, B. M., Pennycook, G., and Rand, D. G. (2021). 'Rethinking the link between cognitive sophistication and politically motivated reasoning', *Journal of Experimental Psychology: General*, Vol. 150, No. 6, pp. 1095–1114.
The Π Research Network (2013). *The Philosophy of Information – An Introduction, Version 1.0*. The Society for the Philosophy of Information.

Thorstad, D. (2021). 'Inquiry and the epistemic', *Philosophical Studies*, 178 (9), 2913–2928.
Thorson, E. (2016). 'Belief echoes: the persistent effects of corrected misinformation', *Political Communication*, Vol. 33, No. 3, pp. 460–480.
Tullock, G. (1967). *Toward a Mathematics of Politics*. Ann Arbor: University of Michigan Press.
Turri, J. (2010). 'On the relationship between propositional and doxastic justification', *Philosophy and Phenomenological Research*, Vol. LXXX, No. 2, pp. 312–326.
Twain, M. (2002). 'My first lie, and how I got out of it', in *The Man That Corrupted Hadleyburg*. New York: Prometheus Books, pp. 159–170 (original work published 1900).
Vermaas, P. E. and Houkes, W. (2003). 'Ascribing functions to technical artefacts: a challenge to etiological accounts of functions', *British Journal for the Philosophy of Science*, Vol. 54, pp. 261–289.
Vrij, A. (2000). *Detecting Lies and Deceit: The Psychology of Lying and the Implications for Professional Practice*. New York: Wiley.
  (2008). *Detecting Lies and Deceit: Pitfalls and Opportunities*, 2nd edition. Chichester: Wiley.
Walsh, J. (2010). 'Librarians and controlling disinformation: is multi-literacy instruction the answer?', *Library Review*, Vol. 59, No. 7, pp. 498–511.
Wardle, C. (2016). '(M|D)isinformation reading list', *First Draft News*. Available at: https://firstdraftnews.com/misinformation-reading-list/.
Wardle, C. (2017). 'Fake news. It's complicated', *First Draft News*. Available at: https://firstdraftnews.com/fake-news-complicated/.
Webber, J. (2013). 'Liar!', *Analysis*, Vol. 73, No. 4, pp. 651–659.
Whitcomb, D. (2017). 'One kind of asking', *The Philosophical Quarterly*, 67 (266), 148–168.
White, R. (2005). 'Epistemic permissiveness', *Philosophical Perspectives*, Vol. 19, pp. 445–459.
Whitty, M. T., Buchanan, T., Joinson, A. N., and Meredith, A. (2012). 'Not all lies are spontaneous: an examination of deception across different modes of communication', *Journal of the American Society for Information Science and Technology*, Vol. 63, No. 1, pp. 208–216.
Willard-Kyle, C. (2023). 'The knowledge norm for inquiry', *Journal of Philosophy*, 120 (11): 615–640.
Williamson, T. (2000). *Knowledge and Its Limits*. Oxford: Oxford University Press.
  (2007). 'Knowledge and scepticism', in F. Jackson and M. Smith (eds.), *The Oxford Handbook of Contemporary Philosophy*. Oxford: Oxford University Press, pp. 681–700.
  (forthcominga). 'Justifications, excuses, and sceptical scenarios', in F. Dorsch and J. Dutant (eds.), *The New Evil Demon*. Oxford: Oxford University Press.

(forthcomingb). 'Epistemological ambivalence', in N. Hughes (ed.), *Epistemic Dilemmas*. Oxford: Oxford University Press.

Worsnip, A. (2015). 'The conflict of evidence and coherence', *Philosophy and Phenomenological Research*, Vol. 96, pp. 3–44.

(2018). 'The conflict of evidence and coherence', *Philosophy and Phenomenological Research*, Vol. 96, No. 1, pp. 3–44.

Wright, C. (2002). '(Anti-)sceptics simple and subtle: Moore and McDowell', *Philosophy and Phenomenological Research*, Vol. 65, pp. 330–348.

(2003). 'Some reflections on the acquisition of warrant by inference', in S. Nuccetelli (ed.), *New Essays on Semantic Externalism and Self-Knowledge*. Cambridge, MA: MIT Press, pp. 57–77.

(2004). 'Warrant for nothing (and foundations for free)?', *Aristotelian Society Supplementary Volume*, Vol. 78, No. 1, pp. 167–212.

Zagzebski, L. (1996). *Virtues of the Mind: An Inquiry into the Nature of Virtue and the Ethical Foundations of Knowledge*. Cambridge: Cambridge University Press.

Zimmerman, M. (1997). 'Moral responsibility and ignorance', *Ethics*, Vol. CVII, pp. 410–426.

Index

belief, 1, 3, 9–10, 14, 16, 21, 25–26, 28–29, 32–34, 38–39, 43–44, 48–49, 52–53, 57–58, 62–63, 65, 70, 79–82, 84–85, 87, 90, 95–96, 98, 101–102, 104–109, 111–113, 117, 119, 121–122, 124–125, 127–129, 132, 134, 138–140, 156–161, 163, 165, 168–172, 174–176, 178, 184, 186, 188, 190
blame, 3, 33, 36, 46, 57, 70, 103, 154, 161, 189
blameless, 46, 122
blameworthy, 46, 161
Brown, xii, 73, 120–122, 126, 167, 171

climate, 1, 3, 10, 13, 48–50, 90, 132, 184, 189–190, 193
closure, 5, 125, 165–167, 176
cognitive architecture, 97, 113–114, 123
cognitive process, 106, 114, 128, 145, 147, 185
cognitive system, 20, 101, 109, 119, 133, 137, 166, 175
cogniser, 10, 16, 27, 30, 34, 69, 96, 113–114, 117, 123, 125, 132, 141

defeat, 2, 4–5, 9, 17, 19, 21, 28, 34, 36, 40, 54–55, 57–58, 63, 65, 67, 95, 103, 107–108, 110, 115, 124–130, 132–133, 135–139, 145, 147, 156–158, 160–161, 163, 165, 167–170, 173–174, 177, 186–188, 190, 194–196
defeater, 19, 48, 124, 126, 130, 134, 174, 176
dilemma, 5, 61, 97, 104, 133, 146, 151–153, 155–158, 160–164
disinformation, 2, 6, 178–192, 195–196
disposition, 34, 50, 69, 79, 109, 154, 161, 185, 187, 190, 192, 195
doxastic, 4, 21, 33, 49, 62, 78, 96, 98, 107, 111, 124, 133, 138, 140–141, 158, 160, 167, 169–170, 172–173, 187, 190
Dretske, 165, 176, 182–184

E = K, 2, 23, 25, 27, 29, 35, 44, 117–118, 120
epistemic, 1–6, 9, 11–17, 19–20, 22–23, 26, 28, 31–32, 34–46, 48, 52–57, 59–66, 68–81, 83–91, 95–97, 99, 101–103, 105–109, 111, 113, 115–117, 119, 121, 124–125, 128–129, 131, 134–136, 138–139, 142–143, 145–147, 151–152, 155–158, 160–167, 172, 174–175, 177–179, 186, 189–190, 192–196
epistemic dilemmas, 5, 151
epistemic norm, 73, 76, 84, 136, 143, 174
epistemic normativity, 2–3, 9, 31–32, 34, 36, 39, 42, 44, 56–57, 80–82, 95, 97, 99, 103–105, 116, 136
epistemic responsibility, 2, 4, 9, 68
evidence, 1–6, 9–12, 14–17, 19–21, 23–34, 36–40, 43–46, 48–50, 54, 58, 60–63, 68–72, 76–77, 79, 82, 85, 87, 89–91, 95–97, 103, 106–109, 111–113, 115–122, 124–125, 128–130, 132–133, 136–145, 147, 151, 156–160, 162–163, 165, 168–170, 172–173, 176, 178, 180–181, 186–190, 192–196
evidence one should have had, 3, 36–38, 136
evidence resistance, 2–3, 9, 12, 16–17, 19, 21, 23–25, 38, 48–50, 54, 60, 68–72, 77, 79, 87, 89, 91, 95, 117, 119, 128–129, 132, 192–195
evidential probability, 112, 119, 130, 137, 174, 187, 196

factive, 2, 23, 28–29, 179–181
function, 2, 4, 6, 24, 71, 81, 95, 99–105, 108–112, 114, 116–117, 119, 122, 132, 134, 136, 138–139, 141, 147, 159, 168, 178, 183, 185–186, 189, 194
functionalism, 99, 104–105

generating knowledge, 101, 103, 105, 117, 119, 122, 137–138, 141, 186
Goldberg, xii, xiv, 1, 3, 36–45, 96, 117, 134, 136, 171
Graham, xii, 84, 99–100, 105, 116, 124, 171, 185

indicator, 3, 23, 30–31, 35, 112–113, 173
information, 6, 13–15, 27, 38, 40–43, 77, 106, 109, 113–114, 125, 130, 146, 169, 171, 178–185, 189–190, 192
input-level malfunctioning, 4, 95
internalism, 29, 35, 78, 80–82, 125

Jenkins-Ichikawa, xii, 1, 96

Kahan, 9, 11–12
Kelp, xii–xiv, 27, 32, 34, 44, 96, 122, 124, 126, 139, 144, 166, 177, 185–186, 192
knowledge, 1–5, 9, 11, 13, 16, 25–26, 32, 35, 45, 48–51, 53–54, 56, 59–61, 63–64, 66, 73, 77, 81–83, 86–88, 90–91, 95, 97, 101–102, 105, 110–114, 117, 119–122, 124–125, 130, 132–133, 137–138, 141, 145, 147, 157, 160, 163, 165–167, 173, 177–178, 182, 184–188, 190, 192, 196
knowledge resistance, 9
Kornblith, 1, 96, 98

Lackey, xii, 1, 54, 73, 96, 117, 167

malfunction, 2, 4, 20, 95, 109, 111, 135, 166, 173, 177, 195
Miracchi, xii, 32, 49, 59–62, 67, 122
misinformation, 6, 14, 178–179, 181–184, 191
Moore, 84, 165–167, 169–177
Moorean, 5, 165–168, 172, 176
moral, 3–5, 21, 36, 45–46, 48, 62, 65, 68, 71–72, 74–77, 83, 86–88, 90–91, 103, 110, 127, 151–152, 154–155, 161, 175
moral norm, 76, 155

norm, 37–38, 40, 49–50, 73–76, 80–81, 83, 85, 99, 104, 106, 135, 143–144, 147, 152–155, 161–162, 175
normative, 1–6, 9, 21, 28–29, 32–33, 35–42, 44–46, 48, 51–52, 54–56, 58, 62–63, 65–66, 72–73, 76–77, 80, 82–83, 87, 89, 91, 95, 97–99, 102–104, 106–108, 111, 115, 117, 119, 124–128, 130–131, 133, 135, 137–138, 142–143, 145–147, 151–153, 155–158, 160–162, 164, 167–169, 171–172, 174, 178
normative defeat, 5, 124, 137

obligation, 96, 106–108, 115–117, 132, 142–144, 146, 151, 174, 177
ought, 74, 77, 84, 96–98, 101, 107–108, 112, 114, 133, 143–144, 172, 174

permissible, 2–3, 5–6, 9, 19, 25, 40, 42, 48–50, 55, 58–63, 66, 68, 73, 75–76, 87, 95, 106–107, 110, 127, 133, 138–139, 141, 143–145, 147, 152, 163, 165, 168, 170
probability, 2, 4, 15, 111–114, 116–119, 123–124, 130–132, 137, 141, 173, 177, 187–188, 191, 196
proper function, 104, 116
Pryor, 5, 165, 167, 169–172, 176

reasoning, 1, 11–12, 16, 21, 31, 43, 96, 99, 101, 124, 138, 142, 158, 165, 167, 193
rebutting defeat, 20, 156–157
reliabilism, 3, 23, 30–31, 35, 38, 59, 62, 80–81, 96
reliability, 13–15, 19, 38, 43, 61, 66, 78, 80–81, 83, 90, 117, 132, 194
reliable, 9, 15, 17, 19–20, 25, 28–30, 32–33, 43, 57–58, 79, 81, 91, 96, 101, 104, 107, 127–129, 132, 156, 158, 163, 165, 171, 177, 192, 194–195
resistance to evidence, 1–2, 4–5, 9, 13–14, 16, 23, 25, 35, 38, 95, 110–111, 147, 165, 169, 193
responsibilism, 70

scepticism, 1–2, 5, 20, 98, 121, 151–152, 164–167, 180, 192–193
seemings, 2, 23–25, 127
social norms, 3, 36, 137, 186, 196
social psychology, 1–2, 9, 11–13, 22, 193
Sosa, ix, xii, 3, 23, 27–28, 31–32, 45, 49–59, 62–64, 66, 115, 141–142
suspension, 2–3, 5, 9, 16, 46, 48–50, 52–57, 59–64, 66, 68, 95, 102, 110, 138–142, 145, 147, 160, 163, 165
Sylvan, xii, 3, 23, 31–32, 49, 59, 62, 85, 140

undercutting defeat, 20, 157, 160–161

vaccine, xiv, 1, 3, 20–21, 48, 131, 193–194
vice, 4, 45, 68–70, 77–83, 87, 91
virtue, 3, 21, 23, 26, 28, 31–34, 36–37, 48–50, 55–56, 58–60, 63, 66, 68–71, 73–74, 76, 78–79, 81, 83, 85–91, 96, 99–101, 105–106, 112, 117–119, 126–127, 132–133, 136, 141, 147, 153, 160, 168–169, 172–173, 180, 184, 194
virtue epistemology, 31, 35, 51, 56, 68, 78

warrant, 4–5, 28, 31, 33, 35, 68, 73, 111, 125, 160, 165–167, 173
warrant transmission, 5, 165–167
Williamson, xii, 2, 5, 23, 25, 27–29, 44, 49–50, 71, 102, 117–118, 122, 126, 154, 160, 165–166, 176–177
withholding, 60, 102, 138–141, 155, 157
Wright, 166

For EU product safety concerns, contact us at Calle de José Abascal, 56–1°, 28003 Madrid, Spain or eugpsr@cambridge.org.